WILLIAM CLARKE QUANTRILL: *His Life and Times*

William Clarke Quantrill
The Guerrilla Chief

William Clarke Quantrill

His Life and Times

by **Albert Castel**

University of Oklahoma Press
Norman

To George Ann

Library of Congress Cataloging-in-Publication Data

Castel, Albert E.
William Clarke Quantrill : his life and times / by Albert Castel.
p. cm.
Originally published: New York : F. Fell, 1962.
Includes bibliographical references and index.
ISBN 0-8061-3081-4 (pbk. : alk. paper)
1. Quantrill, William Clarke, 1837–1865. 2. Guerrillas—Missouri—Biography. 3. Soldiers—Missouri—Biography. 4. United States—History—Civil War, 1861–1865—Underground movements. 5. West (U.S.)—History—Civil War, 1861–1865 Underground movements. I. Title.
E470.45.C3 1999
973.7′42′092—dc21
[b] 98-49039
CIP

The paper in this book meets the guidelines for permanence and durability of the Committee on Production Guidelines for Book Longevity of the Council on Library Resources, Inc. ∞

Published by the University of Oklahoma Press, Norman, Publishing Division of the University. Manufactured in the U.S.A. First printing of the University of Oklahoma Press edition, 1999.

1 2 3 4 5 6 7 8 9 10

Contents

List of Illustrations

Preface

"Except for the men at the head of the respective governments, and some of the leading generals, Quantrill is the most widely known man connected with the Civil War."

So wrote William Elsey Connelley in 1909, in the preface to his biography of William Clarke Quantrill. He was correct then and remains so today. Only Abraham Lincoln and Jefferson Davis among Civil War statesmen, and only Robert E. Lee, Ulysses S. Grant, William T. Sherman, Stonewall Jackson, and Nathan Bedford Forrest among the generals, have been the subject of more books than Quantrill, the guerrilla leader. People who know little about the Civil War, to whom the names of Braxton Bragg and George Meade mean nothing and who confuse Sheridan with Sherman, usually have heard of Quantrill and his exploits. Whether it be in a novel (he is referred to in *Gone with the Wind*) or in a movie (he has been depicted or mentioned often on the screen) there is no need to identify him. For instance, in the film *True Grit*, it is taken for granted that the viewer will understand the significance of Rooster Cogburn (portrayed by John Wayne) describing himself as a former member of Quantrill's band. By contrast, General Sterling Price, the Confederate commander under whom Quantrill sometimes served, merely provides the name for Rooster Cogburn's cat.

Why Quantrill's fame? The answer lies not in his impact on the course and outcome of the Civil War; that was minimal. Rather, it is to be found in what he was and the nature of what he did. He headed the largest, most fearsome gang of freebooting guerrillas to operate anywhere during the Civil War. For nearly four years his bushwhackers terrorized the Kansas-Missouri border, defying all Union efforts to suppress them. On August 21, 1863, they rode into Lawrence, Kansas, and slaughtered nearly two hundred of its male inhabitants, burned down the business district and many homes, and returned virtually unscathed to their Missouri hideouts. It was a deed of murderous carnage unmatched in scale and unsurpassed in ferocity throughout the entire Civil War. It left Quantrill's name inscribed in blood on the pages of history. Less than two months later he underlined his signature with another massacre, this time of nearly one hundred Union troops at Baxter Springs, Kansas. He seemed omnipresent and omnipotent. Yet, for reasons that will be found in this book, he took a holiday from killing in 1864, even though death held high carnival that year in what had become known as "Quantrill country." Not until early 1865 did he resume active operations, this time in Kentucky. There, more than a month after Lee's surrender, a force of irregular Union cavalry surprised and mortally wounded him; twenty-seven days later he died in a Louisville military prison hospital. But his fame lived on and even increased, thanks to the highly publicized exploits of such ex-bushwhackers as Frank and Jesse James and the Younger brothers. Not without cause were these outlaws considered Quantrill's progeny.

Quantrill was the stuff from which legends are made. That is what his first biographer, John Newman Edwards, set out to do. Edwards was a Missouri journalist, a one-time Confederate major, and an unreconstructed Rebel. When not getting drunk on whiskey, which was all too often, he intoxicated himself with words, employing eloquent language to describe grandiloquent deeds. In 1877 he published *Noted Guerrillas, or The Warfare of the Border*. Its hero was Quantrill, and a most heroic one at that, being depicted as a combination of the Count of Monte Cristo, Robin Hood, and Sir Galahad. Along with his followers, whom Edwards portrayed as equally brave, dashing, and romantic, Quantrill waged an epic struggle of revenge and retaliation against the dastardly Kansas raiders known as jayhawkers. His struggle continued until the Confederate cause was lost in Missouri, whereupon he went to Kentucky and to his death, fighting to the last.

Such was the picture painted by Edwards of "Quantrell" and the guerrillas. It pleased Southerners in general and Missourians with Southern sympathies in particular. On the other hand, most

Northerners, and especially Kansans, rejected it. To them Quantrill and his men were demons, not demigods.

In 1910 William Elsey Connelley, a Kentucky-born Kansas historian, published *Quantrill and the Border Wars*. Based mainly on interviews with and written statements from Kansans and Missourians who had known Quantrill before and during the Civil War, its massive documentation toppled the tower of fantasy erected by Edwards. Quantrill was a native of Ohio, not a Southerner; he had been an outlaw in Kansas before he became a bushwhacker in Missouri; and his prime motive was not love of the confederacy but lust for plunder. Far from being the knightly paladins concocted by Edwards, the guerrillas at best were merely tough, young Missouri farm boys engaged in their own private war; at worst they were savage, murdering bandits whose outrages disgusted even the Confederate authorities. Connelley also revealed the dissensions among the bushwhackers, the real reasons why Quantrill was inactive in 1864, and the true story of what happened to him in Kentucky. By providing the most complete and accurate account hitherto written of the Lawrence Raid, the Baxter Springs Massacre, and of guerrilla operations in general along the border, Connelley took Quantrill out of the murky mist of myth where Edwards had enshrined him and put him into the sharp light of history, there to be seen by all except those who prefer not to look.

Valuable as it is, *Quantrill and the Border Wars* suffers from a number of defects, some serious. Connelley, whose father lost both his health and his property while serving in the Union army, often was as anti-Confederate as Edwards was pro. Determined to destroy Quantrill's image as a hero, he went to the opposite extreme of depicting him as a "depraved" and "degenerate" villain. Moreover, most of his followers were little better than he was, and their attacks on Kansas, including the Lawrence raid, were unprovoked and unmitigated atrocities. Connelley thought that the guerrillas' claims of defending and retaliating against Kansas depredations in Missouri were specious, self-serving excuses. To him, the actual, almost sole cause of the guerrilla war was the situation in Missouri itself. The Red Legs, the most notorious of the Kansas jayhawker bands, "were, generally, honest and patriotic men." Senator James H. Lane, "king of the jayhawkers," was a great man, whereas his opponent, Governor Charles Robinson, was a scoundrel who—Connelley implied—helped make the Lawrence raid possible. Franklin B.

Sanborn of Massachusetts, after reading a portion of Connelley's manuscript in 1908, warned him against "extreme statements." Connelley should have heeded him.

In 1958, having had occasion to write much about Quantrill in my first book, *A Frontier State at War: Kansas, 1861–1865*, I undertook to write a biography of him that would strike a balance between Edwards and Connelley. In this endeavor I had four assets. First, I was able to remain objective and avoid partisan writing, unlike Edwards, who was an ex-Confederate officer, and Connelley, whose ancestors fought in the Civil War (mine did not). Second, although a native of Kansas, I had no prejudice against Missouri, where I had relatives and friends, with the sons and grandsons of men who rode with Quantrill being among the latter. Third, I could and did consult sources that either were unavailable to Edwards and Connelley or else not used by them, at least in a systematic fashion. Among these sources are Kansas and Missouri newspapers of the Civil War era, the *Official Records of the Union and Confederate Armies*, and the memoirs of Frank Smith, a young member of Quantrill's band (whose unpublished manuscript I was allowed to transcribe virtually verbatim in 1958 by Smith's grandson, Dr. H. Eugene Smith of Kansas City, Missouri). Smith's memoirs provide valuable information about what might be termed the inner history of the guerrillas not to be found anywhere else.

Fourth, but perhaps most important of all, I am a professionally trained historian who believes that in writing history one should strive to achieve the maximum possible degree of accuracy and objectivity even though you know that, being human, you will inevitably make errors of fact and judgment. To do more is impossible. To do less is not to write history but to promote myth or propagate propaganda.

The result of my endeavor was—and is—this book, first published in 1962 by Frederick Fell of New York. Looking back on it on thirty-six years later, how successful was I in attaining the goals of accuracy and objectivity?

With regard to the first, I found that on the whole, and with regard to major matters, the book stands up well. If I was going to rewrite it completely, I would change little and expunge less. On the other hand, it did contain some irksome typos, embarrassing factual errors, and conclusions with which I no longer agreed. Hence I welcome the opportunity, provided by this new edition, to make corrections and revisions in the text to the extent practical. By doing so I have not eliminated all flaws, but I believe I have reduced them to few in number and minor in nature. Also, I have updated the account (page 214) of the disposition of Quantrill's bones, a process not completed until 1992, when his shin bones and some arm bones were buried in a Confederate cemetery in Missouri. In the same year Quantrill's skull likewise obtained what presumably will be a final resting place, being interred near the main portion of his remains in the Quantrill family plot in Dover, Ohio's fourth street cemetery. Probably no person prominent in American history lies in as many graves as Quantrill does—three of them.

As for objectivity, let me quote what Abraham Lincoln wrote to General John M. Schofield in 1863, when the latter took command of the Department of Missouri and was forced to deal with a bitter, factional struggle between conservative and radical Unionists: "If both factions, or neither, shall abuse you, you will, probably, be about right. Beware of being assailed by one and praised by the other." Ever since the first publication of this book, some have denounced its characterization of Quantrill and the guerrillas as too harsh, whereas others have condemned it for being too lenient. Consequently, while granting that I may be wrong to do so, I like to think that it is "about right."

But let you, the reader, be the judge of this. I am confident that you will find the story of William Clarke Quantrill and his times one well worth reading.

Albert Castel

Hillsdale, Michigan
July 1998

prologue The Border Ruffians

The scene was the chamber of the United States Senate, the date May 21, 1854. Senator William H. Seward of New York, spokesman of the Northern Free-Soilers, had the floor. The South, supported by Northern Democrats, had just passed Stephen A. Douglas' Kansas-Nebraska Bill. Under it Kansas was to be organized into a territory, which as soon as it had sufficient population would be admitted to the Union as either a free or a slave state, depending on how the majority of its settlers voted. The Missouri Compromise of 1820, barring slavery north of 36° 30′, had been swept away, and the doctrine of "Squatter Sovereignty" reigned supreme. Land previously deemed safe for freedom was now suddenly threatened by slavery. The South's "peculiar institution," instead of being confined, seemed ready to expand. Should it move into Kansas, where would it stop? The Southern slavocrats were on the march—they must be halted! So defiantly Seward hurled down the gantlet of battle for the North:

"Come on then, gentlemen of the slave states! Since there is no escaping your challenge, I accept it, in behalf of freedom. We will engage in a competition for the virgin soil of Kansas and God give the victory to the side that is stronger in numbers, as it is in right!"

Even as Seward spoke Northerners were moving to meet the Southern menace. In Massachusetts two antislavery businessmen, Eli Thayer and Amos Lawrence, combined promotion with abolition by organizing the New England Emigrant Aid Society for the purpose of settling Kansas with people dedicated to the "love of freedom." By July, 1854, the society had sent its first party of settler-soldiers across the plains, and more prepared to follow.

Elsewhere throughout the free states similar companies sprang into existence as the "Kansas Crusade" gathered steam. Soon hundreds of Northern men and women streamed westward, singing as they went a new battle hymn written by John Greenleaf Whittier, the Quaker abolitionist poet:

We cross the prairie as of old
  The pilgrims crossed the sea,
To make the West, as they the East,
  The homestead of the free!

The route to Kansas lay through Missouri. In that state the people watched the onrush of Northern immigrants with growing alarm and mounting resentment. Kansas, they felt, belonged to them. They lived next to the territory, their wagon trains to Santa Fe crossed its rolling prairies, and many of them already had staked out claims. For years their representatives in Washington had urged that Kansas be opened to settlement, and they had been the prime movers behind the Kansas-Nebraska Act. Now, all of a sudden, New England "emigrant aid societies" were sending hordes of Yankee abolitionists into Kansas, to grab up the land and threaten Missouri's twenty-five-million-dollars' worth of slave property. Such a prospect was absolutely intolerable. Kansas must become a slave state—a state controlled by and for Missourians. The Liberty, Missouri, *Democratic Platform* did not mince words when it addressed its readers:

> Shall we allow the cutthroats of Massachusetts to settle in the territory adjoining our own state? No! We are in favor of making Kansas a "Slave State" if it should require half the citizens of Missouri, musket in hand, to emigrate there, and even sacrifice their lives in accomplishing so desirable an end!

Most Missourians were Southern in origin and culture. Although relatively few of them owned slaves, and most of these few did not own many, like the vast majority of Southerners they regarded the antislavery crusade in the North as a monstrous threat to their whole way of life. Negro slavery was to them much more than a mere economic matter. It was above all a system of race control and social order, the very basis of White Supremacy and of Southern Civilization. Consequently "abolitionism" was a dread specter which aroused the deepest emotions of fear and wrath in their breasts. "Western savages would be less formidable neighbors than abolitionists," proclaimed a convention at Lexington, Missouri, in the summer of 1854.

Missourians joined the dark passions of the South to the rough turbulence of the West. Violent feelings, violent words, and violent deeds came naturally to them. This was especially true in the western border counties, a region just emerging from the most primitive pioneer conditions. Here dwelt hundreds of tough, restless young men who were engaged in the perilous but profitable overland trade to New Mexico. Their annual treks across the prairies and deserts inured them to physical hardship, imbued them with a rollicking spirit of adventure, and made them highly adept in the use of revolver and bowie knife. Always ready for a "fight or a frolic," and recognizing little or no difference between the two, they set the tone for the entire border country, which as a result had a decidedly "rough-and-ready" flavor.

The Missourians, moreover, possessed considerable military experience and a proud fighting tradition. During the Mexican War they had marched with Alexander Doniphan and Sterling Price to Santa Fe, Sonora, and Chihuahua, conquered Santa Anna's armies, and brought home captured Mexican cannons as glittering trophies of their epic feats. The veterans of these campaigns stood ready to form the cadres of new armies and to follow their old commanders at an instant's notice.

Spokesman of the Missourians was giant-framed, florid-faced, fire-eating United States Senator David Rice Atchison. He had teamed with Stephen A. Douglas to secure passage of the Kansas-Nebraska Bill in the Senate and now he proposed to oversee its execution in Kansas. Like most of his constituents he believed that the bill represented a tacit agreement by which Kansas was to go to the South while Nebraska went to the North. Also, according to some, he planned to make himself political boss of the new territory. During the summer of 1854 he traveled up and down the border haranguing large crowds of rapt listeners on the danger of permitting the abolitionists to take over in Kansas.

Missourians, he urged, must go into Kansas, stake out the best land, and then prepare to make good their claims against the emigrant aid societies—by force if necessary.

Hundreds of Missourians eagerly responded to Atchison's call. They rushed into Kansas, grabbed up choice land, and founded the towns of Fort Scott, Lecompton, Kickapoo, Leavenworth, and Atchison—the last named of course in honor of their leader. Many of them, however, merely marked out claims, then returned to their homes in Missouri. And only a handful of those who actually settled in Kansas brought slaves with them.

The Missouri "squatters" organized themselves into "Blue Lodges" for the purpose of protecting their claims against Yankee interlopers and expelling persons from Kansas who were not "sound on the goose" when it came to the slavery question. The lodge members, just to show that they meant business, wore as an emblem a bit of hemp rope in their buttonholes. Hemp, they avowed as they passed the whisky jug around at their meetings, was excellent for hanging abolitionists.

Next Atchison and his followers moved to get control of the Kansas Territorial Legislature. The first election of members for the legislature was scheduled for March 30, 1855. Although proslavery settlers probably outnumbered Free Staters in Kansas at this time, the Missourians were not taking any chances. On election day over three thousand of them swarmed across the Kansas line, spurred by the promise of "a dollar a day and free whisky" for every voter. They came by ferries, in wagons, and on horses, and with cannons and flaunting banners. Atchison himself, a revolver and bowie knife in his belt, led the largest contingent, eight hundred strong. Claiborne Jackson, Jo Shelby, A. C. Boone, and other prominent Missourians marched at the head of their own bands.

The invaders went into every doubtful district, and even some that were not doubtful, stuffing the ballot boxes full for the proslavery candidates. In many communities more votes were cast than there were residents! Atchison's group marched all the way to Lawrence, forty miles from the line. As a result, this town, although established by the New England Emigrant Aid Society and the stronghold of the Free-Soilers, sent a proslavery delegate to the legislature. One of the Lawrence election officials at first refused to give ballots to Atchison's men, but the cocking of pistols and fierce cries of "Cut his throat!" and "Tear his heart out!" quickly changed his mind. A drunken Blue Lodger, after casting his ballot, was heard to remark that he had as much right to vote in Kansas as any "damned nigger thief" just arrived from Massachusetts. In fact, the tactics of the Missourians were quite in keeping with frontier political ethics. Up in Nebraska the neighboring Iowans were to do the same thing when that territory held its first election. The only difference was that in Nebraska the explosive slavery issue was not involved.

The Missourians returned in triumph to their side of the border. They were confident that they had overawed the Free Staters and secured Kansas for slavery. But as was so often to be the case, their careless, optimistic frontier temperament caused them to overestimate the victory and to underestimate the enemy. The North seethed with moral and political indignation on learning of the Kansas ballot stuffing, and redoubled its efforts to make the territory a free state. Southerners, on the other hand, were hard put to justify the actions of their Missouri henchmen.

As for the Kansas Free Staters, they angrily refused to recognize the validity of the election and the legality of the proslavery territorial legislature. Instead, they boldly formed their own territorial government, wrote a state constitution, and named Charles Robinson of Lawrence, an agent of the New England Emigrant Aid Society, as their governor. At the same time they made preparations to resist another Missouri invasion "to the bloody issue." They surrounded Lawrence with forts and trenches, and sent East for a new breech-loading rifle called the Sharps carbine. Soon large shipments of these potent weapons began moving Kansasward in boxes labeled "Farming Implements."

All through the summer and fall of '55 a condition of cold war reigned along the Kansas-Missouri border and between proslavery and antislavery settlers in the territory. Only a spark in the form of some incident was needed to cause a sudden and deadly thaw. That incident occurred on November 21. A Missouri squatter named Franklin Coleman and a Free Stater named Charles Dow quarreled over a bit of land near Hickory Point, a community ten miles north of Lawrence. The quarrel became bitter, then violent. Dow swung a club at Coleman and missed. Coleman fired a rifle at Dow and did not miss. Dow staggered, fell, and with a groan died.

The sheriff of Douglas County, where Hickory Point was situated, was a tall, lanky, proslavery Missourian named Sam Jones. This official, who spent most of his time in Westport, Missouri, where he was postmaster, did not bother to investigate the killing of Dow or to arrest Coleman. After all, what was one abolitionist, more or less? However, a group of Free State Regulators decided that the slaying must not go unpunished. Led by Jacob Branson, a friend of Dow's, they set out to capture Coleman. When Coleman eluded them by fleeing into Missouri, they took out their frustration by burning a number of proslavery settlers' cabins near Hickory Point.

Sheriff Jones now all at once bestirred himself to enforce the law—against Free Staters. He collected a posse at Westport, went to Hickory Point, arrested Branson, and started to take him to Lecompton, the proslavery territorial capital. But before he could get there a band of fifteen horsemen from Lawrence waylaid him and rescued the prisoner.

Jones, nearly beside himself with fury and embarrassment, returned to Westport and called on his fellow Missourians to supply "a posse of three thousand men to carry out the laws" of Kansas, which he said were being defied by the Lawrence abolitionists. The border men responded with gleeful alacrity. They would teach the Yankees to burn out Southerners and defy legal authority!

By December 3 fifteen hundred of them, heavily armed, were gathered along the Wakarusa River, six miles southeast of Lawrence. This time they had come not to vote but to shoot. They were determined, if given the slightest excuse, to wipe the "abolitionist sinkhole" of Lawrence off the map. "We mean to have Kansas," a border captain declared to a Northern newspaper correspondent, "and we are going to have it, if we have to wade through blood to our knees to get it."

The Lawrence Free State Militia manned the town's fortifications, Sharps rifles ready, grim expressions on their faces. They were resolved, however, not to fight unless first attacked. Charles Robinson shrewdly advised them that "if the Missourians, partly from fear and partly from want of a pretext, have to go back without striking a blow, it will make them a laughing stock."

The entire nation waited with bated breath for the dread news of open, full-scale civil war in Kansas. Atchison, now no longer a Senator, was again in command of the invaders. He brusquely demanded that Lawrence turn over the rescuers of Branson and surrender the Sharps carbines. Robinson replied calmly that none of the rescuers was in town and that the carbines were private property. Both statements were false, but the Missourians had no way of proving it. Therefore they were not quite able to make up their minds to attack "Yankee Town," although the more fiery spirits loudly proclaimed that they had come for a fight and were going to have one, "whether the whisky gave out or not!" So for nearly a week the invaders remained camped beside the shallow Wakarusa, in the meantime sending out detachments to harass the Free-Soil settlers and intercept all supplies and travelers heading to and from Lawrence.

Finally, on December 9, the Territorial Governor, Wilson Shannon, drew up an agreement with Robinson in which the people of Lawrence disavowed the Branson rescue and promised not to impede the execution of the law. Shannon communicated these terms to the Missourians and called on them to return home. The rank and file in the Wakarusa camp raised a howl of protest and demanded to be led against Lawrence. But their commanders realized that an attack without clear legal sanction would do serious harm to the proslavery cause. "Wait a little," advised Atchison. "You cannot now destroy these people without losing more than you gain."

Hence, frustrated and unhappy, the Missourians headed back toward the border. They consoled themselves, however, with the thought that although they had failed to settle things with the Yankees this time, there was bound to be a next time.

The next time came four months later, in April, 1856. Sheriff Jones, with more zeal than discretion, rode into Lawrence alone and began seeking the Branson rescuers, who still remained at large. The townspeople, despite the Shannon-Robinson agreement, were not at all co-operative. One citizen caught Jones by the collar. Another grabbed his revolvers. And still another struck him in the face. Enraged, Jones rode to Lecompton and asked Governor Shannon to lend him some Federal troops. Shannon complied and Jones returned to Lawrence with ten dragoons.

With this force to back him up he managed to make six arrests. Then, while he was standing beside a tent, a bullet whizzed by him. "I believe that was intended for me," he said with a shrug. Soon afterward another shot rang out and a hole appeared in Jones' trousers. "That *was* intended for me!" he cried, and ran into the tent—only to slump to the ground with a nasty wound as a third bullet hit the mark.

First reports had it that Jones was dead. Immediately the Missouri border became alive with angry men clamoring to be led against the arrogant Yankees. "His murder shall be avenged," screamed the proslavery Atchison *Squatter Sovereign*, "if at the sacrifice of every abolitionist in the territory!"

This time the proslavery party determined to have full legal backing before moving against their enemies. First a grand jury at Lecompton voted treason indictments against Robinson, James H. Lane, Andrew Reeder, and other prominent Free State leaders. Next the same grand jury indicted Lawrence's two newspapers, the *Herald of Freedom* and the *Kansas Free State*, for using "inflammatory and seditious language." Finally, the jury condemned as "a public nuisance" the Lawrence Free State Hotel, a large stone building "regularly parapeted and port-holed for use of small cannon and arms." Equipped with these indictments, Israel B. Donaldson, United States Marshal of Kansas Territory and a Missourian, issued a proclamation calling for "a large posse of law-abiding citizens" to assist him in carrying out the grand jury's mandate.

The Missourians were already assembled along the border waiting just such an invitation. Again they marched into Kansas. As before Atchison was at their head. They were reinforced by a sizable contingent from the Deep South led by Major Jefferson Buford of Alabama. Brightly colored flags bearing such legends as "Southern Rights" and "The Superiority of the White Race" waved over their serried ranks. They brought with them a battery of cannons—pieces captured by Doniphan in Mexico.

The invaders now had a distinctive name—"Border Ruffians." Originally Northern newspaper correspondents had tagged them with it as a term of opprobrium. But with customary bravado they had adopted it themselves as a name well calculated to strike terror into Yankee hearts. An Eastern traveler vividly described the appearance of a typical Border Ruffian:

> Imagine a man standing in a pair of long boots, covered with dust and drawn over his trousers, the latter made of coarse, fancy-colored cloth, well-soiled; the handle of a large Bowie knife projecting from one of the boot tops; a leathern belt buckled around his waist, on each side of which is fastened a large revolver; a red or blue shirt, with a heart, anchor, eagle, or some other favorite device braided on the breast and back, over which is swung a rifle or carbine; a sword dangling by his side; an old slouched hat, with a cockade or brass star on the front or side, and a chicken, turkey, or goose feather sticking in the top; hair uncut and uncombed, covering his neck and shoulders; an unshaven face and unwashed hands. Imagine such a picture of humanity . . . and you will have a pretty fair conception of the border ruffian, as he appears in Missouri and Kansas.

On May 21 Marshal Donaldson led his "posse" to Mount Oread, on the outskirts of Lawrence, and trained the Mexican cannons on the town below. But there was no resistance. All the main Free State leaders had either fled to avoid arrest or, as in the case of Robinson, been captured while trying to escape. Moreover, the proslavery forces now had the law as well as overwhelming military strength on their side.

Donaldson contented himself with arresting a few minor Free-Soil leaders, after which he dismissed the posse from his service. At once Sheriff Jones, who had quickly recovered from his wound, stepped forward and summoned the Border Ruffians to act under his authority. With shouts of jubilation they lined up behind the doughty sheriff.

Jones' moment had arrived. First he arrested Jacob Branson, who had been evading him ever since his rescue the previous winter. Then his followers surrounded the Free State Hotel and demanded that the arms and ammunition stored there be surrendered. Samuel C. Pomeroy, an agent of the New England Emigrant Aid Society, turned over some cannons but stuck to the Free State line that the Sharps rifles were private property. Jones thereupon declared that the hotel was to be destroyed in accordance with the grand jury indictment.

Shalor W. Eldridge, proprietor of the hotel, after vainly protesting, asked for and received two hours in which to remove the furnishings from the doomed building. Some of the Border Ruffians even assisted in this work, paying special attention to the hotel wine cellar. Meanwhile other Ruffians enforced the grand jury's charges against the *Kansas Free State* and the *Herald of Freedom* by ransacking their offices, destroying the presses, and dumping the type into the muddy Kansas River.

When the allotted time was up, Jones ordered his men to level the Free State Hotel with cannon balls. Atchison, half-drunk with wine and excitement, claimed the honor of firing the first shot. Shouting, "Boys, this day I am a Kickapoo Ranger, by God!" he touched off the fuse—only to suffer the embarrassment of seeing the projectile entirely miss its mark and plop harmlessly into a distant hillside! Subsequent salvos were more accurate but they failed to shake the thick cement walls of the sturdy structure. The explosion of two kegs of gunpowder in the main doorway likewise had little appreciable effect. Finally, as a last resort, the Ruffians applied the torch. Soon they were cheering and cavorting wildly as crackling flames engulfed the "Free State Fortress."

The Ruffians next spread over the helpless town, pillaging all the shops and a few private homes. Money, clothing, and especially Sharps carbines were their favorite objects of plunder. Some achieved added thrills by sticking books on their bayonets or bedecking themselves fantastically in velvet curtains from the hotel. One gang burned Charles Robinson's house, destroying in the process all of his books and a manuscript history of California. Border Ruffians, obviously, had little love for literature, at least that of Yankee origin.

The following morning the Missourians headed back toward the border. Buford's Southerners, on the other hand, remained in Kansas to hold it against the Free-Soilers. The people of Lawrence doggedly began cleaning up the damage.

The proslavery forces were confident that they had this time completely cowed the abolitionists. But as before they did not reckon with their foe. The sack of Lawrence only increased the North's determination to make Kansas a Free State. More and more Free-Soil immigrants poured into the territory, more and more Northern money went to aid them. And the new Republican Party, with its platform of "Free Soil, Free Men, and Frémont," grew enormously in strength, fed by the fires which raged in the West.

In Kansas itself wrath-filled Free Staters launched a counter-offensive of terror and retaliation. One of their bands ambushed eighteen of Buford's men along the Santa Fe Trail and killed three of them. Another Free-Soil gang looted a Missourian's store near Shawnee Mission. Still another burned out the proslavery settlers along Bull Creek and ordered them to leave the territory.

These affairs, however, were merely a prelude to what was to come.

Near the village of Osawatomie lived an elderly New Englander with a Bible, five sons, and the firm conviction that he held a divine commission to destroy slavery in America. His tall, gaunt body trembled with fury and his blue-gray eyes took on a strange gleam when he heard that the Border Ruffians had sacked Lawrence. In a shrill voice he cried out that those who live by the sword shall perish by the sword—that an example must be made which would strike the Terror of the God of Vengeance into the Missourians.

On the night of May 24 this man, three of his sons, and three other men stole silently through the valley of the Pottawatomie. They stopped at three different cabins occupied by Missouri settlers and forced the male inhabitants to come with them into the darkness. There was a sound of shots, blows, and stifled groans. In the morning the bullet-riddled, sword-hacked bodies of four men lay stark amidst the underbrush along Pottawatomie Creek. John Brown, Agent of the Lord, had struck.

Brown's atrocious massacre shocked, but it did not frighten, the proslavery forces. Captain Henry Pate, one of Buford's lieutenants, mobilized the Lecompton Sharpshooters and set forth to find Brown and kill him. "We are going down to the southern part of the territory," announced one of his men, "expecting to see rattlesnakes and abolitionists, and we are taking our guns along."

The Sharpshooters ranged through the Pottawatomie Creek region looking for Brown. But although they captured two of his sons, they failed to locate the "old man," who lay low in the bush and waited for reinforcements. On May 31 Pate camped in Black

Jack ravine, from which he sent a detachment to plunder the Free State settlement of Palmyra. The following day six of his men rode into Prairie City on a similar mission, only to be greeted with a rifle volley which dropped two of them from their saddles and sent the survivors scampering.

Brown joined the Prairie City defenders and with them marched into Black Jack ravine to attack Pate's camp. The Sharpshooters formed a wagon barricade and held off the Free Staters for several hours of long-range fighting. In the end, after suffering a half-dozen or so casualties, they surrendered. Pate, with a sense of humor rare in those somber times, ruefully remarked, "I went to take Old Brown and Old Brown took me!"

News of the Battle of Black Jack attracted other Free State companies to the area. They had mobilized to meet a threatened invasion by three hundred Border Ruffians under Captain James Whitfield. The combined Kansas forces encountered Whitfield on June 5 near Black Jack. Both armies deployed on the prairie but waited for the other to start something. Then, probably to the secret relief of all concerned, a dragoon squadron rode onto the field. Its commander, bluff, tough Colonel E. V. "Bull" Sumner, ordered the would-be combatants to disperse. At the same time he made Brown release Pate and his men. A United States Marshal who was accompanying Whitfield started to arrest Brown for murder but suddenly discovered that he had lost his warrant and so desisted. On this somewhat ludicrous note both Free Staters and Border Ruffians returned to their respective homes.

Despite the restraining presence of Sumner's dragoons, the border country remained a "seething hell." Proslavery spokesmen called for a war of extermination against the Free-Soilers: "Let our motto be written in blood on our flags, 'Death to all Yankees and traitors in Kansas!' " Free Staters replied with the slogan, "War! War to the knife and the knife to the hilt!"

Border Ruffians infested the Santa Fe Trail, stopping all travelers and asking them across leveled guns whether they were "Free State or Pro-Slave." Those giving the wrong answer were liable to "short shrift and long rope." Similar gangs of Free-Soil militants raided proslavery settlements and forced their inhabitants to leave the territory. Each side accused the other of horrible outrages, always with exaggeration but rarely without foundation. In the words of a contemporary, "Murder and assassination were the program of the day."

Buford's Southerners built so-called forts—log cabins with loopholes—around Lawrence as bases of offense and defense. The main ones were Fort Franklin, Fort Saunders, and Fort Titus. This last bore the name of its commander, Major Henry Titus of Florida, a grizzled veteran of Cuban filibustering raids. He and his followers rapidly became the most feared and obnoxious of all the Ruffian bands.

Early in July Titus decided to eliminate one of the main Free-Soil military leaders, Captain Samuel Walker, by a surprise attack on Walker's cabin near Lawrence. Walker, however, got wind of Titus' intentions, and hence it was Titus who was surprised as his men walked into an ambush of a dozen Free State rifles. The Southerners fled in confusion, leaving behind a dead horse and a bottle of corn whisky, which the rejoicing victors also promptly "killed." The following day the disgruntled Titus posted a three-hundred-dollars reward for Walker's head, "on or off the shoulders."

In August Jim Lane of Lawrence, Major General of the Free State Militia and demagogic leader of the Kansas antislavery radicals, launched a campaign to sweep all proslavery forces from the Kaw Valley. His first blow fell on Fort Franklin. Surrounding the place with eighty-nine men, he called on the garrison to surrender. When it refused, his followers wheeled a wagon loaded with hay against the fort and set it afire. The defenders quickly scurried out with their hands up. Lane proposed hanging their leader as an example "to encourage the others," but in the end was dissuaded by the intended victim's wife, who argued that her husband was such a scoundrel that he should be given an opportunity to reform before dying!

A couple of days later Lane moved against Fort Saunders. His men bombarded the place with artillery and riddled it with Sharps carbines. Then with a loud hurrah they rushed forward to storm it —only to discover, much to their embarrassment, that its garrison was gone! This second "victory" apparently contented Lane, for he suddenly departed for the Nebraska border, taking half of the Free State army with him.

The remainder, under Sam Walker, continued the campaign

with an attack on Fort Titus. Although outnumbered, Titus' Southerners held out until a cannon arrived from Lawrence and began pounding a hole in their ramparts. They then waved a white flag and Titus staggered out through the door streaming blood from gashes in the face, hands, and shoulder. Two wounded and two dead men sprawled on the floor of the fort. One Free Stater had been killed and six others injured in the bloodiest pitched battle so far of the Kansas civil war. Walker cocked his pistol to finish off Titus, but relented when the bleeding filibusterer cried, "You have children, so have I—for God's sake, save my life!"

The Missouri newspapers reported the Lane-Walker campaign and called on proslavery adherents to "arouse themselves and rub out the hired tools of abolition now roaming rampant over the plains of Kansas with fire-brand and sabre." Atchison assembled an army of one thousand Border Ruffians at Little Santa Fe. Acting Territorial Governor Daniel Woodson, a proslavery partisan, declared Kansas to be in a state of rebellion and urged "all patriotic citizens" to rally to the defense of law and order. Once more the Missourians marched into Kansas.

One detachment, headed by General John Reid, moved against the abolitionist stronghold of Osawatomie. Most of the town's male inhabitants were away harassing proslavery settlers, so only forty men were on hand to oppose Reid. They opened fire from an ambush in the timber along the Marais des Cygnes and brought down five Missourians. Reid replied with cannon fire which soon dislodged the defenders. The Ruffians then marched into the town, where they pillaged the stores, burned all except four houses, and killed John Brown's half-wit son, Frederick. A proslavery parson named Martin White, who had been chased out of Kansas by Free-Soilers, shot him. "The ball passed clean through his body," White boasted.

Lane was still up on the Nebraska border when he learned of Woodson's proclamation and of the latest Border Ruffian invasion. He quickly gathered up three hundred men and marched in search of Atchison's column. Near Bull Creek he encountered it and the two armies lined up for battle. But, as at Black Jack, neither side, when faced with the prospect of a full-scale engagement which might plunge the whole nation into civil war, cared to join the issue. Therefore they merely exchanged a harmless long-range volley, then mutually retired from the field.

Atchison's force was a mere advance guard. The Missourians were still mustering their strength for a really large-scale invasion of Kansas. The new Territorial Governor, John Geary, while on his way by Missouri River steamboat to assume his duties, witnessed these preparations himself. At Glasgow, Missouri, sixty Border Ruffians under Claiborne Jackson boarded the boat. "Each man," noted the governor's secretary, "carried some description of fire-arm, not any two of which were alike. There were muskets, carbines, rifles, shot guns, and pistols of every size, quality, shape, and style." Only a few of them "had any definite idea of the nature of the enterprise on which they were embarked. The most they seemed to understand was that they were going to Kansas to hunt and kill abolitionists."

John Reid, fresh from his success at Osawatomie, took command of this latest army of invasion, which numbered over three thousand "desperate men" and had a battery of six-pounders. Atchison, Jackson, Jones, and most of the other border captains rode at Reid's side. The Missourians began crossing into Kansas during the second week of September. They ignored a proclamation by Governor Geary ordering all armed activity in the territory to cease. On the fourteenth they encamped, as previously, along the Wakarusa.

Lawrence was practically defenseless. Lane again was off to the Nebraska border and the various local military companies were away conducting unco-ordinated and purposeless raids on proslavery settlements. It was saved from total destruction only through the timely personal intervention of Governor Geary. As soon as he heard of the Border Ruffian invasion he hastened there from Lecompton with a detachment of dragoons. He assured the townspeople that they would be protected and cautioned them not to use their guns except as a "last resort, to protect their lives and property, and the chastity of their females." He then set out for the Missouri camp. On the way he met three hundred red-shirted Ruffians, the vanguard of Reid's army.

"Who are you?" he demanded.

"We are the Territorial Militia, called into service by His Excellency, the Governor of Kansas," answered their leader. "We are marching to wipe out Lawrence and every damned abolitionist in the country."

"I am the Governor of Kansas and Commander-in-Chief of the Territorial Militia," thundered Geary, who stood six foot six inches and was not a man to tolerate trifling. "Countermarch your troops and conduct me to your commanding general."

The governor found Reid at the Wakarusa camp, over which black flags were waving. He ordered Reid to disband his army. An attack on Lawrence, he warned, would lead inevitably to national civil war. Moreover, the dragoons would defend the town.

Jones and some of the other hotheads cursed Geary and advocated "pitching into" the dragoons if they tried to stand in the way of wiping out the Free State citadel. Atchison and Reid, however, heeded the governor's words, and their counsels prevailed. Once again the Border Ruffians turned away from Lawrence and marched back to Missouri, resentment and frustration rankling in their breasts.

The withdrawal of Reid's army marked the defeat of the proslavery cause in Kansas, although few on either side realized it at the time. Never again did the Border Ruffians attempt a major invasion of the territory. Henceforth the sway of the Free Staters was almost complete. During the succeeding months they dominated the territorial legislature, elected the congressional delegate, and wrote a state constitution which forever barred slavery from Kansas. Their triumph was not the result of superior fighting ability or of superior strategy, it was simply one of superior numbers. The North by 1856 had won the war of immigration proclaimed by Seward and launched by Thayer and Lawrence. For every Southerner in Kansas there were four Northerners. Although the Robinsons and Atchisons, the Lanes and Joneses, the Browns and Pates, made the headlines, the plain, everyday Northern settler won the victory.

The Missourians, despite their proximity to Kansas, were severely handicapped in the race of settlement. Their main weakness was slavery itself. In order to make Kansas a slave state slaves were needed. But few slaveowners cared to undertake the arduous and expensive task of transporting their valuable chattels to a raw territory swarming with "abolitionists," subject to constant strife, and probably not suited to slavery in the first place. Consequently at no time did the actual number of slaves in Kansas come to more than four hundred. If through the exercise of sheer violence the Border Ruffians had won, Kansas would have presented the strange spectacle of a slave state without slaves!

Some of the Border Ruffian chieftains, however, did not realize that the battle was lost. On the other hand, certain Kansas antislavery zealots declared that it had not yet been won—that all proslavery settlers must be driven from Kansas and a crusade launched against slavery in Missouri itself. This last element organized bands of reckless young adventurers and abolitionists who combined a hatred of slavery with a love of plunder. They soon became famous and feared along the border as "the jayhawkers."

Their outstanding leaders were James Montgomery and Charles Jennison. Montgomery, a forty-seven-year-old Ohioan, was a part-time evangelical preacher and a full-time abolitionist fanatic. Tall and slender, "his eye had the uneasy glare peculiar to haunted men, and his hollow laugh aroused the constant and unpleasant suggestion of a mind diseased." Jennison, who began as Montgomery's lieutenant but who soon headed his own gang, was a young, bushy-haired New Yorker, whose thin mustache and short, pointed goatee gave a satanic cast to his already cruel visage.

Except for a few minor clashes peace prevailed along the border during most of 1857. Then, late in that year, George Clarke's Border Ruffians swept through southern Kansas destroying crops, stealing horses and cattle, and burning Free-Soil cabins. They "took everything they wanted, and I think they took things they didn't want, to keep their hands in," reported one victim, who while losing his property at least retained his sense of humor.

Montgomery personally undertook to find out the names and residences of the raiders so that they could be punished. He traveled through Missouri posing as a schoolteacher, which he had been at various times in his checkered career, and soon acquired the information he desired. He then returned to Kansas, got his jayhawkers together, and in a quick dash across the border proceeded to strip twenty of Clarke's men of all their removable property, which he turned over to their Kansas victims.

A short lull in the border strife followed. Then came horror and tragedy. Charles Hamilton, a fiery young Georgian whose cabin near Fort Scott had been attacked by Montgomery, decided to answer terror with terror. On May 19 he led a gang of Border Ruffians in a sweep of the Free-Soil settlements along the Marais des Cygnes. His men took nine captives and marched them at gun point into a gulch. There they lined them up against a dirt embankment.

Their intention was obvious. "Gentlemen," said one of the prisoners, "if you are going to shoot, take good aim."

The Ruffians fired, but their aim was not good. Although five victims fell dead, the other four were only wounded, and were able to save their lives by feigning death. The murderers quickly frisked the bodies, then rode away.

The massacre along the Marais des Cygnes was the proslavery counterpart of Brown's murders along the Pottawatomie. Whittier indicted Hamilton's crime in words of chilling beauty:

> A blush of roses,
> Where roses never grew!
> Great drops on the bunch grass,
> But not of the dew!

News of the Marais des Cygnes atrocity shocked most Missourians and infuriated most Kansans. The former hastily repudiated the deed and promised to bring Hamilton and his men to justice —something, however, which was never accomplished. The latter, on the other hand, condemned Hamilton as a "monster" and cried loudly for revenge.

Montgomery endeavored to supply it. Along with a dozen jayhawkers he swooped down on "that infamous nest of border ruffianism" at Fort Scott and attempted to set it afire. The citizens rushed to their arms and a furious gun battle ensued. Finally the jayhawkers fell back frustrated in their purpose but promising to come again and with more men.

Before this threat could be carried out, the more sober, responsible, and intelligent Free State and proslavery leaders got together and agreed to a truce of mutual amnesty. This action, designed to prevent complete chaos in southern Kansas, resulted in an uneasy peace through the summer and early fall. Montgomery and his jayhawkers, however, grumbled that the truce was nothing but a proslavery trick and they eagerly sought the first plausible excuse for breaking it.

They did not have long to wait. Early in November a jury at Mound City made the mistake of indicting Montgomery for the destruction of some ballot boxes the previous January. Montgomery at once yelped that the promise of amnesty had been violated; soon he was off on a new jayhawking spree through Linn County. The proslavery settlers, feeling betrayed in their turn, retaliated by arresting a jayhawker named Ben Rice and jailing him at Fort Scott.

Then, as if things were not sufficiently tumultuous already, John Brown chose this moment to reappear on the border after a long sojourn in New England. With him was a small but fanatical band of followers whom he proposed to train in guerrilla warfare in the West as a prelude to larger operations in the East. He joined forces with Montgomery and Jennison, and together they prepared to attack Fort Scott and liberate Rice.

Early on the morning of December 16 one hundred jayhawkers stormed into a slumbering and strangely unsuspecting Fort Scott. They freed the prisoner, plundered the store of Marshal Blake Little, killed his son, and in general shot up the town. Jennison, as was his wont, distinguished himself by "some big stealing on his own hook." Before riding away one of Brown's men turned to the townspeople and said, "The time is nigh when you will see Missouri overrun with blood."

A week later Brown set forth to make this prophecy come true. He marched his band to the Missouri border, divided it into two squads, then moved down the Little Osage River, plundering houses, destroying farm equipment, and liberating slaves. When he turned back into Kansas he brought with him eleven Negroes and a large number of horses, as well as much miscellaneous loot. Behind him he left the body of David Cruise, "a plain and unoffending farmer," who had died attempting to defend his property.

Brown's raid severely jolted the Missourians. Their worst fears concerning Kansas-based abolitionist attacks on slavery appeared more than justified. Many excited slaveowners hotly demanded that the militia be called out at once to defend the border. The state legislature considered a bill putting Missouri on a war footing.

Fortunately the moderates again won out among the Missourians. The legislature confined itself to offering a three-thousand-dollar award for Brown, dead or alive, and the governor merely appealed to the Kansas territorial authorities to suppress the jayhawkers. The nation generally applauded the temperate action of the Missourians in the face of such great provocation. But would they always be so restrained?

A dragoon squadron pursued Brown but he managed to escape into Nebraska. From there he went on to fulfill his destiny at Harpers Ferry. His sole contribution to the cause of freedom in Kansas had been to arouse forces which might easily have destroyed it.

Despite efforts by the Federal authorities to suppress them, the jayhawkers continued to ride amuck throughout 1859 and 1860. Many Kansans condemned them as outlaws, but many others praised them as heroes, and there were enough of the latter to prevent any effective action against them by the former. Lane in particular was their advocate and abettor. Some even charged that he shared in their spoils.

Jennison gained increasing notoriety during this period. His most sensational exploit was the lynching of Russell Hinds for allegedly returning a fugitive slave to his Missouri master. He cited as his authority for this deed the sixteenth verse, twenty-first chapter of *Exodus*: "And he that stealeth a man, and selleth him . . . he shall surely be put to death."

Lesser jayhawker chieftains, such as Eli Snyder of Osawatomie and John Stewart of Lawrence, also conducted frequent raids into Missouri in quest of Negroes and horses. Kansas law-enforcement agencies were either too weak or too apathetic to check them. Missourians grew more and more angry over their depredations and began to threaten retaliation in kind.

The long struggle between the antislavery and proslavery parties came to an official end on on January 29, 1861, with the admission of Kansas to the Union—a free state, overwhelmingly dominated by the Republican Party and headed by men of pronounced antislavery views. Yet never, not even in 1855 and 1856, had the prospects for peace along the border been dimmer than they were at the beginning of 1861. On the Kansas side the jayhawkers eagerly sensed in the storm which was gathering over the nation a chance to extend the scope and effectiveness of their operations. On the Missouri side the same men, or type of men, who had formed the Border Ruffian armies of Atchison and Reid were ready to ride again behind the same or different leaders. And on both sides there was implacable hatred, intense bitterness, and a burning desire to revenge past wrongs and settle old scores.

Thus, as the fateful spring of 1861 drew near, the border country constituted a giant stage set for a tragic melodrama of death and devastation. The parts were assigned, the roles rehearsed, and the performers were on hand. In fact, although none realized it, the man who was to be the leading actor had already made his initial appearance.

chapter I "The Devil Has Got Unlimited Sway"

Sometime in the spring of 1860 a lone man disembarked from the Lawrence ferry and walked with quick, light strides down Massachusetts Street to the Whitney House hotel. His lean body was attired in a rough woolen shirt and corduroy pants tucked into high leather boots. A slouch hat was pulled low over his face and he carried a cheap oilcloth grip. He entered the hotel, went to the desk, and asked for and obtained a room for the night. In the register he signed the name "Charles Hart."

After he had gone upstairs the hotel proprietor, Nathan Stone, called Holland Wheeler, one of the residents, over to the desk. Pointing to the back page of the register, Stone whispered confidentially, "That's Hart's real name." Wheeler leaned forward and read: "Wm. C. Quantrill." "He's a detective for the Delaware Indians," Stone added, as if to explain the discrepancy.[1]

Within the next two years the name scribbled on the back page of Stone's guestbook was to be spelled out in giant letters of fire and blood along the entire border. It was to become a name hated and feared by thousands, loved and admired by thousands more. It was to become a name linked to the bloodiest deeds of the Civil War, and to some of that war's most dashing and sensational exploits. It was to become a name synonymous with desolation, terror, and murder. It was in the end to become a name around which myths clustered and legends developed. It was the name of a man on the threshold of becoming the "bloodiest man in American History."

William Clarke Quantrill's life began, unsensationally enough, in the quiet little town of Canal Dover, Ohio, where he was born on July 31, 1837.* His father was Thomas Henry Quantrill, a tinsmith, who in time became a teacher, then principal of the Canal Dover school. His mother's maiden name was Caroline Cornelia Clarke. Both she and her husband were natives of Hagerstown, Maryland, whence they had moved following their marriage in 1836. Seven other children were born to them, four of whom died in infancy. A sister, Mary, one year younger than William, had curvature of the spine and passed away in 1863. Two brothers, Thomas and Franklin, survived both him and the notoriety he gave their family name.

We no longer believe in the hereditary transfer of character traits. But if we did, we could make much out of Quantrill's immediate ancestors. For instance, a great-uncle named Thomas Quantrill achieved a certain fame as a pirate along the Louisiana-Texas coast during the rollicking days of Jean Lafitte. His father's brother Jesse, on the other hand, led a long and eventful career in and out of prisons as a forger, confidence man, and six-time bigamist. Indeed, the father himself once embezzled school funds in order to pay for the printing of a booklet on tinsmithing which he had written. And when a member of the school board exposed the fraud, the senior Quantrill endeavored unsuccessfully to kill him. But, in noting these things, we should also in fairness

* Quantrill never told the truth about his life, his apologists have never attempted seriously to discover it, and his detractors have been incapable of presenting it. Most of what we know reliably about his early career is the result of the researches of W. W. Scott, a schoolmate who after the Civil War undertook the task of gathering data for a biography of his former, now notorious friend. Scott, however, never got beyond the collection stage and died before writing his proposed work. William E. Connelley, Secretary of the Kansas State Historical Society, acquired Scott's materials, and supplemented them greatly by interviewing the then still numerous persons who had known Quantrill both before and during the war. All of this information, together with data from general printed and documentary sources, Connelley published in his book, *Quantrill and the Border Wars* (Cedar Rapids, Iowa, The Torch Press, 1910). This work, while extremely valuable for the information it contains, is seriously impaired by Connelley's extreme pro-Union, pro-Kansas, and moralistic bias, which made it impossible for him to deal objectively, accurately, and fairly with so controversial and emotion-charged a subject as Quantrill and the border wars. Fortunately, however, Connelley reprinted in the book most of the documentary material and interviews he had obtained—data which in its original form have apparently since been lost. Except where otherwise indicated, this information provides the basis for this chapter.

point out that the rest of the rather numerous Quantrill clan apparently led normal, decent, humdrum lives. His mother seems to have been nothing more nor less than that—a mother. And his father, despite the theft and attempted assassination, retained both his position as principal and his respectable standing in Canal Dover.

The meager records which have come down to us concerning Quantrill's childhood depict a juvenile monster. He is supposed to have delighted in shooting pigs through the ears, nailing live snakes to trees, stabbing horses and cows, and other equally sadistic rural sports. Moreover, his favorite pastime allegedly was wandering through the woods alone shooting small game, and he is described as having had few friends and no close ones.

Such accounts should be received with more than a little skepticism. As in the case of all men who achieve fame of any sort, the events of later life are reflected back upon their early years. In addition, deeds which on the part of any other youth would have been completely forgotten no doubt took on a sinister quality in the case of Quantrill. Finally, one can readily imagine that the post-Civil War inhabitants of Canal Dover were not exactly bursting with pride over this particular home-town boy and how he had "made good."

Quantrill was a superior student academically and acquired a better than average education for his time and place. At the age of sixteen he ceased to be a pupil and became a teacher in the Canal Dover school. Such youthful pedagogues were not at all unusual in those informal days.

In December, 1854, Quantrill's father, for whom he is said to have had little love, died of consumption—a common disease in the family. The Quantrills now found themselves in straitened circumstances. Mrs. Quantrill took in boarders, sister Mary did sewing, and Quantrill continued teaching. There are many indications that he bitterly resented his home being turned into a boardinghouse and the resultant loss of social status.

Like so many other young men before and since, Quantrill decided to try his luck in the West. There, surely, he would soon make a great fortune. In the summer of 1855 he left Canal Dover and with some friends went to Mendota, Illinois. But the best he was able to do there was just another teaching job. Although he supplemented his income by selling copies of his father's tract on tinsmithing and by hunting ducks and geese, he found it impossible to send any money home. By November he regretted leaving Canal Dover, and informed his mother that he planned to come back and "turn over a new leaf entirely." "This will be the last winter," he assured her, "that you will ever have to keep boarders."

However, he failed to carry out either his intention or his promise. Instead of returning home he remained on at Mendota until January, working in a lumber office following the expiration of his school job. According to a totally unsubstantiated historical rumor, he at this time shot and killed a man who attempted to rob him at the lumberyard. If this be so, then at the age of eighteen he "got his man"—the first of what someday was to be a numerous company.

Upon leaving Mendota he headed back east, but went only as far as Fort Wayne, Indiana. Near there, in the spring of 1856, he took another teaching post. His school, he wrote home, was a "very good one, with from 35 to 40 schollars [*sic*]" and "20 dollars a month and boarded [*sic*]." Moreover, the people of the neighborhood said he was "the best teacher they ever had." In his spare time he studied bookkeeping with the intention of taking up that occupation, as he could "make more money at it" than teaching. During the summer he attended a school at Fort Wayne where he took courses in "Chemistry, Physiology, Latin, and Plane Trignometry."

By fall he was back in Canal Dover. Once again he taught school, this time in the country south of town. The venture into the world in quest of wealth and success had failed. His mother still took boarders, his sister continued to sew other people's clothes, they all remained poor. As the bleak winter days passed, he sat in his little backwoods schoolhouse bored and restless, and filled with a spirit of longing.

Then came a chance to escape, and with it the golden prospect of success and adventure. Two Canal Dover men, Colonel Henry Torrey and Harmon V. Beeson, planned to join the thousands of other Ohioans who were migrating to Kansas Territory. Beeson's son, Richard, a schoolmate of Quantrill's, was accompanying his father. Quantrill eagerly asked to be included in the party. Mrs.

Quantrill also requested that he be allowed to go along. Perhaps in Kansas he might acquire a farm where all her family could settle and begin life anew. In the end Beeson and Torrey agreed to pay Quantrill's way to Kansas, he in turn to work for them after arriving.

Late in February, 1857, the two Beesons and Quantrill set out for Kansas. Torrey took a separate route and met them in St. Louis. Together they went by steamboat up the Missouri River to Independence. Along the way Quantrill posted a letter home in which he related that the boat was crowded with Kansas-bound settlers and soldiers, that they all had to sleep on the deck, and that he had not been able to remove his clothes more than once since leaving Ohio! At Independence—a town destined to figure prominently in Quantrill's later career—they purchased two ox teams, loaded up with bacon, flour, beans, and other frontier basics, and then took the Santa Fe Trail to Stanton, Kansas. Here, along the banks of the Marais des Cygnes, they decided to settle. Beeson and Torrey each purchased claims, and in addition took out another claim under Quantrill's name. Quantrill received sixty dollars to hold the claim for them.

Two months of back-breaking toil and rugged living followed. But the outlook for the future seemed good. Quantrill wrote his mother urging her to sell their Canal Dover house and send him part of the proceeds so that he could buy a claim on which the whole family might settle. By so doing, he argued, "we all will be square with the world & able to say our soul is our own. . . . Is not this worth sacrificing something for?"

Quantrill lived with the Beesons and Torrey, who all occupied the same cabin, and helped them roll logs, clear the land, and plant corn. When not working, he hunted and visited with John Bennings, a neighbor, with whom he became very friendly. After a while Bennings convinced him that Beeson and Torrey had not paid him enough for holding their claim. Therefore he insisted that they give him a larger amount. Apparently his demand was justified, for a local "squatter's court," which arbitrated the dispute, awarded him sixty-three dollars additional, to be paid in two installments of thirty-three dollars and thirty dollars.

Beeson and Torrey, however, did not settle up at once. Perhaps they did not have the money—sixty-three dollars was a big sum in Kansas in those days—or perhaps they felt that young Quantrill was displaying a disgusting lack of gratitude. Finally Quantrill, impatient and irritated, stole a yoke of oxen from Beeson and a blanket and two pistols from Torrey in order to force payment. Beeson naturally suspected Quantrill of the thefts and went in search of him. This was not the first time he had been troubled by a member of the Quantrill clan. It was he who had exposed the embezzlement of Quantrill's father and whom the elder Quantrill had attempted to kill!

Beeson spotted Quantrill out on the open prairie. Quantrill turned to run, but Beeson aimed a rifle at him and yelled, "Bill, stop! I want to see you!"

Quantrill faced around toward Beeson, who then shouted, "Lay your gun down in the grass!"

As soon as Quantrill obeyed this order, Beeson told him, "You must bring my oxen back by three o'clock this afternoon, or I shall shoot you on sight!"

Quantrill replied that he would do so, and Beeson let him go. Shortly after the time specified he returned the oxen, also the pistols. The blanket was not found until long afterward, rotted in a hollow log. Beeson and Torrey eventually paid Quantrill at least thirty dollars of the money owing him. Despite this incident, which is the first authenticated indication of criminal tendencies on Quantrill's part, they remained on generally good terms with him.

During the summer Beeson returned to Canal Dover for the purpose of bringing his and Torrey's families to Kansas. His enthusiastic account of the opportunities present in the Territory inspired a number of other Canal Dover men to migrate there also. The newcomers took out claims near Stanton at a place which they named Tuscarora Lake in honor of their home county in Ohio. Since many of them were former school chums, Quantrill soon joined their settlement.

Before long the Tuscarora Lake group began missing blankets, provisions, clothing, and other articles. Quantrill loudly denounced the Cedar Creek settlers as being responsible, but his accusation merely directed suspicion to himself. The others kept a close watch on him, and ultimately they caught him in the act. Inquiries among neighboring communities developed the fact that he had been selling the stolen goods. Completely disgusted, they ordered Quantrill to leave the settlement. They spared him a harsher punishment only out of consideration for his mother and because he was a boyhood friend.

Quantrill remained in the vicinity for several weeks, staying either with Bennings or Torrey. Then he went to Fort Leavenworth and joined an army expedition which was fitting out for Utah as a teamster. The commander of the expedition was Brigadier General Albert Sidney Johnston, destined to die in a few years leading the Confederate Army at Shiloh. Its purpose was to assert United States authority over the polygamous Mormons of Brigham Young's state of Deseret.

Johnston's column marched across the vast plains, mountains, and deserts, and arrived in Salt Lake City the first of October. Quantrill wrote his mother from the "City of the Saints" describing the country and the customs of the Mormons, and announcing his intention of going in the spring to the Colville gold mines of Canada. "You need not expect me home till you see me there, but bear in mind that I will do what is right, take care of myself, and try to make a fortune honestly, which I think I can do in a year or two."

Quantrill's second letter to his mother from Utah, written on December 1, 1858, is much less optimistic. In it we learn that he had suffered a three-week siege of "mountain fever" but had recovered fully and was soon to begin work as a quartermaster's clerk for fifty dollars a month, "which is no more than 25 at home." He still did not know when he would return to Ohio, but he was not going to do so "without some money." *

* In 1904 R. M. Peck, an ex-Union soldier who served along the Kansas-Missouri border during the Civil War, wrote a sensational account of Quantrill in Utah, where he claimed to have known him (see Connelley, *Quantrill*, pp. 75-76). According to Peck, Quantrill was a swashbuckling professional gambler, wagering and winning high stakes, and flourishing his revolvers in a style which would do credit to the most dashing dime-novel hero. In fact, Peck's description reads a little too much like a dime novel. While it is possible that Quantrill gambled (indeed, it would be unlikely that he did not), and perhaps resorted to pistols on occasion, it is hardly believable that the twenty-one-year-old schoolteacher and blanket thief suddenly developed into the poker-playing, gun-wielding marvel depicted by Peck. This story is just another contribution to the Quantrill myth.

Slightly more than a month later he wrote a third letter home. He had been having a "rather hard time of it." Through his own fault he had lost the quartermaster job and been reduced to cooking for a mess of twenty-five men. He asked his mother not to "greeve [*sic*] any more than possible" about him. Someday he would "be worth something—don't fear."

In the spring Quantrill carried out his intention of going to the gold fields. But instead of Canada he went to Colorado, where the Pike's Peak strike had just been made. The trip across the mountains from Utah was a nightmare of cold, starvation, and Indian attacks. He became snow-blind, and twelve out of the nineteen men in his party died. Once in the "diggings" his luck did not change. Forty-seven days of hard pick-and-shovel work netted a mere $54.34—barely enough to pay expenses.

Early in the summer, convinced that Pike's Peak was "undoubtedly *the* Humbug of the Humbugs," he headed back to Kansas. On the way Indians stole his horse and shot his traveling companion. When he arrived in Lawrence he was so "weather beaten & rough looking" that people judged him to be at least twenty-five years old. From Lawrence he wrote his mother asking her not to lose confidence in him. "I expect everybody thinks & talks hard about me but I cannot help it now—it will be all straight before another winter passes."

By autumn Quantrill had returned to Stanton and his old profession of schoolteaching. Four years of wandering through the West and still he was where he had started—teaching farm children in a back-country schoolhouse at so much per "scholar" and "boarding around" among their parents.

During odd moments in the schoolroom he penned long letters to his mother and sister. Certain passages in them provide interesting insights into his mood at the time and into his character generally. One bespeaks a sense of guilt at having left home and failing to provide for his mother. Another announces an abandonment of his hopes for a great fortune and resignation to a life of hard work and modest achievement. Still another states that he is tired of "roving around" without any tangible goal in sight, and that "such a course must end in nothing" and hence "must be changed, and that soon or it will be too late." Finally, there is an expression of belief that his survival amidst so many hardships and perils means that "there must have been something else for me to do."

All in all, these letters convey the impression of a man discontented with his past but unsure about his future—of a man, in short, undergoing a personal crisis and about to make a vital decision. In view of what that decision ultimately was, a passage from the next-to-last letter he ever wrote his mother bears a special significance:

> There is no news here but hard times, and harder still coming, for I see their shadows; and "coming events cast their shadows before," is an old proverb. But I do not fear that my destiny is fixed in this country, nor do I wish to be compelled to stay in it any longer than possible, for the devil has got unlimited sway over this territory.

The school term ended late in March. Immediately afterward Quantrill went to Lawrence. He remained there a short while, then took up residence among the Delaware Indians, a semicivilized tribe who occupied a reservation across the Kansas River from Lawrence. Insofar as it is known he engaged in no regular occupation. He made frequent trips into Lawrence, where as we have seen he went by the name of Charles or "Charley" Hart and posed as a "detective" for the Delawares. Only a few of the townspeople, such as Nathan Stone of the Whitney House, knew his real name. The fact that he adopted an alias is suggestive of his intentions.

He spent most of his time loitering about the north ferry landing opposite Lawrence. There he became friendly with a bunch of Border Ruffians and toughs who made this spot their rendezvous. Among the more prominent of this ilk were Jake Herd, Frank Baldwin, Esau Jager, Hank McLaughlin, and the McGees, consisting of Old Man McGee, his two sons, and a cousin with the interesting sobriquet of "Cuckold Tom." These characters engaged in the nefarious business of kidnaping free Negroes in Kansas and selling them into slavery in Missouri. Sometimes indeed, they would even "liberate" a slave and then hold him for ransom. Superficially both Border Ruffian and jayhawker, they basically were freebooters who exploited the antislavery and proslavery conflict along the border to their own personal advantage.

Quantrill's personal sympathies were proslavery. This was true in spite of his Ohio background and his having been raised, according to the later testimony of his mother, "as an abolitionist." To be sure, when he first arrived in Kansas he wrote letters praising Jim Lane, denouncing the Democrats, and asserting that it was a "pity" that every Missourian at Fort Scott was not shot. But by 1860 a complete shift had occurred in his political views. He then wrote as follows to his mother:

> You have undoubtedly heard of the wrongs committed in this territory by the southern people, or proslavery party, but when one once knows the facts they can easily see that it has been the opposite party that have been the main movers in the troubles & by far the most lawless set of people in the country. They all sympathize with old J. Brown, who should have been hung years ago, indeed hanging was too good for him. May I never see a more contemptible people than those who sympathize for him. A murderer and a robber, made a martyr of; just think of it.

Bennings, Torrey, and many others whom Quantrill knew around Stanton were pro-Southern, and no doubt they influenced the change in his opinions. But it is unlikely that his political sentiments were ever more than an incidental or supplementary motivation throughout his career. In essence, as one of his associates at the ferry landing remarked, his interest was in "anything that had a dollar in it for Charley Hart."

Quantrill ran foot races, wrestled, gambled, and drank with his new-found friends, who soon accepted him as one of their own kind—which, in fact, he soon became.

One day a young Negro, exhausted, frightened, and obviously a fugitive, appeared at the ferry landing and asked the way to Jim Lane's house. Quantrill and Frank Baldwin, after exchanging winks, stepped forward and said that they would take him there. The Negro followed them, thanking them profusely for their help as he did so. But instead of going to Lane's, they went to Old Man McGee's cabin. When night fell, Quantrill, Baldwin, and McGee tied the fugitive on a horse and took him to Westport, Missouri. They then contacted the master who agreed to pay a five-hundred-dollar ransom for his return. The following day they delivered the unfortunate Negro back into bondage and collected their "blood money."

Quantrill's criminal tendencies, first hinted at in the Beeson-Torrey affair, then manifested by the Tuscarora Lake thefts, had now been confirmed in a most contemptible manner. In all likelihood he became a bandit as much out of deliberate choice as accidental circumstance. The life of a freebooter must have appealed to him as a chance to get out of his dreary rut of failure, to experience a life of pleasure and excitement, to obtain big money easily, and above all to *be* somebody.

Quantrill used his share of the ransom to buy a race horse named White Stockings. Accompanied by Baldwin and another friend he took the steed to Westport. There he challenged and beat Mulky Colt, a famous local runner, in a stake race. He remained in Westport about three weeks trying to promote some more races but had little success. At last seeing that there was no prospect of further "sport" he took White Stockings down to southern Kansas. A week or two later he was back in Lawrence—without the horse.

He next began associating with the notorious jayhawker, Captain John Stewart. Second in reputation only to Montgomery and Jennison, Stewart operated out of a fort a few miles south of Lawrence. Before coming to Kansas he had been a Methodist minister in New Hampshire, where he had "preached to good acceptance." His frequent forays across the border resulted in the Missouri legislature placing a price on his head, and he was suspected in Kansas of "entertaining loose notions with regard to property in horses as well as negroes." But as in the case of the other jayhawkers his professed zeal for abolitionism caused a large proportion of the settlers to wink at his activities.

Along with Walt Sinclair, Barclay Coppoc, and others of Stewart's followers, Quantrill during the summer conducted a series of raids against alleged proslavery settlements in Leavenworth and Atchison counties. The horses and cattle stolen on these expeditions he took to Stewart's fort, then sold to people who were not particular about bills of sale or other such minor technicalities.

Ultimately he made the mistake of rustling eighty head of cattle from the Kickapoo settlement near Leavenworth. The citizens of Kickapoo were renowned for their pugnacity and they did not take this outrage lying down. A party of them trailed Quantrill to Lawrence, then secured the aid of Sam Walker, now sheriff of Douglas County, in recovering their stolen stock. Walker had already noted "Charley Hart" and another man driving a herd across the Kansas River in the direction of Stewart's fort. Therefore he and the Kickapoo men went to Stewart's, where they found all the cattle except two, which had been butchered. Stewart alibied for Quantrill, who was present, by claiming that a "couple of strangers" had left the herd at his place for "safekeeping" until they returned, and that he had purchased the slaughtered steers. Although this yarn was obviously ridiculous, Walker did not arrest Quantrill or any of the other jayhawkers. He did, however, make them restore the surviving cattle to the owners.

Quantrill next began playing a dangerous double game. Late in the summer he tipped off Jake Herd, Hank McLaughlin, and Esau Jager that Stewart had a number of fugitive slaves concealed in his cabin who if captured would fetch fine ransoms. He then joined these ruffians in an attack on the fort, staying in the background so that Stewart would not recognize him. Stewart, however, armed the Negroes and with their help beat off the attackers in an all-night gun battle. Quantrill and his friends managed to jayhawk only one Negro from the jayhawker.

Although Stewart did not learn of Quantrill's double-cross, he nevertheless became suspicious of the ex-schoolteacher. When Quantrill proposed that they make a joint raid into Missouri he refused to have anything to do with the scheme. In view of events which were soon to transpire, Stewart later believed that Quantrill hoped to induce him into a trap and thereby collect the reward which the Missourians were offering for his capture or death.

In November Quantrill got together a small gang of his own and led it into Missouri on a cattle-stealing excursion. The raiders rounded up a large herd and headed back for the border. Quantrill, however, slipped away in the darkness, aroused the countryside, and then led a large party of irate Missouri farmers in pursuit of his own men. The jayhawkers were brought to bay near the Kansas line but after a brisk fight they escaped with most of the livestock, which they subsequently sold to settlers living along the road to Lawrence.

A few days later Quantrill appeared in Lawrence and claimed his share of the proceeds from the raid. He explained his absence by stating that he had got lost in the dark and had been forced to make a long detour in order to avoid the pursuing Missourians. The others were openly skeptical of this story but they paid him his portion of the spoils.

This, however, was merely the beginning of his impudence. For he next returned to Missouri and made arrangements with the owners of the stolen cattle to locate and restore their property at so much per head! He indeed was playing both ends against the middle, or rather making the best of two possible worlds. Obviously, however, such a course could not be followed very long with impunity.

During the fall of 1860 he committed a number of other crimes. Chief among them was stealing some ponies from the Delawares, robbing a store in Lawrence, and kidnaping another fugitive slave, in the process of which he burned down a house. All this was too much even for the lax law authorities of Kansas. Late in November the Douglas County court issued a warrant for his arrest on charges of horse and cattle rustling, kidnaping, burglary, and arson. But he only laughed at the indictment and boasted that Sheriff Walker would never take him. In the meantime he continued to ride openly about Lawrence.

One day early in December Walker spotted "Hart" calmly strolling down Massachusetts Street. Calling another man to his assistance he set out after him. Quantrill, instead of standing to fight as he had claimed he would do if threatened with arrest, ran down the street and dashed into the wagon shop of John Dean, a friend, who closed and barred the door behind him. By the time Walker broke the door down, Quantrill had escaped through the back way and found refuge in a near-by house. Walker searched the Whitney House and Quantrill's other known hangouts, but failed to find him. The following day Quantrill slipped out of town and holed up in the country, where friends kept him well supplied with food and whisky.

The man who helped Quantrill escape, John Dean, represented an element in Kansas known as the "practical abolitionists," men who believed that only direct and militant action could eradicate slavery and who acted on this belief. Such persons, while utterly unscrupulous as to their means, were sincere antislavery zealots, and belonged to the Brown class of fanatic.

Quantrill first met Dean in the spring of 1860 and immediately offered to aid him in running off slaves from Missouri. Dean naturally was at first suspicious, but in the end Quantrill gained his confidence and became a member of his jayhawker gang. Sometimes, to be sure, Dean would ask him why he associated with such notorious Border Ruffians and outlaws as Herd and the McGees, but Quantrill reassured him that he did so only to learn their "secrets."

The two eventually became so close that Dean assigned Quantrill the task of assassinating a Lawrence Negro named Allen Pinks, who had committed the detestable crime of selling one of his own race back into slavery. Quantrill, however, instead of killing Pinks, tried unsuccessfully to kidnap him for ransom purposes. Dean thereupon shot Pinks himself, but merely wounded the wretch. Ultimately and fittingly a mob of Leavenworth Negroes lynched Pinks for his treachery to their race.

Among Dean's associates were four youthful and fanatical abolitionists named Charles Ball, Chalkey T. Lipsey, Edwin S. Morrison, and Albert Southwick. They were all from Springdale, Iowa, and were all of Quaker background, although no longer members of that church. Their participation in the militant antislavery cause dated from a visit to Springdale by John Brown and his men in the winter of 1857-58. Brown set up a "mock legislature" or debating society, wherein Richard Realf, John Kagi, and others made eloquent speeches denouncing slavery and depicting the horrors committed by the Border Ruffians in Kansas. The orations inspired Ball, Lipsey, Morrison, and Southwick, who were already members of the Underground Railway, to go to Kansas and fight for freedom. They settled at Pardee, in Atchison County, and soon joined up with Dean.

Sometime in the late fall of 1860 three refugee Negroes came to Pardee and asked the four abolitionists to aid them in rescuing their families from slavery in the Cherokee Nation. The young zealots agreed to do so, and accompanied by the Negroes they went to Lawrence for reinforcements, arriving there shortly after Quantrill's escape from Walker. They got in touch with Dean, who in turn contacted Quantrill and another Lawrence jayhawker named John S. Jones, both of whom readily agreed to join in the rescue expedition. Dean, however, felt that more men still were needed. Therefore, he, Quantrill, Jones, the Pardee abolitionists, and the Negroes traveled to Osawatomie for the purpose of enlisting additional recruits in that antislavery stronghold.

At Osawatomie they conferred with Captain Eli Snyder, the jayhawker who had burned four Border Ruffians to death in their cabin while on a raid in Missouri with Montgomery. They asked Snyder to furnish some of his men and offered to give him command of the expedition. Snyder, however, declared that their scheme was impractical because of the cold weather and their lack of money. Nothing, he pointed out, could be accomplished in such matters without money. On his advice, therefore, they reluctantly abandoned the project.

At this juncture Quantrill expressed the opinion that it was a shame to go to so much trouble and have nothing to show for it. Why not, he asked, jayhawk the slaves of Morgan Walker, the wealthy Jackson County, Missouri, farmer?

Snyder vehemently opposed this idea also, and told the others that Quantrill would only get them in trouble if they followed him. Jones, Southwick, and the three Negroes heeded Snyder's warning, but Dean and the others, after some hesitation, agreed to make the raid. Later Dean induced Southwick to change his mind.

Several days later, on a brisk mid-December morning, Quantrill, Ball, Lipsey, and Morrison set out on foot for Missouri. Snyder made a last-minute effort to persuade the latter three not to go, even walking with them a short distance, then bade them good-by. His final words to them were, "I don't expect to see any of you alive again."

Dean and Southwick followed sometime afterward in a wagon. Although their part in the enterprise is obscure, apparently they were to meet the others after the raid and help haul away the slaves and plunder.* Excellent mounts for all would be found at

* Most accounts of the Morgan Walker raid do not include Dean and Southwick among the participants. I am following Connelley, who produced good evidence to show that they were present, although he is unable to establish their exact roles.

Walker's, whose large stone barn contained "some of the best mules and horses to be had in Jackson County."

After a two-day hike Quantrill and his three companions made camp in a dense thicket one mile from the Walker farm. It was now that Quantrill began carrying out the treacherous plot which undoubtedly was his motive in proposing the raid.

"Boys," he said, "you lay low here while I take a look-see at Walker's place. I'll be back soon."

The others nodded agreement to this reasonable-sounding proposition and Quantrill went off alone to the Walker farm.

Morgan Walker was not at home, but his son Andrew lived near by and Quantrill accordingly went there.

The younger Walker eyed with suspicion the unkempt and unshaven stranger who knocked at his door. "Yes, I'm Morgan Walker's son. Who are you and what do you want?"

"My name's Charles Quantrill," replied Quantrill, dropping part of his alias. "I'm part of a gang of Kansas abolitionists who plan to kill your father and run off his slaves tonight. Three others besides me are camped out in the woods."

"If you're one of them, why are you here telling me this?"

"I don't have time to explain. But trust me and you won't regret it."

"All right, Quantrill, but what should I do?"

"Set a trap at your father's place. When it gets dark we'll be coming up on the porch. As soon as I get away from the others, shoot 'em down—that's what they plan to do to your father! Just don't shoot me, that's all I ask."

"I'll get together some of the boys and get things ready, then. And I'll see to it that you don't get hurt none. But you better be telling the truth, Quantrill."

"I am—you'll see. Just don't shoot me. Now I got to go or the others'll get suspicious."

Quantrill returned to the camp. What thoughts ran through his mind as he faced the three men he was about to betray? Certainly his manner did not give him away, for they suspected nothing.

Meanwhile, Andrew Walker rounded up four neighbors, John Tatum, Lee Coger, Clint Williams, and Clark Smith, to help him prepare the trap. He and Tatum got behind a loom on the front porch of the Morgan Walker residence, the other three hid in a harness room which adjoined the house. Each man was armed with a double-barreled shotgun loaded with buckshot. Morgan Walker himself arrived home only a few minutes before darkness fell. On learning what was up, he agreed to meet the raiders when they came to the door.

Night came, cold and moonless. The Missourians tensely waited in their places of ambush. Finally there was a sound of footsteps. The shadowy forms of four men appeared. They went up onto the porch and pounded loudly at the door. Morgan Walker opened it and Quantrill, Ball, and Lipsey rushed in with drawn pistols, while Morrison remained standing outside.

"We're here to take your slaves," announced Ball, "and also your horses, mules, and any money you got."

"Have you talked to my slaves," replied Walker, "and do they want to go with you?"

"Yes," lied Ball, "and they all are anxious to go. So don't give us no trouble."

"All right, then, but don't take any slaves who don't want to go."

At this point Quantrill spoke up. "Boys, you go take care of the niggers and horses. I'll stay here and keep an eye on the old man."

Ball answered, "All right, Charley, we won't be long." He and Lipsey thereupon turned and stepped out onto the porch. As they did so John Tatum rose up from behind the loom and fired his shotgun. Morrison fell dead instantly, riddled with nine buckshot. But Tatum's blast had been premature. Before the others could open fire, Ball and Lipsey began running. A storm of buckshot followed them as they dashed through the yard. Ball was unscathed but Lipsey received a nasty wound in the groin. However, he kept going, and both men escaped into the brush. The Missourians made no attempt to pursue them in the darkness. Dean and Southwick, who were near by with the wagon, fled back toward Kansas as soon as they heard the sound of gunfire. A stray bullet struck Dean in the foot.

Two days later, a neighbor of Walker's, George Rider, went into the timber with a slave to cut some wood. The slave accidentally discovered Ball and Lipsey in a camp concealed amidst some thickets. Lipsey was lying in great agony on a bed of leaves. Ball had slaughtered a hog and was cooking it over a small fire. A horse stolen by Ball stood close by tied to a sapling.

The slave informed his master of what he had seen—a cruelly ironical act of betrayal. Rider in turn notified Morgan and Andrew Walker. The Walkers and Quantrill, who was staying with them, at once hurried to Ball's and Lipsey's refuge. Ball went for his revolver when he saw them coming but was cut down instantly by Morgan Walker's shotgun. Quantrill ran up to the helpless Lipsey and shot him through the head with a pistol. Now there would be no embarrassing revelations on his part!

Word of the bloody events at the Walker farm threw the people of Jackson County into a near-panic. Men began standing guard over their farms at night and patrols scoured the countryside for suspicious strangers. The alarm increased as rumors of fresh jayhawker outrages floated about.

The Jackson County sheriff brought Quantrill to Independence for questioning. Quantrill gave a statement of his part in the Walker affair which satisfied the sheriff and no charges were made against him. Some of the townspeople, however, advocated stringing him up anyway, on the general grounds that he was a Kansan and had been in the company of the abolitionist raiders. After the sheriff released him, a large and threatening mob gathered outside the hotel where he was staying with Andrew Walker. Only a declaration by Walker that if Quantrill were hanged, it would have to be over his own dead body, prevented a lynching.

Morgan Walker expressed his gratitude to Quantrill by giving him fifty dollars, a saddle, and a powerful coal-black horse of pure Kentucky stock, but blind in one eye, named Black Bess. At the same time, however, he asked Quantrill not to remain at his place, for fear that the remainder of his former gang might come back seeking revenge and burn the house down. Quantrill agreed, and during the next several weeks stayed with various neighbors. He was something of a local celebrity, and would ride frequently into Blue Springs, where the people would ask him to tell the story of the Walker affair. Here a young Missourian who was later to serve under Quantrill saw him for the first time in the general store. "He seemed to be a very pleasant sort of fellow. He was laughing and joking with the men in the store and his appearance was any other than that of a killer." [2]

It was on such occasions as these that Quantrill told the story which served to explain his betrayal and to gain him the confidence of the Missourians. According to this tale, he was born at Hagerstown, Maryland, in 1836 and went to Ohio at the age of sixteen with a Colonel Toler (Torrey?). In the summer of 1856 he joined an elder brother in Kansas and together they started across the plains for California. One night, while they were camped along the Cottonwood River, a gang of jayhawkers attacked them, killing the brother and leaving Quantrill badly wounded to die on the prairie. However, an Indian named Spiebuck rescued him and nursed him back to health. He then dedicated himself to avenging his brother's murder. In order to discover the slayers, he joined the jayhawkers. Whenever he found one of the guilty parties, he would kill him. The three men he led to Morgan Walker's were the last to be so punished.

The Missourians accepted this story, which Quantrill obviously based on various actual incidents and aspects of his life, and to this day many sincerely and firmly believe it to be true. As elaborated by John N. Edwards in his *Noted Guerrillas; or, The War of the Border*, it forms an integral part of the Quantrill legend, surrounding him with the romantic aura of the man driven by noble hatred to revenge unforgivable wrongs.*

* John N. Edwards was a Missouri journalist who during the Civil War served as a major in Jo Shelby's Confederate cavalry brigade and wrote Shelby's reports—undoubtedly the most flamboyant in military annals. At the end of the war he went with Shelby to Mexico, then returned to Missouri where he became editor of the Kansas City *Star*. In the midst of his newspaper work, and in between drunken sprees, he found time to write three books: *Shelby and His Men; or, The War in the West* (Cincinnati, Ohio, 1867); *Noted Guerrillas; or, The War of the Border* (St. Louis, Mo., 1877); and *Shelby's Expedition into Mexico*, published posthumously.

Noted Guerrillas was based in large part on stories told by members of Quantrill's band, including Frank and Jesse James. With such sources Edwards could have produced an authoritative, if not definitive, account of the guerrilla war in Missouri. But unfortunately he was extravagantly romantic in temperament, bitterly pro-Southern in outlook, and completely devoid of a sense of historical objectivity and integrity. Therefore he described the deeds of the Missouri guerrillas in a torrent of colorful prose in which the truth was all but drowned. Every one of his guerrillas is a Byronic hero; in every battle they slay their

Quantrill's treachery was undoubtedly designed to ingratiate himself with the Missourians. Probably its immediate cause was his outlawry in Kansas, which made continued operations there extremely hazardous. There is considerable evidence, however, to indicate that he had long contemplated such an act. According to later accounts by Dean and Stewart, he had urged making a raid on the Walker farm as early as the previous summer. Also there is the case of his betrayal of his own men during the foray into Missouri in November, and his subsequent collection of fees from the Missourians for locating their stolen stock. Finally, there is the fact that he began his freebooting career in company with Border Ruffians and by returning a Negro to slavery. Thus it would seem apparent that all along his basic predilections, to the extent he had any, were proslavery, and that there was a certain substratum of truth in his story to the Missourians that he joined the antislavery forces merely to cause them injury. Just as a jayhawker is best defined as a bandit with abolitionist leanings, Quantrill might be best described as a bandit with pro-Southern sympathies.

Why did he become a bandit? Some effort has already been made to answer this question. There can be, however, no definite explanation, unless of course we wish to accept the thesis of fundamental depravity advanced by Connelley in his *Quantrill and the Border Wars.* In general we can only point out that many other men besides Quantrill degenerated from respectability to criminality within a few years after coming West. The frontier everywhere, and nowhere more so than in Kansas, was a crucible which, if it often extracted the best from men, frequently revealed their baser metals as well. Or, in other words, the American West was not only a land of new beginnings; it was also one of bad endings.†

---

puerile Union foes in wholesale numbers; and they are almost always victorious, losing only to the most overwhelming odds. Actually Edwards probably did not intend to write history but rather to create a legend. If so, then he succeeded magnificently. There are few books on the Civil War more exciting than his—or less reliable.

† A striking case illustrating this point is that of C. B. Zulavsky. This young Hungarian was a nephew of Louis Kossuth and possessed an excellent education. He became the protégé of the wealthy Boston abolitionist George Luther Stearns and in 1861 went to Kansas to join the Union Army and fight against slavery. Shortly after his arrival he wrote Stearns a letter indignantly denouncing

More particularly, in Quantrill we have the rather common case of a young man whose ambitions outran his accomplishments; who desired wealth and success, but who was impatient and impotent in their quest; and who came to resent his failure and the world which caused it. Furthermore, it appears obvious that he deemed himself to belong to a superior order of being, above and immune to the laws which govern others. Yet, while contemptuous of the herd, he desired its applause. Thus the experience of failure could only fill him with bitterness and frustration, and make him desperately anxious to prove his superiority to himself and to the world.

We have described a paranoid. And paranoids make history—which is unfortunate for mankind. No human force matches the power generated by a man who feels himself to be great, but who is denied greatness; who regards himself as superior, but who is made to feel inferior; and who can never rest until his greatness and superiority are established for others to see and admire. This terrible force raged in Quantrill. The years of wandering and drifting, of ill-paid teaching and futile aspirations, gave it birth, and the turbulent Kansas-Missouri border inspired it to express itself in terms of robbery, treachery, and murder.

What did this man look like? How did he impress others?

Although in fact he was about five feet nine inches, thanks to high-heeled boots he stood close to six feet tall, and weighed approximately 160 to 170 pounds. His hair was blond and long exposure to the prairie sun had bronzed his naturally sallow complexion. He possessed a rather handsome face, with a Roman nose and thin, down-curling lips which suggested both cruelty and determination. But of all his features, the eyes were by far the most noticeable. They were of a strange gray-blue color, and the lids had a peculiar droop which gave him a somnolent, yet dangerous, appearance.

Holland Wheeler, the man to whom Nathan Stone revealed Charley Hart's true identity, became well acquainted with Quantrill, the two often sharing the same room at the Whitney House. In after years he remembered Quantrill as being "somewhat of a

---

the thievery of the Kansas jayhawkers. Then, a few months later, he was arrested and jailed at Lawrence, Kansas, for horse-stealing!

horseman" and a "fair shot," but generally speaking without any "particular talent or ability." Other persons who knew him during his Lawrence days described him as having been quiet, aloof, and secretive.[3]

He liked to gamble, was a moderate drinker, and had a pronounced but not abnormal interest in women. In a letter to his sister early in 1860 he stated that he "had seen a great many pretty girls" since leaving home and had had "considerable sport sometimes." While at Lawrence he squired several of the local girls and supposedly helped perpetuate the reputation of "Cuckold Tom" McGee. Also, following the Morgan Walker affair, he was seen sitting on a porch "sparking" a Missouri damsel. On one occasion, however, when out walking with a girl in Stanton, he pointed to a tree and said, "I could hang six men on that limb." The girl told her parents of this decidedly unromantic remark and they forbade her to have anything more to do with the strange young man from Ohio. Similar incidents, and a sinister quality about him, caused many others to shun him or regard him with suspicion. Even his occasional roommate, Wheeler, would place a pistol under the pillow before going to bed at night. Why, not even Wheeler himself could explain.

Quantrill's year of banditry in Kansas was his apprenticeship. During it he acquired many tricks of the trade which were to be extremely useful later on. Furthermore, he displayed a high degree of ruthlessness, boldness, cunning, and unscrupulousness, as well as a certain talent for personal leadership. But, all in all, those remarkable qualities which he subsequently manifested in Missouri did not reveal themselves, other than latently, in Kansas. At the close of 1860 he was essentially just another border outlaw, only perhaps somewhat more vicious, imaginative, and daring than the average.

Quantrill remained in the vicinity of Blue Springs throughout the winter of 1861, living off the hospitality of the still grateful Walkers and their neighbors. Late in March, however, he returned to Kansas to visit his old friend John Bennings at Stanton. This was an extremely hazardous venture which nearly ended in disaster. His part in the Walker raid had become known to the Kansans and they were on the lookout for him—especially Eli Snyder, who was anxious to avenge the murder of his fellow jayhawkers.

Snyder, who lived only a few miles from Stanton, soon learned that Quantrill was at Bennings'. Immediately he got together some of his men and went to the office of the Stanton justice of the peace. There he swore out a warrant for Quantrill's arrest on the general charge of horse-stealing. His hope was that Quantrill would resist arrest and thereby provide a legal cover for killing him. The justice, however, suspected Snyder's motives and so insisted that the local constable, E. B. Jurd, serve the warrant. Snyder grumblingly assented to this arrangement and Jurd swore in Snyder and his men as a posse.

The posse surrounded Bennings' cabin and Jurd called on Quantrill to surrender. Quantrill replied that Snyder, whom he quickly spotted, would kill him if he did, and that he preferred to die fighting. Jurd then promised him that he would be protected from harm, backing up the promise by deputizing a half-dozen more men, including some of Quantrill's friends. Thus assured of safety, Quantrill handed his revolver to Jurd.

On the way to the justice's office Snyder tried to provoke Quantrill into some act which could be used as an excuse for killing him. Failing in this effort, he started to shoot him anyway, but one of the posse knocked his gun aside just as he fired. This courageous and creditable action saved a man whose life was to mean death for hundreds.

At the justice's a hectic, confused scene took place. Snyder and his men constantly threatened the prisoner, and it was only with great difficulty that his appointed defenders prevented him from being shot. Once, in fact, he escaped only because a would-be slayer's gun misfired. Quite understandably he was "very pale and nervous."

Meanwhile one of Bennings' sons rode to Paola, the county seat, to get help for Quantrill. Paola was a proslavery center and Quantrill had numerous friends and sympathizers there, including Colonel Torrey, who was now operating a hotel. As soon as they learned of Quantrill's predicament sixteen men, all heavily armed, set out for Stanton on horseback and in wagons and buggies. Their arrival nearly touched off a pitched battle with Snyder's gang, but in the end the jayhawker captain backed off, while the justice agreed to commit the prisoner to the county jail at Paola for safekeeping. His rescuers then took Quantrill to Paola, where they lodged him in a cell and gave him a revolver and bowie knife in order that he might defend himself against lynchers.

Quantrill remained in the Paola jail several days. Then on April 3 he applied for a writ of habeas corpus on the grounds that his arrest was "malicious, false, and illegal." The county judge, although a Republican, found no just cause for holding him and accordingly ordered his release.

A group of friends jubilantly escorted him to Torrey's hotel, where the ladies hastily packed him a lunch of sandwiches and cake. As he stuffed the food into his pockets his friends advised him to stay in Missouri until there was no longer any danger in Kansas. This he agreed to do. He then went outside and mounted Black Bess, who was saddled and waiting for him. Just as he started to ride away, Snyder and his gang entered the town, bearing a warrant for his arrest issued by the Douglas County court in Lawrence. Quantrill leaned forward in his saddle and patted his buttocks in a "vulgar gesture" of contempt for Snyder. Then, waving a pistol over his head, he galloped off toward the border.

chapter II "Playing War Is Played Out"

A dozen grim-faced horsemen pound furiously through the night down a dirt road in western Missouri. They draw rein beside a fence gate, open it, and trot up the wagon path toward a small frame house. Inside the house a man and his wife are awakened by the clattering of hoofs. Shaking loose his wife's frantic grasp the man springs out of bed, takes a loaded shotgun from the wall, and goes into the front room. As he does so, a rock crashes through the window and a voice from outside shouts: "This is your last warning—clear out of the county by tomorrow night! We don't want no nigger-loving Black Republicans around here!"

There is then a flurry of yells and shots, followed by the sound of departing hoofbeats. The man stands silently in the room, shotgun in hand. He has recognized the threatening voice as that of a neighbor whom he has known for years, with whom he has hunted and fished, played poker and drunk whisky, laughed and joked. His wife comes to his side and they look at each other in mute despair. Then, without a word, they dress and begin to pack their belongings. By morning, in a wagon piled high with household goods and farming implements, and with the older children driving along a small herd of cattle, they are heading for Kansas and safety. Behind them they leave their crops, their fields, their home. . . .

Throughout West Missouri during the spring of 1861 scores of similar scenes were being enacted. Sometimes the victims defied their persecutors, often there was violence and bloodshed. But everywhere "Union men"—those who opposed secession or who were suspected of harboring antislavery views—were being, as one of them later described it, "outraged, proscribed, derided, persecuted and lastly hunted like wild beasts." [1] The worst and most vicious kind of civil war had broken out—neighbor against neighbor, friend against friend, even kin against kin.

Divided: that one word alone best describes Missouri early in 1861. Like the other border states, it was politically as well as geographically neither North nor South, but rather both. At one extreme stood the "Unconditional Unionists," a small but powerful minority. They insisted on full support of the Federal Government and declared that secession by Missouri would not only be illegal but disastrous. Their stronghold was St. Louis, with its large German population, and their leaders were Frank Blair, Jr., of the politically powerful Blair family, and Captain Nathaniel Lyon, the tough little red-bearded commander of the United States Army garrison in St. Louis. Blair organized the St. Louis Germans into Home Guard regiments, equipping them with army muskets furnished by Lyon.

At the other extreme were the Secessionists, men laboring either overtly or covertly to lead Missouri out of the Union and into the Confederacy. Their main support came from the hemp-growing, slaveowning planters of the Missouri River counties, and from the old Border Ruffian element along the Kansas border. Governor Claiborne Jackson, the former Border Ruffian captain, was their principal leader. As yet he did not openly favor secession, but instead maneuvered secretly to bring it about. When, following the bombardment of Fort Sumter on April 12, President Lincoln called on the states to furnish troops for suppressing the Southern rebellion, Jackson answered that Missouri would not provide a single man for so "wicked and diabolical" a purpose. Soon afterward, declaring his determination to resist any Federal invasion, he mobilized the State Guard.

The majority of Missourians fell somewhere in between the Unconditional Unionists and the Secessionists, and were commonly known as "Conditional Unionists." As a rule they were people who possessed strong sympathy for the South because of family and cultural ties, but who were also devoted to the Union and did not want to see it disrupted.[2] Generally, too, they were Douglas Democrats who blamed both the Northern Republicans and the Southern fire-eaters for bringing on the war. In particular they condemned the abolitionists as the source of all the nation's woes. Many of them in fact were slaveowners and for this very reason opposed secession. As their spokesmen pointed out, "So long as we remain loyal, the General Government is bound by every motive and obligation, not only to respect, but to maintain and defend our slave property." Secession, on the other hand, would merely "bring the Canada line down to our borders," and leave Missouri exposed to the "murderers and bandits of Lane and Montgomery." [3]

The Conditional Unionists hoped against hope that Missouri could follow a "neutral" course between North and South. In this way the dangers of secession would be avoided, yet they would be spared the odious necessity of fighting against their Southern brethren. But if there are any absolute laws in history, one of them must be that any group which tries to take the middle road in time of revolution—and the American Civil War was a revolution—is almost certainly doomed to failure and tragedy. And such was to be the fate of the Missouri Conditional Unionists. Constantly and with ever-mounting impatience the Unconditional Unionists and the Secessionists demanded that they take a definite stand, one way or another. And at the same time the even greater pressure of events made such a decision increasingly difficult to evade or postpone.

Most of the State Guards called out by Governor Jackson concentrated on the outskirts of St. Louis at "Camp Jackson." From the first Blair and Lyon regarded these troops as a serious menace to the Union cause in the city. Their fears increased as they learned that the company streets in the camp bore such names as "Beauregard" and "Davis," and that the State Guards were receiving military equipment from the Confederacy. Finally, feeling that to do otherwise would be to invite disaster, the two Union leaders decided to break up the encampment.

On the morning of May 10 Lyon marched forth at the head of four regiments of German Home Guards and a battalion of regulars. After surrounding the camp he called on the State Guards to surrender. Much to everybody's surprise, and to the consternation of St. Louis Secessionists, they did so with scarcely a protest. But as Lyon's troops escorted the prisoners into the city, a large mob gathered along the sidewalks shouting: "Damn the Dutch!" and "Hurray for Jeff Davis!" These yells were soon followed by a shower of clods and stones. Then someone shot and wounded a Home Guard officer. Another officer thereupon ordered his men to open fire. A fusillade of musket balls swept the streets, scattering the mob in panic-stricken flight. When it was all over, twenty-eight persons, including a small child, lay dead along the walks and curbs.

News of the "Camp Jackson Massacre" set Missouri afire with excitement and brought on a strong reaction in favor of the Secessionists. All except the Unconditional Unionists roundly condemned Blair and Lyon, and many Conditional Unionists now sided with the pro-Confederates, among them ex-Governor Sterling Price, a former Mexican War general and the most popular man in the state. Jackson at once appointed Price commander of the Missouri State Guard. At the same time an infuriated legislature in Jefferson City, its members wearing revolvers and bowie knives, hastily enacted a Military Bill placing the state on a war footing.[4] Everywhere, and especially in North and West Missouri, recruits flocked to the State Guard camps, where, significantly, they took an oath to uphold the Missouri Constitution but not the Federal. Also, newspapers began featuring advertisements of "military meetings" and special sales of powder, lead, caps, rifles, and shotguns.[5]

Major General William S. Harney, the elderly and conservative commander of United States troops in the West, considered the capture of Camp Jackson rash and unnecessary. In his opinion a policy of tactful but firm pressure would be best calculated to keep Missouri in the Union. Therefore he moved to head off a major clash between the Federal and state forces. On May 21, after several days of negotiation, he made an agreement with Price under which the State Guards would be disbanded in return for the Federal Government's recognizing the neutrality of Missouri.

Missourians generally applauded the agreement as meaning peace for their state. Lyon and Blair, however, suspected Harney's loyalty and believed that he was playing into rebel hands. They communicated their fears to Lincoln, who responded by secretly sending Blair an order dismissing Harney and placing Lyon in command of Missouri with the rank of brigadier general. Blair withheld the order until May 30, then delivered it when Harney started to remove the German regiments from St. Louis.

Matters now rapidly came to a climax. On June 11, in a room at the Planters House Hotel in St. Louis, Jackson and Price met in an eleventh-hour conference with the two Union leaders. Jackson demanded that the Home Guard regiments disband and that all United States troops in Missouri pull out immediately. Blair insisted that the State Guards be sent home and that Missouri co-operate with the Federal Government in suppressing the rebellion. Neither side conceded a point to the other, neither side really desired a compromise. The meeting came to an abrupt and dramatic end when Lyon stood up, shouted, "This means war!" and strode out of the room, his saber clanking.

Jackson, Price, and their staffs hastened back to Jefferson City, stopping only to cut telegraph wires and burn railroad bridges. On arriving in the capital Jackson wrote a florid proclamation calling for fifty thousand volunteers to resist the "Northern invasion." For the time being, however, Price's forces were too weak to stand against Lyon's pursuing column. Consequently, accompanied by Jackson and the legislature, they retreated to the southwest corner of the state below Springfield. There they obtained the support of the Confederate Army in Arkansas, and began preparing for a counterattack.[6]

Full-fledged civil war was now under way in Missouri. In many sections neighborhood gangs of Unionists and Secessionists battled viciously for local supremacy. Brawls, brutal whippings, shootings, and lynchings became common daily occurrences. The civil authorities were either powerless or afraid to intervene, and when they did it was usually to aid one side against the other. Generally speaking, the Secessionists prevailed throughout the northwestern part of the state and especially in the Missouri River counties west of Jefferson City. Thus, at St. Joseph, the city council passed an ordinance making it illegal to fly the United States flag.[7]

An unusually tense and complex situation existed in Jackson County. Here the Unionists were concentrated in Kansas City, where the population was predominantly of Northern origin and where there was even a sizable Republican Party. The Secessionists, on the other hand, controlled the hinterlands, being particularly strong around such communities as Hickman Mills, Lee's Summit, Westport, Independence, Blue Springs, and Liberty, over in Clay County. Earlier in the year they had even raided the United States arsenal at Liberty, taking a large quantity of small arms and several cannons. Many of them were former Border Ruffians.

In the beginning these "prairie wolves," as they were called by the Kansas City Unionists, had things pretty much their own way. Thus on April 30 a large number of them, heavily armed and full of "bust-head whisky," marched into Kansas City carrying a rebel banner and accompanied by a brass band playing Southern songs. They proceeded to beat up a Union man, shoot a German, demolish a saloon, and raise a large Secessionist flag in the square. Then their leaders made inflammatory speeches condemning the "Black Republicans" and warning them to get out of town.

These threats, and the apparent helplessness of the Union faction in face of them, caused a number of Republicans to seek refuge in Kansas. Those who remained soon received letters, signed by "The Committee of Fifteen," warning them to leave Missouri within ten days. Appeals for police protection were worse than useless, since the police commissioner was a rabid Secessionist, as were most of his force.

Just as it seemed that the Secessionists were about to triumph by sheer terrorism, the situation suddenly and dramatically reversed itself. Mayor R. T. Van Horn, a staunch Unionist and a leading businessman, went to St. Louis and asked Lyon to send Federal troops to Kansas City and authorize the recruitment of a battalion of Home Guards. Lyon promptly agreed to both requests.

On June 11 (the day of the Planter House conference) five companies of regular cavalry and infantry from Fort Leavenworth, under the command of Captain William Prince, marched into Kansas City, where they were greeted by the enthusiastic cheers of the majority of the townspeople. Prince established a post on the outskirts of the town called Camp Union and immediately set about mustering in Home Guard companies. Kansas City Unionists ceased fleeing and now began persecuting the dismayed Secessionists, who in their turn resorted to flight.[8]

The "prairie wolves" set up a howl over the "illegal invasion" of the "Black Dutch, their beards foaming with lager beer, and reeking with the fumes of sauercrout [*sic*]." On orders from Governor Jackson, a large force of State Guards gathered at Independence for the announced purpose of defending their "sacred hearths against the mercenary hirelings of Lincoln." Several companies from Clay County crossed the river to help them.[9]

Prince heard of this concentration and sent Captain John Stanley with a cavalry detachment to look into the matter. He instructed Stanley to persuade the Missourians that neither they nor their property were in danger, and that they should disband peacefully. In particular he cautioned Stanley not to fight, but to withdraw immediately to Kansas City if attacked.

Stanley marched out from Kansas City on the morning of June 13. Several miles west of Independence he encountered about two hundred State Guards drawn up in line of battle. He halted his command and asked the leader of the Missourians, Captain Holloway, what were their intentions. Holloway, however, refused to give a direct reply. As they talked, Stanley noticed signs of hostility among the Secessionists. Remembering his instructions to avoid a fight, he ordered a retreat. But before the order could be executed, Holloway's men, mistaking the movement, opened fire. Instinctively the troopers replied. A brief general engagement ensued, during which the Missourians employed the cannons taken from the Liberty arsenal. In the end Stanley broke off the battle and fell back to Kansas City. Two soldiers were slightly wounded and three State Guardsmen, including Holloway, were killed.* Obviously neither side had their blood up. But this was merely the beginning. In the future there would not be so much restraint.[10]

The outbreak of civil war in Missouri gave the Kansas jayhawkers the chance of their lifetime. Not only would the divided and strife-torn Missourians be unable to offer them any effective resistance, but they would now be able to steal horses, plunder farms, and liberate slaves in the name of the Union and under the guise of suppressing rebellion. Soon Jennison, Montgomery, Stewart, Snyder, Marshall Cleveland, H. H. Williams, and a host of

* According to John McCorkle, *Three Years With Quantrill* (Armstrong, Mo., 1910; reprint, University of Oklahoma Press, 1992), p. 7, Holloway was killed by the fire of his own men. McCorkle was present at the skirmish, a member of a State Guard company.

petty jayhawkers were busy "playing hell" along the border. Indeed, Jennison even accompanied Prince's force on its march to Kansas City!

Most of Kansas applauded the jayhawkers. Their raids, they felt, were "well-calculated to quell the rebellious dispositions of our evil-disposed neighbors in Missouri." The numerous Missouri Unionist refugees who continued to stream into Kansas also encouraged jayhawking. They told heart-rending stories of outrage and suffering, and begged the Kansans "on bended knees" to help them recover their plundered property and secure revenge against their persecutors. Some of them even joined jayhawkers or formed raiding gangs of their own.[11]

Early in July the Federal troops began extending their control throughout West Missouri. As part of this movement the Fifth United States Reserve Regiment left Kansas City on the ninth and proceeded by steamboat down the Missouri River to Lexington. Along the way it occupied various towns, seized rebel supplies, and broke up several Secessionist camps. At Lexington it erected fortifications around the Masonic College. From there it made a number of expeditions into the country for the purpose of rounding up hidden stores of guns and powder. Small bands of guerrillas attacked the Federal search parties and even made several futile attempts to capture or burn the steamboats. A Union officer reported that "the most vindictive feeling exists towards our men," especially among the women. Hundreds of Union adherents were fleeing the region, and those who remained stated that if the troops pulled out their lives would not be "worth an hour's purchase." [12]

Despite this and other Union expeditions the Secessionists remained strong and active throughout West Missouri. In fact, if anything their strength and activity increased. The entry of Federal troops into the state turned large numbers of pro-Southern Conditional Unionists into out-and-out Secessionists. Persecution of Unionists was rampant and guerrilla attacks on Union troops and supply lines increased. Late in August the Kansas City *Journal* reported that there was an "organized force of 1,000 rebels" in Jackson County alone.[13]

Probably the worst conditions, from a Union standpoint, reigned in North Missouri. The Federal commander of that district, Brigadier General John Pope, declared the "whole country in commotion, bridges and railroad tracks destroyed, or in danger of being so, and the entire population in a state of excitement and apprehension." Pope blamed this tumultuous situation on small bands of roving guerrillas and declared that it was virtually impossible to suppress them. Whenever troops were sent against them, they merely returned to their normal occupations, with the result that the soldiers "found only men quietly working in the field or sitting in their offices." No one except Secessionists was safe from outrage and persecution, and the Union men were either "too timid or too few" to offer the "least resistance." [14]

Meanwhile Price, following his retreat into Southwest Missouri, organized the State Guard into the semblance of an army. Then, early in August, he moved northward against Springfield in conjunction with a regular Confederate force from Arkansas. Lyon, although heavily outnumbered, decided not to wait for Price. Instead he launched, early on the morning of August 10, a hard-hitting surprise attack at Wilson's Creek south of Springfield.

The thrust nearly defeated the Confederates, but Lyon lacked the strength to carry it through to complete success. Price quickly rallied his followers, and the two armies settled down to a savage slugging match amidst the hills and thickets of Wilson's Creek. The farm boys and raw recruits who composed the majority of troops on both sides fought like veterans as hundreds died in the bloodiest battle so far of the war. Finally Price's superior numbers began to tell. Lyon fell dead leading a desperate counterattack, and with their great leader gone the Union troops streamed off the field in full retreat. The exhausted and badly battered victors made no attempt to pursue. It was, they readily admitted, a "might mean-fowt fight." [15]

Wilson's Creek produced the supreme crisis of the war in Missouri. All the western part of the state lay open to Price's army. Thousands of exulting Secessionists eagerly awaited his northward march. They were all confident that complete triumph was at hand. As for the Unionists, they were gripped by alarm and filled with foreboding. Frantically they labored to shore up their crumbling defenses, desperately they strove to prevent a mass uprising of Southern sympathizers. Both sides knew that the coming weeks were likely to prove decisive.

Nearly three weeks elapsed, however, before Price's army recovered sufficiently from its victory to resume its advance. Then, just as it began moving, Price received word that "marauding and murdering bands" of jayhawkers from Fort Scott were infesting western Missouri. Therefore he decided to make a detour and "chastise" the Kansans before going on after bigger game.

The commander of the Union troops at Fort Scott was none other than Jim Lane, who had chosen this propitious moment to reappear on the border. The "Grim Chieftain" was now a United States Senator and Republican political boss of Kansas. His forces, which he called the "Kansas Brigade," consisted of some twelve hundred badly organized, poorly equipped, and totally undisciplined cavalry and infantry. No less a personage than Montgomery was second-in-command, and the jayhawker gangs of Jennison and Stewart were on hand as auxiliaries. Lane openly proclaimed that he intended to march his "army" into Missouri, "and when I do so, I'll not object to seeing an army of slaves marching out."

But when Lane learned that Price was moving on Fort Scott he hastily evacuated the town and retreated to Fort Lincoln. Near there, on September 2, at a place called Drywood Creek, a portion of his brigade encountered Price's advance guard. In the skirmish which followed there was "much shooting and little execution on both sides." The Kansans finally gave way but Price did not pursue. He threatened, however, to "lay waste the farms and utterly destroy the cities and villages" of Kansas unless the jayhawkers stayed out of Missouri.

Price's army resumed its northward march, heading for Lexington. Hundreds of eager recruits flocked to its banners. At Lexington it besieged Colonel James Mulligan's Chicago Irish regiment in the fortifications about the Masonic College. Fierce, no-quarter fighting raged for the possession of strategic points. The Missourians cut the garrison off from its water supply, but still it held out, hopeful that a relief column would come in time. Then one of Price's officers got an idea. Why not use hemp bales as a moving barricade behind which to advance in safety on the fort? The stratagem worked—bullets failed to penetrate the bales, cannon balls merely caused them to teeter back and forth. Slowly but inexorably the Missourians closed their "hemp noose" about the Masonic College. At last the garrison realized that further resistance was as futile as it would be fatal, and so struck its flag. Price gallantly declined the proffered sword of the courageous Mulligan and soon paroled all the Union prisoners. The Secessionist cause in Missouri reached its zenith.[16]

Meanwhile Lane cowered behind the breastworks of Fort Lincoln until he was sure that Price had moved on northward. Then, instead of pursuing, he sent Jennison on a raid against Papinsville, Missouri. Jennison returned with two hundred cattle and a number of "contrabands," current slang for liberated slaves.[17]

This foray was a mere warm-up for what was to come. On September 12, with his "smart little army," Lane crossed into Missouri. Immediately his followers went on a gigantic spree of arson and looting. "Everything disloyal," their leader cried, "from a Durham cow to a Shanghai chicken must be cleaned out!" Soon the invading column, as it wended its way through the Osage Valley, was literally staggering with the weight of its accumulated plunder.

Near Morristown the Kansas Brigade clashed with a small detachment of State Guards. It drove the Missourians away and took several prisoners, who were promptly sentenced to death by a drumhead court martial. The condemned men were made to dig their own graves, then shot and hastily covered up. The executions were in retaliation for the murder of seven Kansans a few days previously by guerrillas. But even to one of Lane's own followers they were "sickening evidence that we were fighting under the black flag."

Lane's march reached its climax at Osceola on September 23. Not only did his men rob the banks, pillage the stores, and loot the houses, but they even took the county records from the courthouse! Many of them got so drunk that they could not march but had to be placed in wagons and carriages. Before leaving they set the town afire, almost completely destroying it. Their spoils were immense, including as Lane's personal share a piano and a quantity of silk dresses. The former he subsequently placed in the parlor of his home in Lawrence. The latter he eventually distributed among certain female friends.

Lane's "self-sustaining army" next swung northward and on September 29 it reeled into Kansas City. Observers there described it as "a ragged, half-armed, diseased, mutinous rabble, taking votes whether any troublesome or distasteful orders should be obeyed or defied." Whites, Indians, and even Negroes mingled in its ranks. All boasted of their plundering and offered various items of loot, varying from napkin rings to horses, for sale. Lane brazenly defended the conduct of his brigade: "When you march through a State you must destroy the property of the men in arms against the Government—destroy, devastate, desolate. This is war." [18]

The Union generals fully expected Price to follow up his success at Lexington by further thrusts. General John C. Frémont, Federal commander in the West, even ordered the troops at Kansas City to retreat to Fort Leavenworth. But Price lacked adequate provisions and equipment to sustain his offensive. Moreover, although many youths joined his army, their number was far from being as great as he had expected, and many of them soon left in disgust on finding that no arms were available. Consequently Price began withdrawing southward again. Thus his invasion became nothing more than a raid, and the high hopes of the Missouri Secessionists zoomed downward, never again to ride so high. Frémont, who at first refused to believe that Price was retreating, began a ponderous and super-cautious pursuit.

The Kansas Brigade joined Frémont's army as it advanced on Springfield. Once more Lane's rapscallion followers distinguished themselves by large-scale plundering and small-scale pilfering. "Our trail through Missouri," boasted one of them, "was marked by the feathers of 'secesh' poultry and the debris of disloyal bee-gums."

Frémont, despite overwhelmingly superior numbers, failed to overhaul Price or to defeat him in battle. In addition, his whole military administration threatened to collapse from sheer incompetence and corruption. Lincoln finally could stand it no longer. On November 2 he ordered Major General David Hunter to relieve Frémont. Hunter abandoned the bootless pursuit of Price and dispersed the Union Army into winter quarters. The Kansas Brigade returned to Fort Scott, accompanied by a "Black Brigade" of six hundred Negroes collected in the Springfield region.[19]

The march of the Kansas Brigade, and especially the wanton destruction of Osceola, caused Missourians to boil over with wrath and resentment, and turned many Conditional Unionists into Confederate adherents. In fact, according to the conservative St. Louis *Republican*, "The presence of Lane, and the atrocities he and his troops have committed, have contributed more to make secessionists out of loyal citizens than almost all other causes combined.[20]

Jennison did not accompany Lane to Springfield. Instead he remained behind to take command of his own regiment, "The Independent Mounted Kansas Jayhawkers," or as it was officially designated, the Seventh Kansas Cavalry. His second-in-command was Daniel R. Anthony, publisher of the Leavenworth *Daily Conservative*. Anthony, a brother of Susan B., was a hot-headed abolitionist and his paper, despite its name, was the most radical publication in Kansas. He, rather than the semiliterate Jennison, was to exercise actual control of the Seventh Kansas during most of its subsequent operations.

The regiment contained a large number of Missouri Unionist refugees burning for revenge against their erstwhile neighbors. It included also a company of fanatical Ohio abolitionists headed by none other than John Brown, Jr., the slightly insane son of the hero of Harpers Ferry. Additional seasoning for this already potent mixture was provided by Company H, an outfit composed entirely of border bandits, ex-convicts, and jayhawkers!

The Seventh was not ready for field service until the first week of November. Until then it prepared for future action by sacking the saloons of Leavenworth and raiding Parkville, Missouri, in steamboats. But as soon as it was mustered the Federal commander at Fort Leavenworth ordered it to West Missouri for the purpose of protecting Union supply trains against guerrilla attacks, which were becoming increasingly irksome.

On November 12, led by Anthony, the jayhawker regiment entered Kansas City, where it marched through the streets "in silent pageantry, such as usually marks a funeral procession." The following day it moved out in the direction of Independence, Company H in advance. Soon farmhouses, barns, and wheatfields for miles on either side of its line of march were in flames. Hundreds of panic-stricken Missourians fled for safety into the woods.

Near Independence, on the banks of the Little Blue, a force of about 150 irregulars under the "notorious" guerrilla leader, Upton Hayes, made a stand against Anthony's column. For an hour a hot fight raged. Both sides lost over a dozen men killed and many more wounded. But the Kansans, although they captured Hayes' camp and most of his supplies, were unable to dislodge the Missourians from their strong position. In the end they fell back to the outskirts of Kansas City.

A few days later lack of food forced Hayes to retreat. Anthony promptly moved out again and occupied Independence without resistance. Here he was joined by Jennison, who made his only appearance of the campaign. It was, however, a memorable one.

First Jennison herded every white male in the town into the public square. Then he rounded up all the Negroes, dressed them in Federal uniforms, placed them under a colored officer, and had them march in military formation around the captive whites. Next he read a proclamation addressed to people of western Missouri which had been written for him by Richard Josiah Hinton, a radical abolitionist reporter from the Leavenworth *Conservative*. The proclamation stated that the Seventh Kansas was in Missouri to throw a "shield of protection and defense around all men who are loyal." It would not commit "excesses," but "every man who feeds, harbors, protects or in any way gives aid and comfort to the enemies of the Union will be held responsible for his treason with life and property.

"For," concluded the proclamation ominously, "playing war is played out."

As if to underscore this last statement, Jennison's men burned the house of an alleged Secessionist, plundered several stores, and took all the "useful" horses they could locate. They then marched back to Kansas City, first warning the townspeople not to touch the United States flag they had nailed to a pole in the square. But no sooner were they gone than the citizens tore the pole down and trampled the flag in the dirt. It would take much more than flamboyant proclamations and insulting demonstrations to scare free-born Missourians!

Early in December Price threatened another advance to the Missouri River. In order to help guard against this possibility the Seventh Kansas moved to West Point, Missouri. Again, as it marched, it cut a swathe of devastation. "Every house along our line of march but one was burned," recorded a soldier in John Brown, Jr.'s company, "and off on our left flank for miles, columns of smoke from burning houses and barns could be seen." Its route, wrote the noted Kansas City artist George Caleb Bingham to a friend, could be "traced by the ruins of the dwellings of our citizens, which being mainly of wood, are now but heaps of ashes, above which the tall chimneys remain in their mute solitude."

Price did not make his anticipated move, but the Seventh remained in the vicinity of West Point and Morristown until early January. Just prior to Christmas, Anthony took 250 men on a sweep through central Jackson County. This expedition netted 150 mules, 40 horses, and 129 Negroes. The latter he placed in wagons and carriages, which were "all loaded down with Household furniters [*sic*]," and sent in a fantastic caravan over a mile long into Kansas. "In our march," he wrote Sister Susan, "we free every slave . . . and arm or use them in such manner as will best aid us in putting down the rebels. We hope to stir up an insurrection among the negroes."

Anthony celebrated New Year's Day by burning Dayton, Missouri. Then, a week later, he put the little village of Columbus to the torch. General Hunter read his report of these deeds with surprise. It contained no evidence, Hunter wrote him, "of a state of facts sufficient to warrant these extreme measures."

Major General Henry W. Halleck, who replaced Hunter as commander of the Department of the West, shared his predecessor's sentiments. "A few more such raids," he declared, "will make Missouri as Confederate as Eastern Virginia." Accordingly he threatened to drive Jennison's jayhawkers out of Missouri unless they returned immediately to Kansas, and "to disarm and hold them prisoners" if they refused to leave.

Faced with this ultimatum the Seventh quickly pulled back into Kansas. But despite bitter denunciations of their activities in the Missouri press, both Jennison and Anthony went unpunished. The same was true of Lane. When Halleck wrote Lincoln a letter criticizing the Kansas Senator, Lincoln merely wrote on the margin, "I am sorry that General Halleck is so unfavorably impressed with General Lane."

Kansans, with few exceptions, hailed Lane, Jennison, and Anthony as heroes and saviors. To their way of thinking the jayhawkers were merely paying the Missourians back in their own coin—although perhaps with just a little interest. Moreover, they were suppressing rebels, protecting Kansas from the Border Ruffians and guerrillas, and striking mighty blows against slavery. "Jayhawking," wrote one Kansas editor, "works well; we believe in it, we are going to have it." [21]

The citizens of the Sunflower State, however, were badly mistaken in thinking that jayhawking intimidated the "secesh" or doused the flames of rebellion in West Missouri. Actually its effect was quite the reverse. This fact can be demonstrated as well as illustrated by the case of Upton Hayes, leader of the guerrillas encountered by Anthony on the Little Blue. At the beginning of the war Hayes was operating a freighting business out of Little Santa Fe. Although not a Unionist, neither was he a Secessionist. Rather he hoped to remain neutral and so took no part in political or military affairs. Then a gang of jayhawkers captured one of his wagon trains, burned his house, and made off with his horses, cattle, carriages, and slaves. It is no wonder that he thereupon turned guerrilla.[22]

Many other Missourians did the same thing for identical causes. Theirs was the natural and inevitable reaction of a proud and militant people to the depredations and outrages of the jayhawkers. Through guerrilla warfare, and through it alone, they felt, could they protect themselves against future wrongs and secure revenge for past sufferings.

Jayhawking, however, was not the sole cause of guerrilla war in Missouri; in fact, it perhaps was not even the main cause. For instance, there were no jayhawking raids into northern or southeastern Missouri, yet both regions were scenes of heavy partisan activity throughout the war. At least as important as jayhawking in bringing about guerrilla warfare was the fierce hostility existing between Missouri Unionists and Missouri Secessionists. The Secessionists, wherever they held the upper hand, formed guerrilla bands to terrorize and drive away their Unionist neighbors. On the other hand, if they were subject to Unionist domination and persecution, they likewise "took to the bush" in order to protect themselves and retaliate against their oppressors. In either case the result was the same: bitterness, strife, chaos, and desolation. By the end of the war there was to be far more killing of Missourians by Missourians than by Kansans.

The outbreak of guerrilla warfare in Missouri was not an isolated or exceptional phenomenon. Partisans sprang into existence in all the Southern border states, from North Virginia where the "gray ghosts" of Mosby rode, through Kentucky and Tennessee and down into Arkansas, Louisiana, and Texas. In fact, they eventually were to be found in every region of the South where large numbers of people, as in Missouri, refused to accept Union rule and struggled against military occupation. One would think that they were a definite and important factor in the over-all course and conduct of the war. However, contrary to what Virgil Carrington Jones had claimed, they never became an important factor in the overall conduct of the war.[23] Most of the Union troops employed against them were local militia or low-quality regulars, and their raids had little or no impact on the operations of the main armies. When, at the end of the war, Confederate President Jefferson Davis, in a last desperate effort to maintain the struggle for Southern independence, proposed ordering Lee and Joseph Johnston to lead their armies into the mountains for the purpose of waging a large-scale guerrilla campaign, his cabinet unanimously and rightly replied that this was an impracticable strategy that would merely prolong the South's agony.

The main immediate effect of the jayhawker raids was to increase the hatred of Missourians for Kansans and instill in them a passionate desire for vengeance. On October 14 three hundred mounted Missouri State Guards crossed the border and burned every building and house in Humboldt, Kansas. Later that month Sheriff Clem's band from Cass County dashed through the Mound City region, killing three settlers and pillaging several stores. In December he returned to gut the little town of Potosi. The people of Kansas in their turn howled about "atrocities" and screamed for "reprisals." [24]

By the winter of 1861-62 partisan warfare was rife along the border. Efforts by the Union military authorities to suppress the "bushwhackers," as the guerrillas became commonly known, achieved little or no success. Instead, as the weeks went by, reports of scouting parties being ambushed, of wagon trains being plundered, and of Union adherents being killed or forced to flee became ever more frequent. Finally, out of sheer exasperation,

General Halleck on December 22 issued a general order outlawing all guerrillas and irregulars. Such men, he declared, were to be "immediately shot" whenever captured.[25]

Halleck's order formed the basis of Union policy toward bushwhackers in Missouri during the remainder of the war. In large measure it was a natural, even inevitable, reaction on the part of the Federal commander. No form of fighting is more aggravating than guerrilla war, especially to the professional soldier, who tends to regard it as an illegitimate violation of the "rules of the game." Also, as Halleck himself correctly pointed out in issuing the order, the death penalty for partisans had the legal sanction of many centuries of military precedent.

Nevertheless, by thus outlawing the Missouri guerrillas, Halleck in effect, insofar as the bushwhackers were concerned, raised the black flag. Their response to his order also was natural and inevitable: if the Federals were going to show no quarter, then they would receive none themselves. Let it be a fight to the finish.

Jennison had been right. Playing war was indeed played out.

chapter III **First Blood**

Quantrill, following his narrow escape from Snyder's gang, returned to the Blue Springs neighborhood. Kansas was now closed to him and he had no alternative but to exist on the hospitality of the still grateful Missourians. It is interesting to speculate what his eventual course in life might have been had not, as for so many men of his generation, the coming of the Civil War determined his destiny.

Most of the time he stayed at the house of Mark Gill, one of Morgan Walker's neighbors. He also had an affair with Walker's daughter, Anna, a young woman described as having possessed sensual beauty and easy morals. She previously had been married to a Blue Springs merchant named Slaughter, who had divorced her after finding her in bed with a local physician. In subsequent years she was to become the mistress of George Todd, Quantrill's chief lieutenant, then to marry Joe Vaughn, another guerrilla leader, and finally, at the end of the war, to open a brothel at Baxter Springs, Kansas.

Late in the spring Gill, as did many other prudent Missouri planters at the time, took his slaves down to Texas, where they would be safe from jayhawkers. Quantrill, perhaps for want of anything better to do, accompanied Gill on this expedition. Then, after a brief stay in Texas, he went to the Indian Territory, where he lived with Joel Mayes, a half-breed Cherokee chieftain who was captain of a company of Confederate cavalry. Quantrill fought with this company at the Battle of Wilson's Creek, after which he joined Price's army as a cavalry private and served at Drywood Creek and the siege of Lexington. According to a highly imaginative account by Edwards, he displayed conspicuous daring at Lexington, where mounted on a splendid horse, armed with a Sharps carbine and four revolvers, and wearing a red shirt and a sweeping black plume, "he advanced with the farthest, fell back with the last, and was always cool, deadly, and omnipresent." However, when Price retreated southward, he deserted and returned to the Blue Springs region, arriving there about the first of October.[1]

Conditions around Blue Springs were peaceful. So far there had been no jayhawking incursions, and neither was there any bushwhacking. The people, although strongly pro-Southern, had no desire to get mixed up in the war. Only a few of the younger men had gone off to join Price's army.

All this, however, was soon to change.

Shortly after Quantrill's return, a band of Kansas jayhawkers appeared a few miles north of Blue Springs and began pillaging the farmhouses. Quantrill brought word of the raid to Morgan Walker's, then joined eleven others under the leadership of Andrew Walker, in pursuit of the Kansans. Walker's party tracked them to the Strawder Stone farm, which had been plundered and set afire. Mrs. Stone ran up to them and showed where one of the jayhawkers had struck her on the head with a pistol. Now thoroughly enraged, they continued on rapidly to the Billy Thompson farm one-half mile beyond. Here they came upon the marauders just as they were leaving the burning house and were preparing to mount their horses. Walker and his men charged immediately, opening fire as they did so. Their bullets killed the man who had hit Mrs. Stone, but the rest of the Kansans escaped into Independence.

The next day the marshal at Independence arrested Strawder Stone and Billy Thompson for the murder of Mrs. Stone's assailant. Quantrill thereupon went to Independence and swore out an affidavit before the justice of the peace in which he assumed full responsibility for the shooting, at the same time describing the circumstances. His statement apparently satisfied the authorities, for they released Stone and Thompson and made no charges against him. The Unionist militia at Independence, however, threatened to "get him," and he was forced to go into hiding.

During the following weeks Andy Walker and his impromptu

posse continued to patrol the countryside on the outlook for new jayhawker raids. But after a while Walker, at the insistence of his father, returned to his normal occupations, as did several of the other men. Quantrill then took command of those who remained, and thus in this informal and unsensational way the organization that soon was to be famous as "Quantrill's guerrilla band" came into being.[2]

Quantrill's becoming leader was only natural. To begin with, he was an accomplished horseman and a good shot—the two skills most prized along the frontier—and in addition he was, so to speak, an expert in irregular warfare by virtue of his experience in Kansas. Furthermore, he had participated in Johnston's Utah expedition and had served in Price's army, and so had a certain knowledge of military organization and tactics. Finally, although an outsider, he had gained the confidence, sympathy, and perhaps even the admiration of the people around Blue Springs by the false story he told them in order to explain his part in the Morgan Walker affair, and by his action in exonerating Thompson and Stone. All of these factors, plus his superior education, obvious intelligence, and winning personality, made him a logical choice for the commander and, as time was to show, an excellent one as well.

We can easily imagine that Quantrill received enormous personal satisfaction out of becoming the leader. Here at last was recognition and power, and a chance to achieve even more.

The original members of Quantrill's gang were Bill Hallar, Jim and John Little, Ed and John Koger, Harrison Trace, Joe Gilchrist, Bill Gregg, Joe Vaughn, and George Todd. Others of note who joined in the early days and were counted among the "old men" were Ol Shepherd, George Maddox, Perry Hoy, and Fletch Taylor. Insofar as can be determined they were all Jackson County farm boys, mainly from around Blue Springs and Independence, with the exception of Todd. According to the scant and contradictory information on Todd's prewar career, he was a native of Canada and did not come to Missouri until 1859. When the war broke out he was working as a stone mason in Kansas City. Although one authority states that he joined Quantrill after getting in trouble with the law at Independence, people who knew him in Kansas City were at a loss to explain why he turned guerrilla. Only twenty years old in 1861, he was a ruggedly handsome blond, had cold blue eyes, was illiterate, hot-tempered, callously brutal, a deadly shot, and absolutely fearless. Quickly he became Quantrill's right-hand man; eventually he supplanted him as leader.[3]

Quantrill's closest friend in the band was Jim Little, who in turn was devoted to Quantrill. If at all possible, Little would fight by Quantrill's side and never permit him to go into a "tight spot" alone.[4] Hallar and Gregg, along with Todd, became Quantrill's chief lieutenants. The former, however, was killed in late 1862, and Gregg joined the regular Confederate Army early in 1864. Long after the war Gregg, by then a deputy sheriff in Jackson County, wrote a detailed account of Quantrill's band which is one of the best sources on its operations through 1863, despite a tendency on the part of the author to magnify his own role.

Shortly before Christmas, right after Quantrill assumed command, a deserter from Price's army named George Searcy robbed several people near Blue Springs and also tried to bushwhack Quantrill. Quantrill's band tracked him down, hung him in the timber along the Little Blue, and returned the horses, mules, and other property he had stolen to their rightful owners, some of whom were Union men. This was the opening episode in the history of Quantrill's bushwhackers, and strangely enough it involved action against an ex-Confederate.

A few days later Quantrill and his men had their first clash with Union troops. At Manasseth Gap near the Little Blue they ambushed a Federal patrol on the road to Independence. They wounded several of the soldiers and forced them all to surrender. Quantrill relieved the prisoners of their arms and ammunition, then paroled them.[5]

On Christmas day Quantrill temporarily disbanded his company because of the cold weather. Most of the men returned to their homes or established camps in the bush. Quantrill made no effort to combat Anthony's depredations, which were then at their height in Jackson County. Indeed, a jayhawker detachment nearly captured Gregg, Hallar, and another bushwhacker in a farmhouse where they were staying. The three, however, shot their way out, accompanied by an unarmed civilian named Barnhill, who promptly joined up with Quantrill.[6]

In January a man named Riley Alley announced that he was going to hold a ball at his farmhouse east of Blue Springs. He invited all the young people of the region and in particular asked Quantrill and his men to attend. Quantrill, however, suspected a trap and hence stayed away. His hunch proved correct. Alley had notified the Union post at Independence that the bushwhackers would be at his place the night of the ball, and when the dancing was at it height—"Cider and gingerbread, four hands around and down the middle, first couple out"—a squadron of Federal cavalrymen burst into Alley's parlor with drawn revolvers. The soldiers confined all the men and boys in the upstairs rooms, the women downstairs, and permitted no one to leave until the following night, hoping that Quantrill and his men might show up after all.

During the night a half-dozen wagonloads of Union infantry arrived from Independence, then in the morning went out into the countryside. When they returned all of them were mounted on confiscated horses except the wagon drivers. In the wagons were a large number of prisoners, among them Jim Tatum, a returnee from Price's army. By the second night all the Federals had gotten "beastly drunk" on peach brandy acquired at the near-by house of "Aunt" Rhoda Harris. They finally released the women, but took all the men to Independence in the wagons. In order to cover his treachery, Alley was included among the prisoners, but before reaching Independence the soldiers released him and he returned to his home. Quantrill and Todd, who had learned of what had happened, were waiting for him, but he escaped into the darkness, then went to Kansas City, never again to show his face in the Blue Springs neighborhood.

Ultimately the Federal authorities released all the prisoners from the Alley ball with the exception of Sol Basham, who was sent to Rock Island Penitentiary in Illinois, where he remained until the end of the war. One of the captives, fifteen-year-old Frank Smith, was told by the Union commander at Independence: "You damn little rebel, I'm going to let you go, but if I hear of you getting into anything down there at Blue Springs, or taking any part in assisting the rebel cause, I'll send down and have you brought in here and will cut your damn head off."

Ed Koger, the minstrel of Quantrill's gang, wrote a parody on the Alley ball which he sang to the accompaniment of his banjo:

Old Rile Alley gave a ball,
The Feds came down and took us all
Over the ice and over the snow—
Sing-Song Kitty, won't you kiss-me-o!

Old Rile Alley gave a ball,
Planned to catch Quantrill and bushwhack all,
But Quant was smart and didn't go—
Sing-Song Kitty, won't you kiss-me-o! [7]

When Quantrill's band came together again late in January it numbered nearly two dozen men. Notable among the newcomers was a tall, broad-shouldered eighteen-year-old named Cole Younger. Cole was the son of Colonel H. W. Younger of Cass County, a slaveholder and pronounced pro-Southern man, but an opponent of secession. During the fall Kansas jayhawkers raided Colonel Younger's livery stable and house at Harrisonville, taking all the horses and a large quantity of liquor. Then, that winter, while at a dance in Harrisonville, Cole "cut in" on Captain Walley of the Fifth Missouri Federal Militia, who became incensed and said, "I'll make no disturbance here, Mr. Younger, but I'll kill you the first opportunity I get." Since Walley was notoriously vicious and "not afraid of blood," Cole decided to take to the bush—a move he would have made sooner or later in any case. Walley, unable to catch Cole, thereupon robbed and brutally murdered Colonel Younger—a crime which resulted in his arrest by the Union commander in the area. Later, after Cole had become one of the most famous of the bushwhackers, the Federals imprisoned his sister and drove his mother out of the family home, which they plundered and burned.[8] Thus the war was strictly a personal affair with Cole Younger; it was to be a long, long time before it ended for him. . . .

The Quantrill guerrillas rapidly became an object of special concern to the Union troops stationed at Independence. On February 3, Captain W. S. Oliver, commander of the garrison there, reported that "the notorious Quantrill and his gang of robbers" were daily robbing the mails, stealing horses, and driving Union men and their families from the country. Stressing the obvious, Oliver declared that "Quantrill will not leave this section unless he is chastised and driven from it." [9]

On February 22, Quantrill and fifteen followers rode boldly into Independence itself. However, a whole regiment of Ohio cavalry had just passed through the town, and stragglers reported the presence of the guerrillas to their colonel, who at once ordered the regiment to turn back. Taken completely by surprise by this overwhelming force, Quantrill's men fired a few scattering shots, then wheeled their horses about and hightailed it down the Spring Branch road. The Ohioans pursued them hotly, but had inferior horses and so abandoned the chase after a couple of miles. Two bushwhacker recruits, Gabriel George and Hop Wood, were shot dead from their saddles, and Bill Gregg received several saber slashes on his arm. Quantrill himself had his horse shot out from under him and was forced to flee on foot into the bush. A couple of days later he appeared at George's funeral limping on a wounded leg and using a cane.[10]

Less than two weeks after the Independence fiasco Quantrill was ready to make his most daring venture yet: a raid into hated Kansas. His objective was Aubry, present-day Stilwell, a village near the border on the Kansas City-Fort Scott road. It was to be sacked, Quantrill told his men, in retaliation for Anthony's burnings of Columbus and Dayton in Missouri.

Forty bushwhackers charged into Aubry at daybreak on March 7, "screaming and swearing like devils," and riddling everything in sight with their revolvers. Two overnight lodgers at the village inn, Abraham Ellis and Second Lieutenant Reuben A. Randlett, hastily tossed on their clothes and went to their second-story window to see what was happening outside. They gasped with horror as they saw a group of guerrillas chase five unarmed men across an open field and shoot every one of them. Quantrill, astride his horse on the street below, looked up and noticed Ellis and Randlett at the window. At once he whipped out a pistol and sent a bullet crashing through the window casing and into the forehead of Ellis, who slumped to the floor bleeding profusely and apparently dead. It was, as Quantrill himself later remarked, a "damn good shot."

Another man ran into the room and excitedly proposed to Randlett that the lodgers fight it out with the raiders. Randlett asked him how many guns were available. When he heard that there were only three, he declared that resistance would be suicidal. He then went downstairs, where he handed his pistol to a guerrilla and asked to be treated according to the rules of war. The guerrilla merely laughed, as if such a request were a joke. He then took Randlett out onto the porch where he turned him over to two other raiders. Both of them began swearing at Randlett, one of them pushed the barrel of a revolver into the Union lieutenant's mouth, and the other poked a pistol muzzle into his ear! But at this critical moment Bill Gregg came up and ordered the two not to injure the Yankee, as Quantrill wanted him alive. Gregg then took Randlett back inside and into a room where Quantrill was sitting. Quantrill asked the lieutenant if he had a horse, and when Randlett replied that he had a good one out in the stable, he ordered one of his men to saddle it and bring it to the front door.

Before Quantrill could ask Randlett any more questions, the supposedly dead Ellis staggered into the room, covered with blood. By a strange coincidence Ellis had been superintendent of schools when Quantrill had taught at Stanton in 1859, and had even examined the future bushwhacker chieftain for his teaching certificate. Therefore, despite the blood, Quantrill immediately recognized him. "Why, Ellis," he cried out, "is that you?" Ellis replied that it indeed was he, and that Quantrill himself had shot him. Quantrill thereupon got a cloth and some water and washed away the blood on Ellis' face. While doing this he remarked, "Ellis, I am damned sorry I shot you—you are one of the Kansas men I do *not* want to shoot!"

Ellis was struck by the change in Quantrill's appearance. Formerly Quantrill had been slender, light-haired, and beardless. Now he was a tough-looking ruffian, with a reddish mustache and side whiskers. His followers impressed Ellis as "the most desperate Demons that ever disgraced the name of man."

The bushwhackers plundered all the stores and houses in Aubry, robbed every male inhabitant, and set fire to one building. They then galloped back into Missouri, easily eluding the Union pursuit parties.[11]

The Aubry raid was not the first such incursion by the Missouri guerrillas, but it was by all odds the most brutal and devastating one to date. News of it alarmed and enraged the people of Kansas, and the "strange, barbaric" name of Quantrill began to be heard frequently along the border.[12]

Quantrill took Randlett with him on leaving Aubry. He planned to use the lieutenant as a hostage to secure the release of one of his men who had recently been captured and was being held prisoner at Fort Leavenworth. After returning to his Jackson County hideout, he wrote several letters to the Union commandant at Fort Leavenworth demanding an exchange of prisoners, at the same time threatening to kill Randlett if such did not take place. The commandant, however, as did all Federal officers, considered Quantrill to be nothing more than an outlaw and so refused to hold any communication with him. Quantrill then had Randlett himself write asking for an exchange, but again there was no reply. Finally Quantrill took Randlett to Independence, which was temporarily ungarrisoned, and freed him on parole. Randlett promised to try to arrange for the release of Quantrill's man, and to return voluntarily to Independence should this prove impossible.

Randlett faithfully carried out his strange mission. But the Union generals at Kansas City and Fort Leavenworth scornfully refused to have any dealings with the "Bandit Quantrill." Instead, they urged Randlett to lead troops to the bushwhackers' camp, and when he refused to do this, they told him not to keep his promise to Quantrill. Randlett, however, felt that it would be dishonorable as well as dangerous to violate the parole, and so went back to Independence. Although the town was now occupied by a Federal regiment, he managed to get in touch with a guerrilla spy and inform him that he had been unable to make the exchange. Then, feeling that he had fulfilled his part of the agreement, he returned to Kansas City, perhaps the only Federal officer ever to be captured by Quantrill who lived to tell the tale.[13]

Quantrill instinctively realized the essence of guerrilla warfare: stay always on the offensive, striking first here and then there, and never giving the enemy a chance to concentrate his forces against you. On March 18, he crossed the Missouri River on skiffs with about forty men and attacked an eight-man Union garrison at Liberty. The Federals held out in a brick building for three hours before surrendering. Their captain was badly wounded, and on entering the town the bushwhackers had killed a soldier who refused to tell where the post was located. Quantrill paroled all the prisoners and did not permit any looting. Liberty was strongly pro-Southern and the people welcomed Quantrill and his boys.

The bushwhackers recrossed the Missouri and went into camp at the Little Blue Baptist Church, twelve miles southeast of Independence. Here, on the night of March 19, Quantrill got hold of a copy of the St. Louis *Republican* containing Halleck's order outlawing guerrillas and calling for their extermination. In the morning he assembled all of his men and read the order to them, explaining as he did so its implications and consequences. Then he marked a line on the ground, rode his horse to the other side of it, and said, "Now, boys, I accept the challenge. All of you who wish to remain and fight with me ride over on this side of the line. All of you who wish to leave the outfit go ahead and nothing will be held against you. Every man now will make his own choice."

All except about fifteen crossed the line. Those who refused were new men from Cass County. They returned to their homes and endeavored to live peacefully. But the suspicion of their Unionist neighbors and the persecution of the Federal troops made this impossible. Within a month they were back with Quantrill. They had learned, as many others were to find out, that once a bushwhacker, always a bushwhacker.

Quantrill burned to strike immediately at the Federals in retaliation for Halleck's extermination order. At first he proposed attacking a small Union detachment at Independence, but had to abandon the idea when three hundred additional troops entered the town. Finally, on March 22, he led his men, now nearly a hundred strong, to a bridge on the Little Blue southeast of Kansas City. Here they captured a "Dutch Federal Sergeant." Quantrill drew a Colt dragoon revolver and in cold blood shot the helpless soldier down.

The sound of the shot echoed starkly through the hills. Holstering his smoking revolver, Quantrill looked around him, his eyes glittering beneath their heavy lids, a twisted smile on his bearded face. Suddenly, in a fierce, shrill voice, he cried, "They issued the order, but we draw the first blood!" His men exchanged quick glances; they knew now what fighting under the black flag meant.

The tollkeeper of the bridge was also taken prisoner. Some of the guerrillas accused him of being a Union spy. He was given a speedy trial, found guilty, and shot down on the spot before the eyes of his young son.[14]

After the war the survivors of Quantrill's band all claimed that prior to Halleck's extermination order they usually took prisoners but that afterward they did so only rarely. Outside evidence tends to confirm their contention, as instanced by the Manasseth Gap ambush and the Liberty fight (although it is apparent from the Aubry raid that they were not disposed to show much mercy to Kansans even before March 20). They denied, however, that they ever took an "iron-clad oath" to kill all Union soldiers. As one of them explained, such an oath was unnecessary: "Any new recruit coming into the organization was aware of the type of warfare that Quantrill's followers waged and he just naturally fell into line and adapted himself to this method of fighting." [15]

The bushwhackers burned the bridge, then resumed their march, proceeding eighteen miles southeastward to a farmhouse, where they took lunch. They rested there until evening, whereupon Quantrill and about twenty-five men rode to the David Tate farm three miles south of the Little Santa Fe near the state line, and the others dispersed in small groups to various houses in the same general area. Quantrill's detachment, after feeding the horses and eating supper, bedded down for the night at about eight o'clock. Quantrill and Todd shared the only available bed, while the rank and file stretched out on the floor. Soon all were sound asleep.

In the meantime Colonel Robert B. Mitchell's Second Kansas Cavalry had been scouring the countryside looking for the murderers of the sergeant and the tollkeeper. On arriving at Little Santa Fe Mitchell sent a squadron under Major James M. Pomeroy to arrest David Tate, who was a known friend and abettor of the guerrillas, and bring him back for questioning.*

* According to Frank Smith, who states he got his information from one of Quantrill's men who was present at the Tate house on the night of March 22, Tate himself slipped away when the guerrillas were asleep and betrayed them to the Federals. But there is nothing to this effect in either Mitchell's report

Quantrill had posted two sentinels a hundred yards from the Tate house, but they must have dozed off, for Pomeroy's men came up on them so suddenly that they did not have time to sound an alarm and were barely able to escape into the timber. (It is not known whether they ever dared rejoin their comrades.)

Pomeroy, obviously unaware that the house contained more than two dozen heavily armed bushwhackers, went to the door and knocked loudly, demanding entrance. Quantrill, who along with his men had been awakened by the clatter of the Federal horses in the yard, whispered to the others to remain still. Then, quietly sneaking to the door, he suddenly fired a shot through it. The bullet, however, missed Pomeroy, who ran back to his troops and ordered them to begin firing. Their first volley produced frantic screams on the part of the women and children of Tate's family. Pomeroy thereupon had his men hold their fire while all the noncombatants evacuated the house. As soon as they were out of the way the soldiers opened up again, splattering the thick log walls with a hail of rifle bullets. The trapped bushwhackers blazed back from the upstairs and downstairs windows with revolvers and an occasional shotgun.

After a while Pomeroy, who now realized that he had flushed none other than the notorious Quantrill himself, ordered his men to cease firing. Then, cupping his hands to his mouth, he shouted: "Quantrill! I have you surrounded with five hundred men! Come out and surrender or I'll burn the house down over your head!"

The only reply was a flurry of revolver shots from the guerrillas. Pomeroy's troops then tried to set fire to a shed adjoining the house. The attempt failed, and during it one soldier was killed and Pomeroy received a nasty leg wound.

So far the bushwhackers had not suffered any casualties. The walls of the house were made of thick logs, and they had barricaded the doors and windows with piles of furniture and mat-

---

or Gregg's account, and in view of the fact that Tate's family was in the house with the guerrillas it would seem very unlikely that he would have done as Smith's source alleged. The account in John McCorkle, *Three Years With Quantrill*, pp. 38-40, is of no value, as McCorkle was not with Quantrill until August 11, 1862, and yet he describes the fight at the Tate house as taking place after that date.

tresses. They were determined not to surrender. To do so, they knew, meant sure and speedy death.

Then the Federals made a second and this time successful effort to set the house afire. Soon it was "fuming briskly." The guerrillas began to show signs of panic. Two of them, unable to stand the horrible prospect of roasting alive, crawled out of a window and gave themselves up—only to be cut down ruthlessly by the exulting soldiers.

Quantrill alone remained completely calm. "Boys," he shouted above the crackling of the flames, "we are in a tight place. But don't anyone lose his head, and listen to me. Our only chance is to bolt out the door and cut right through them. Follow me in single file, stoop low, and shoot right and left, and stay right in line."

Outside the Federals were standing in the yard, thickly bunched and close to the flaming house, eagerly waiting to shoot down the doomed bushwhackers as they emerged. When everybody was ready, Quantrill yelled, "Steady, boys, follow me," then threw open the door and sprang out firing rapidly. The others followed immediately behind him, also blasting away with their guns. The soldiers, startled and surprised by this wild charge, fell over each other as they tried both to get out of the way and to shoot at the fast-running guerrillas. But before they could fire more than a few scattered shots, Quantrill and his men had broken through to the safety of the near-by timber. The Federals could not follow them there on horseback, and dared not pursue on foot. Only one bushwhacker, Joe Gilchrist, was killed in the breakout.

Despite their light losses, the bushwhackers had suffered a severe setback, and they knew that they were fortunate to have escaped at all. For having done so they could and did thank Quantrill, who had displayed unusual coolness and ingenuity in a desperate predicament. The Tate house fight, which became one of the most famous episodes in bushwhacker annals, increased Quantrill's prestige among the West Missouri guerrillas and strengthened his leadership.[16]

After escaping from the Tate house, Quantrill made his way on foot through the timber to the Dave Wilson farm in lower Jackson County. He was so exhausted when he arrived that he could barely stand up, and his clothes were in tatters. From Wilson's he sent word to the various scattered detachments of his band to meet him at the headwaters of the Little Blue. When all the men were together again, he instructed them to disperse long enough for those who lost their horses to secure new mounts, then to rendezvous at Sam Clark's farm near Pink Hill.[17]

By March 30, some thirty bushwhackers, including Quantrill, Todd, and other leaders, were assembled at the Clark farm.* It was Sunday, and the men were taking it easy. Bill Gregg was out in the front yard, cutting a comrade's hair. John Koger had just ridden up and was hitching his horse to the rail fence. Then, all of a sudden, a squadron of blue-jacketed cavalry thundered out of the woods, shooting as they came! The bushwhackers had allowed themselves to be surprised again.

The attacking force consisted of Company D, First Missouri Cavalry, sixty-five men, under Captain Albert Peabody. It had heard that Quantrill was in the Pink Hill area, and after diligently searching the countryside had come upon him unawares. However, the startled guerrillas quickly rallied. Knocking loopholes through the chinks in Clark's log house they beat off several Union charges. One group of bushwhackers fought from the upper story under the direction of Sam Clark himself, an old-time deer hunter, who brought down several attackers with his shotgun. Another bunch, under Quantrill, held the first floor while still more under Gregg held out in some Negro cabins in the rear. The rest, led by Todd, who distinguished himself with his deadly revolver fire, took cover behind a corner of the house. In addition, as the battle progressed, dozens of local farmers appeared on the surrounding hillsides and sniped away at Peabody's men at long-range with Sharps carbines.

* According to accounts published in the Kansas City *Journal* for April 2, 1862, and the Liberty *Tribune* for April 4, 1862, some two hundred bushwhackers under Quantrill attacked the Union garrison at Warrensburg on March 26 and were repulsed. It is extremely unlikely, however, that Quantrill and his men were present at this engagement. None of the bushwhacker memoirs mention it, and it would have been close to impossible for Quantrill's band to reorganize in time after the Tate house fight to march nearly fifty miles and assault Warrensburg on the date stated. No doubt bushwhackers or Confederate cavalry attacked Warrensburg, but probably already the Unionists were coming to identify all partisan forces as being Quantrill's.

Quantrill realized that he must escape before the Federals brought up reinforcements. Therefore, accompanied by the men inside the house, he tried to make a dash to the barn, two hundred feet away, where the horses were stabled, but was instantly driven back to cover by the heavy fire of the troopers. He then proposed that half of the men, led by himself, run to the barn while the other half, under Todd, covered them from the house. This plan was put into execution, but just as Quantrill's party started to leave, the soldiers rushed the house and it was necessary to remain in order to help beat them back.

His next scheme for escaping was much better, even though it meant abandoning the horses. Six guerrillas sprang out of the house as if they were going to make a dash for the barn but immediately jumped back inside again. This ruse caused the besiegers to fire, thereby emptying their single-shot carbines. Before they could reload, the bushwhackers ran out of the house and into the timber, horseless once more but at least still alive. Their only casualty was Koger, who had been wounded when Peabody's company first attacked. However, Quantrill lost a powerful spyglass which he had found extremely useful in watching Federal troop movements around Independence from a high point near Blue Springs, and which was very hard to replace.

Upon reaching the timber, Quantrill detailed three men to take care of Koger, then with the remainder of his force proceeded by a short cut to Ball ford on Sni Creek. Here his men concealed themselves in the brush atop the bluff overlooking the creek. In a short while fifty-one soldiers, on their way to join Peabody, entered the ford, where they stopped to water their horses. The guerrillas opened fire and promptly emptied a number of Union saddles. The survivors rallied and attempted to counterattack. But they were unable to dislodge the bushwhackers from their position until Peabody's pursuing squadron arrived. Quantrill's band thereupon once again fled into the protecting timber, happier now that they had gained a certain amount of revenge against the Bluebellies.[18]

The bushwhackers dispersed for several days in order to secure new horses. This they had little difficulty in doing. The region abounded in splendid horseflesh, and most of the inhabitants were more than willing to help out Quantrill's boys. Even those who opposed the guerrillas dared not refuse them if they "requested" a mount. Otherwise, it might mean losing more than a favorite mare.

The band reassembled at Reuben Harris', ten miles south of Independence, then moved to Job Crabtree's farm, eight miles east of that town, when Union patrols got dangerously close. At first Quantrill planned to attack Harrisonville, but he abondoned the project when his scouts reported that the garrison was much too strong. He next marched to the Jordan Lowe place, an abandoned farmhouse near Little Santa Fe, arriving there on the evening of April 15. Instead of taking up quarters inside the dwelling, the guerrillas slept in the adjoining woods. But a rainstorm came up during the night and drove them into the shelter of the house. Confident that there would be no Federal patrols out on such a bad night, they posted no guards. They left their horses tied to a fence in the back yard.

Again the bushwhackers were destined to pay the penalty of carelessness. A Federal scouting party, thirty men of the First Missouri Cavalry, commanded by Lieutenant G. W. Nash, had been tipped off to their whereabouts and was moving in for the kill under the cover of darkness and the storm. Just as dawn broke, Nash's troopers surrounded the farmhouse, quickly secured the horses, and opened fire.

The bushwhackers by now were becoming almost accustomed to such rude awakenings. There was no panic as Quantrill told his men to shoot their way out. Since they outnumbered the attackers they quickly broke through to the timber. Then Cole Younger noticed that Todd and Andy Blunt were missing. They had been firing away from the upstairs loft and had not heard Quantrill's order. Younger ran back to the house and succeeded in getting Todd away. Blunt, however, was not so lucky. The soldiers captured and shot him, and left him for dead. However, he recovered sufficiently to make his way to a farmhouse, where friends nursed him back to health. In a short while he was back with the gang. Two other guerrillas, William Carr and a young recruit, were killed. Lieutenant Nash did not report any Union casualties and the bushwhackers did not claim any.[19]

Frank Smith relates that Quantrill's "old men" never talked about the Lowe house affair. Little wonder. For the third time in less than a month they had been surprised, lost their horses, and almost been wiped out. Only Quantrill's quick thinking had saved them from the firing squad or the hangman's noose—that and the incredible ineptitude of the Federal troops, who had thrice trapped them and thrice allowed them to escape with only minor losses. But the bushwhackers profited from these near-disasters. Never again did Quantrill fail to post adequate sentries around his camp, never again did a Union force catch Quantrill's band completely unawares—that is, not until a certain rainy spring morning in Kentucky, several years hence.

As before, the guerrillas scattered for the purpose of remounting and re-equipping themselves. Such a dispersal, however, did not mean that they ceased to be active. Rather, they operated in smaller groups and on a lesser scale, ambushing Union scouts, waylaying mail carriers, holding up stagecoaches, and driving Unionists from their homes. Such operations, in fact, were the stock-in-trade of the bushwhackers, and their cumulative effect was perhaps greater than their more ambitious and sensational exploits. Certainly they wore on the nerves of the military authorities and created a state of chronic terror among the Union adherents in West Missouri.

Following the escape from the Lowe house, Quantrill used the enforced lull in his operations to replenish the band's dwindling supply of pistol caps.* He and Todd journeyed to Hannibal, Missouri, and purchased 500,000 caps. They then returned west by railroad to St. Joseph, and from there proceeded in a wagon to the Missouri River, which they crossed in a skiff. They were gone approximately a month, and according to Edwards, during the trip they masqueraded as Union majors and even stayed three days at Federal headquarters in St. Joseph.[20]

Soon after returning, Quantrill sent out word for all the men to come together. Within a few days the band was reunited once more. It contained many new recruits who more than made good all losses, and the men were mounted on some of the best horses

* The single-package percussion cartridge was just coming into use in the early 1860's. Most of the bushwhackers used revolvers which fired cartridges that had to be exploded by a spark set off from a separate cap placed on a "nipple," one for each chamber.

that they had yet possessed. Quantrill was now ready to resume big-scale operations.

Late in June, Upton Hayes, who had become a colonel in the regular Confederate Army, marched up into Missouri from Arkansas for the purpose of recruiting a cavalry regiment in Jackson County. He sent word ahead to Quantrill asking him to aid in this venture by diverting the attention of the Federal troops in the region. Quantrill accordingly led his band southward into Henry County. The stratagem worked, as most of the Federal units in Jackson County set out in pursuit, thus opening the way for Hayes. Also, at Hayes' request, Quantrill detailed thirty men under Todd to escort Hayes' recruiting parties.

Quantrill was still engaged in carrying out his diversionary movement when, on July 8, the Federal commander at Clinton, Major James O. Gower, learned that he was camped on Sugar Creek near Wadesburg. Gower promptly sent out a ninety-man detachment which at dawn on the ninth attempted a surprise attack on the guerrilla camp. But this time the bushwackers were not caught napping. They easily beat off the Union assaults and wounded several soldiers. In the end, the Federal detachment returned to Clinton, mission unaccomplished.

Major Gower, disgusted by this failure, took personal charge of operations against Quantrill. He led eighty troopers to the Lotspeich farm in Cass County, where on the morning of the tenth he was joined, on his orders, by 130 soldiers from Harrisonville under Captains William H. Ankey and William A. Martin, and by sixty-three men from Warrensburg under Captain Martin Kehoe. He then made a cautious approach on Quantrill's Sugar Creek camp with his combined force, only to find it deserted. However, his men soon picked up the guerrillas' trail, and during the remainder of the day they followed it relentlessly. After marching nearly fifty miles under the torrid July sun, they bivouacked for the night near Pleasant Hill. Gower was confident that he would overtake Quantrill on the morrow.

In the morning, Captain Kehoe got his company up and saddled before the other units were ready. Thinking that they would soon follow, or perhaps anxious to secure the glory of wiping out Quantrill's gang singlehandedly, he did not wait, but went on ahead alone. Six miles west of Pleasant Hill he discovered the guerrillas encamped in a clearing near a farm. He sent a courier back to Gower with this intelligence, then drew up his troopers in a column with drawn sabers and ordered them to charge.

The bushwhackers had spent an uncomfortable night in the rain, and were busy drying out their blankets in the warm morning sun when the firing of the sentinels announced the presence of an enemy force. Seeing at a glance that Kehoe's company was about equal in strength to his own band, and unaware that many more Union troops were on the way, Quantrill decided to stand and fight it out. He had the horses taken to a near-by ravine, then posted part of his men behind a fence facing the road down which the Federals were advancing, and the remainder in some timber bordering the road.

The overeager Kehoe failed to perceive the ambush. When his men reached point-blank range, Quantrill shouted, "Let 'em have it, boys!" Six cavalrymen toppled to the ground dead, nine more reeled in their saddles wounded, among them Kehoe, who received a bullet through his shoulder. The surviving Federals frantically drew rein, then with cries of "Let's get out of here!" wheeled their horses around and retreated pell-mell back down the road. Only the six riderless horses continued to charge ahead. At Gregg's suggestion, Quantrill opened the fence gate and let them gallop on into the yard, where they were quickly secured by the jubilant bushwhackers. Other guerrillas ran out onto the road and obtained the guns and ammunition of the dead soldiers—which was standard bushwhacker practice.

Kehoe's company, once it regrouped, did not attempt a second charge. Instead it opened up a long-range carbine fire on the guerrillas. Since most of Quantrill's men were armed with revolvers they could not reply effectively. In a short time, one bushwhacker had been killed and two others wounded. Moreover, the rest of Gower's force began to appear on the scene. Quantrill now saw that he was heavily outnumbered and that it would be suicide to remain where he was. Therefore, he ordered the bulk of his men to fall back to a ravine, one-half mile distant. He and a small rear guard covered the retreat with a quick hit-and-run charge which killed two soldiers.

The Federals pursued the bushwhackers closely. One company,

sixty-five men of the Seventh Missouri Cavalry, under Captain Martin, dismounted on coming to the ravine and attacked in an extended line on foot, firing as they advanced. When their guns became empty they leaped down into the ravine and engaged the guerrillas in a fierce hand-to-hand struggle. Pistol butts and bowie knives countered rifle stocks and sabers amidst dense, smoke-wreathed thickets. The bushwhackers finally broke free of their determined assailants and started to retreat through the other side of the ravine. But Gower, anticipating such a move, had sent a force around to cut them off, with the result that they ran head on into fresh hordes of blue-uniformed Yankees.

A terrible melee ensued. Both bushwhackers and soldiers battled desperately. No quarter was asked and none was given. The only sounds heard were the bark of pistols and carbines, the groans of the wounded and dying, and the heavy breathing of men locked in mortal combat. Most of the guerrillas were forced to abandon their horses and some even fought with rocks and clubs when their ammunition gave out.

The vicious struggle raged for over an hour. Quantrill, bleeding from a bullet wound in his thigh, realized that the ravine would become a grave for his men unless they escaped soon. Therefore, on his orders, Gregg led all the men who still had horses—about twenty-one in all—in a wild charge which broke through the Union lines on one side. At the same time Quantrill and the dismounted men cut their way out in the opposite direction. They then scattered into the timber in small parties, carrying their wounded comrades with them. The Federals were so exhausted by the long pursuit, the intense heat, and the fierce fighting that they made no attempt to follow. Major Gower claimed that his troops killed eighteen of Quantrill's men and wounded twenty-five to thirty more, at the cost of eleven dead and twenty-one wounded. But the bushwhackers admitted losing only four or five slain and ten to twelve wounded.[21]

With good reason Quantrill's followers always spoke of the fight with Gower's troopers as the hardest one the band ever had. In it they proved themselves capable of holding their own in an open, stand-up battle against trained and disciplined soldiers, even though heavily outnumbered. But while their performance might be termed magnificent, it was not bushwhacking. By remaining to fight it out with Gower's command they violated one of the cardinal rules of guerrilla warfare: Never do battle against a superior force on its own terms unless absolutely necessary. Quantrill and the other bushwhacker leaders realized their mistake and, as in the case of the surprises at the Tate, Clark, and Lowe houses, profited from it. Henceforth, they always carefully reconnoitered the enemy, fought only under the most favorable possible circumstances, and constantly endeavored to make surprise attacks. By the same token, they avoided battle in open country, attempted to keep personal risks to a minimum, and scattered into the bush whenever hotly pursued by large Union forces. Such tactics were not a matter of courage or cowardice, but rather of necessity and common sense. The guerrilla's purpose is to kill, not be killed. And by the summer of 1862, Quantrill's bushwhackers had become accomplished killers.

chapter IV Shooting Them Down

The terrible fight in the ravine with Gower's troopers forced the bushwhackers to disband for several weeks in order to procure fresh horses and new equipment. During this period Quantrill hid out in a secluded farmhouse with several followers and nursed the leg wound he had received in the battle. Meanwhile, Todd successfully carried out his mission of escorting Upton Hayes into Jackson County. Hayes set up headquarters in the strongly pro-Southern Independence-Blue Springs region and began enrolling the local youths into the Confederate Army. In a short time he had some three hundred men.[1]

The Federal commander at Independence, Lieutenant Colonel James T. Buel, made little effort to interfere with Hayes' activities or, for that matter, to combat the bushwhackers, who continued to harass the countryside. However, late in July, Jim Knowles, Town Marshal of Independence, tipped Buel off that Quantrill's men frequently used a certain crossing on the Little Blue. Acting on this information Buel sent a detachment under Lieutenant Thomas to the place indicated. Thomas concealed his men around the ford and then waited in high hopes of bushwhacking some bushwhackers. After a while three guerrillas—George Todd, John Little, and Ed Koger—rode into the stream and stopped to let their horses drink. Instantly, at point-blank range, the soldiers poured a volley into them which killed Little and Koger outright. But miraculously Todd was not even scratched. Dashing up the bank, he galloped off into the surrounding timber. The Federals, content with a good day's work, did not pursue. This was highly fortunate for Todd. By some freak his horse ran in between two large rocks and became so tightly wedged that it could not move either forward or backward! Todd, cursing like a madman, jumped from his hapless steed and scurried on foot back to the guerrilla camp. Sometime later the horse was found dead of starvation, still stuck tightly between the rocks.

The highly emotional Todd bitterly resented the ambush slaying of John Little and Ed Koger. Not only were they original members of the band, but they were also his close friends. Henceforth he was filled with a raging blood lust against all Union soldiers. Already notable for his ruthlessness and courage, he now fought with a murderous ferocity and contemptuous disdain of danger that had few if any equals. His sole object became to kill Yankees and he was happiest when doing so. Moreover, despite a recklessness in battle which bordered on the suicidal, he seemed to bear a charmed life. "I have seen him," one of his followers later wrote, "in more tight places than any other man in the outfit, where it looked impossible for him to escape, but he always came through unscathed." Because of his great bravery he became the idol of the bushwhackers, especially the younger, wilder ones, who followed him unhesitatingly wherever he led.

As time went on, Todd would take orders from only one man —Quantrill—and even this was not to be the case forever. Quantrill, in turn, came more and more to rely on Todd. The two men were direct opposites in temperament, and in a sense complemented each other. Quantrill never became excited—in fact, "the greater the danger, the calmer he was"—and he carefully planned every operation, always keeping in mind just how and where he was going to retreat. Todd, on the other hand, was always excited, and he "knew no fighting but to charge." Together they formed a perfect team—"Quantrill did the planning, Todd did the executing."

Quantrill, however, was not completely immune to strain when in a "tight spot." During fights his followers noticed that he was always smiling, and that he frequently laughed—a sort of gay, nervous chuckle. Sometimes this strange giggle would be heard right after he had killed a man. The guerrillas themselves found it rather eerie and even a little frightening.[2]

Big things were happening all over Missouri in the summer of

1862, and bigger things were on the way. Groups of specially selected Confederate officers had entered the state from Arkansas for the purpose of enlisting recruits, attacking Federal posts and communications, and if possible fomenting a mass uprising of Southern adherents. Among these officers were Colonels Joseph Porter, J. A. Poindexter, John T. Hughes, Gideon W. Thompson, and, as has been noted, Upton Hayes. They were all prominent Missourians who could be counted on to rally the young men of the state around the Confederate banner. Their missions had been assigned to them by General Tom Hindman, the fiery Confederate commander in the Trans-Mississippi, who was busy organizing an army in Arkansas for an eventual invasion of Missouri—an invasion which he hoped would reverse the tide of war in the west in favor of the South.

Under the leadership of Hindman's colonels, parties of Confederate irregulars ran rampant through Missouri, burning bridges, cutting telegraph wires, ambushing Union patrols, and attacking exposed military posts. By July, their activity and success had become so alarming that the Federal commander in Missouri, the young but able Brigadier General John M. Schofield, decided that only drastic measures could prevent a general insurrection. Therefore, on July 22, he issued General Order No. 19. This required every able-bodied man in Missouri to enlist in the Union state militia "for the purpose of exterminating the guerrillas that infest our state." Already he had renewed Halleck's directive to give no quarter to captured partisans—they were to be "shot down upon the spot."

The first effect of Schofield's order was to worsen rather than to improve the Union military situation. Hundreds of pro-Southern Missourians who so far had taken no active part in the war, now suddenly found themselves called on to fight against their friends and relatives. Rather than do this, they either went into hiding or else joined up with Porter, Poindexter, Quantrill, or some other partisan leader. In addition, many ex-members of Price's army, men who had been allowed to return home with the assurance that they would not be required to serve in the Union Army, felt that this promise had been violated and hence took to the bush. As a consequence, the strength and number of the guerrilla bands increased enormously, and it seemed for a while that they would drive the Yankees out of the state and open the way for Hindman.

Schofield's order, however, accomplished its primary purpose: fully arousing and mobilizing the Missouri Unionists to meet the Southern challenge. Following its issuance heavily reinforced militia companies combined with regular Federal forces to launch a determined counteroffensive against the Confederate irregulars. Bloody, large-scale fighting then took place in northern and western Missouri, the main centers of partisan activity. In the former region, Joe Porter, who had raised nearly a thousand men and wiped out several Union detachments, was endeavoring to march southward and link up with Hindman's army. Schofield blockaded the Missouri River and concentrated every available unit against Porter. In a series of extremely bitter battles, Porter's followers fought with the ferocity of men who knew that the only alternative to victory was death. For a while the outcome hung in the balance; Schofield even complained that the rebels gathered recruits faster than he could kill them. But in the end Porter's forces were defeated and dispersed, and Porter himself was eventually slain while leading a forlorn hope. By early August, despite continued depredations by Poindexter and other Confederate leaders in the area, the Federals once more were firmly in control north of the Missouri River.[3]

Meanwhile, the stage was being set for more furious fighting in western Missouri. Colonel John T. Hughes, with seventy-five men, followed Hayes into Jackson County and established a camp at Lee's Summit, a few miles east of Independence. Hughes, a popular hero of the Mexican War, planned to cross over to the other side of the Missouri and raise a brigade in the northern counties. However, he realized that his prospects for success were dim unless he could secure his escape route back to the south bank. Therefore, he decided to capture and temporarily occupy Independence. Since his own force was much too small for this job, he called on Hayes and Quantrill to assist him. Hayes readily agreed, and on August 10 joined Hughes at Lee's Summit. Shortly afterward Quantrill and twenty-five bushwhackers also rode in. Hughes assumed command of the combined Southern forces, altogether about four hundred men.

The Union garrison at Independence consisted of three hundred infantry and cavalry. Most of this force was stationed in an unfortified tent camp on the western outskirts of the town. Buel's headquarters was located in the Southern Bank at the southwest corner of the courthouse square. Posted in the building across the street was the headquarters guard company; a block to the north the provost marshal's detachment occupied the county jailhouse. Buel was aware that a considerable number of Confederate irregulars had gathered in his district, but he was confident that they would not dare attack Independence. Consequently he did not alert his troops, he neglected to send out scouting parties, and he scoffed at all warnings of danger. The townspeople, on the other hand, were not so skeptical. By climbing to the top of the courthouse they could look out across the prairies to the south and see a large, brightly colored Confederate banner flapping proudly in the breeze at Lee's Summit. Many of them, therefore, decided to "skedaddle before all hell busted loose."

One of Quantrill's men, Morgan Mattox, entered Independence on August 10, disguised as a farmer selling onions and pies, and obtained complete and accurate information on the layout of the Union garrison. On the basis of his report, Hughes drew up a plan of attack which assigned Quantrill's bushwhackers the key role.

They were to lead the Confederate advance into Independence, cut Buel off from his troops in the camp, and picket the town after it was taken. When Quantrill expressed concern over the big job given his small band, Hughes reassured him: "You will be well supported. In fact, I shall be right behind you when you enter the public square."

Just before daybreak on Sunday, August 11, Hughes' partisans galloped into Independence from the east along the Spring Branch road. Quantrill's vanguard surprised and killed the Federal pickets at the edge of town before they could sound the alarm, then swept on to the square, closely followed, as promised, by the main body under Hughes. A sentinel in front of the guard building across the street from Buel's headquarters first saw the Confederates. He fired his rifle, then rushed inside to arouse his sleeping comrades. The men of the headquarters guard grabbed their muskets and cartridge boxes and began firing from the second-floor windows—only to stop abruptly when a wily bushwhacker below cried out, "For God's sake, don't fire; it's your own men!"

Captain William Rodewald, commander of the guard company, thinking that perhaps a mistake might have been made, led his troops down to the street to investigate. The first person he saw was a Confederate soldier well known to him. Covering him instantly with a pistol, he shouted to his troops that they were being attacked by rebels and to open fire. Most of the partisans by now had passed through the square on the way to attack the Union camp, but Rodewald's men did manage to fire a volley into their rear ranks. They were then attacked by Quantrill's guerrillas, who had remained behind to carry out their mission of holding the town.

Colonel Buel was rudely awakened from a sound slumber by the sudden burst of firing on the street outside the Southern Bank. As soon as he grasped what was happening, he sent word to Rodewald to bring his men over to the headquarters building. Rodewald complied, but it at once became apparent that this move was a mistake. Quantrill's men surrounded the bank and from the adjoining buildings and other vantage points poured a hail of bullets through its windows. This fire pinned down the soldiers inside and prevented Buel from getting in touch with the rest of his command.

Up the street a squad of bushwhackers led by Todd quickly overcame the provost marshal guard at the county jail, then smashed open the cell doors with sledge hammers. Among the prisoners in the cells was none other than Town Marshal Jim Knowles, the man who had supplied Buel with the information which led to the ambush deaths of John Little and Ed Koger. He was being held in the jail on charges of killing a citizen in a brawl. When he saw him an expression of fiendish glee came over Todd's face. Drawing both of his pistols, Todd shot Knowles again and again until the guns were empty and Knowles' body was a riddled hulk. A little later another party of bushwhackers had the satisfaction of slaying Lieutenant Thomas, leader of the ambushers. They found him in a hotel room, shot him, and then kicked his body down a flight of stairs.

Meanwhile, Hughes was attacking the Federal camp west of

town. His first onslaught took the soldiers completely by surprise. Many of them were killed or captured in their tents, others fled in wild panic, in some cases not stopping until they reached Kansas City. However, a doughty Union captain named Jacob Axline, who had joined the garrison just the previous day, rallied a portion of the troops and formed them in a line behind a stone wall. Hughes, who was having trouble keeping his young and poorly disciplined followers from plundering the Union tents in disregard of more important business, led a charge against Axline's position. But the Federals repulsed the assault, during which Hughes fell from his saddle with a bullet through the forehead. Colonel Gideon W. Thompson then assumed command of the Confederates and ordered another attack. This too failed, and Thompson also was hit, but not fatally. Still another colonel, this time Upton Hayes, took over—only soon to be wounded in his turn in the foot. So all in all it was a bad day for Southern colonels: one killed and two wounded.

Several hours now had gone by, and it was beginning to look as if Captain Axline's stubborn stand behind the stone wall might snatch victory from defeat for the Federals. Such, however, was not to be the case. Back in the town, Quantrill grew tired of peppering away at Buel's headquarters and decided to adopt more drastic measures. He had his men set fire to the building next door to the Southern Bank, then yelled up to Buel, "Surrender or roast!"

Buel speedily decided that the first alternative was preferable to the second. He shouted back that he would surrender, but that he wanted assurance that his men would be protected from the bloodthirsty bushwhackers. Colonel Thompson, who had ridden back to town after being wounded, promised him that they would be treated as regular prisoners of war. Buel thereupon hauled down the Union flag flying from the roof of the Southern Bank and sent word to the troops with Axline to surrender also. Axline at first angrily declared that he would not obey this order, but in the end was persuaded to do so by several less determined officers. Colonel Thompson promptly paroled all the Union prisoners, including Buel. Quantrill's men did not molest them.

Federal casualties were officially reported as twenty-six killed and seventy-four wounded, while according to Union sources the Confederates lost twenty-three dead and a large but undetermined number wounded, many mortally. The battle was the worst Northern defeat in Missouri since the fall of Lexington, and it produced shocked alarm among Union adherents throughout the border country. Major credit for the victory undoubtedly belonged to Quantrill and his bushwhackers. They led the attack, bottled up Buel and his guard company, and finally forced the hapless Union colonel to surrender his entire command when it appeared that the rest of the Confederate army would be unable to finish the job.[4]

The Confederates remained in Independence, gathering captured Union equipment and other spoils, until late in the afternoon, then marched back to their base at Lee's Summit. Although they sent several parties across the Missouri to get in touch with the partisan bands on the other side and let them know that an escape route southward was open, the death of Hughes ended the plan to raise a large force north of the river. Quantrill's men left the main body and went into camp at the Morgan Walker farm, where they remained until the evening of August 12. They then marched to the Ingraham farm, six miles west of Lone Jack, where, on August 15, Colonel Thompson officially mustered them into the Confederate service. Henceforth, from a legal standpoint, Quantrill's band was part of the Confederate military establishment—but the actuality of the matter, as will be seen, was something quite different.

Following their mustering in, the bushwhackers formally elected their officers. Quantrill was named captain, Bill Hallar first lieutenant, Todd second lieutenant, and Gregg third lieutenant. Thompson then commissioned Quantrill a captain of Confederate Partisan Rangers. He did this under authority from General Hindman and on the basis of the Confederate Partisan Ranger Act, which empowered field commanders to issue such commissions.[5]

Todd resented Hallar being selected first lieutenant. An open quarrel ensued between the two men which ended only when Hallar left the band.* Actually, however, the organization set up at the Ingraham farm meant little. Lacking true military disci-

* Soon after leaving Quantrill, Hallar was killed. Bushwhacker memoirs rarely mention him, and it is hard to understand why he was elected first lieutenant.

pline, serving with boyhood friends in their own neighborhoods, ever-varying in numbers, frequently operating in small parties, and constantly scattering and regrouping, the bushwhackers found it impossible to maintain a regular, rigid military organization. In practice, therefore, the real leaders were whoever became so by virtue of personality, daring, and ability—men such as Todd, Cole Younger, Andy Blunt, Gregg, Dave Poole, Fletch Taylor, and Dick Yeager, to name only the more prominent of Quantrill's followers. Quantrill relied on these subchieftains to carry out his orders and they in their turn exercised considerable operational independence except when Quantrill was in direct personal charge.

On August 16, Quantrill took sixty men to Independence, which had not yet been reoccupied by the Union forces, and loaded several wagons with barrels of captured gunpowder. He then took the powder to the Morgan Walker farm, where it was hidden in the cellar. There it remained until after the war, undiscovered and undisturbed by the numerous Federal patrols which scoured the area.

The remainder of the band, some ninety in number, stayed behind at the Ingraham farm under the command of Hallar. Before going to Independence, Quantrill instructed Hallar not to leave the camp until he returned. But while he was away a large-scale battle broke out at the near-by village of Lone Jack. Hayes and Thompson, who had been reinforced by a thousand Confederates from Arkansas under Colonels Vard Cockrell and John T. Coffee, attacked a column of eight hundred Federals commanded by Major Emory Foster. This force had marched down from Lexington as part of a general movement of Union forces against Southern partisans in western Missouri. The battle which followed was extremely bitter and hard-fought. Foster's command, although heavily outnumbered, beat off charge after charge, and even delivered some rocking counterattacks. The troops on both sides were Missourians, many of them boyhood chums and members of the same church congregations, but if anything, this only caused them to fight all the harder.

When it became obvious that Foster was not going to be defeated without a long, tough struggle, Hayes sent a messenger to the bushwhackers' camp asking them to come to his assistance.

Hallar, bearing in mind Quantrill's instructions, refused. Later in the day another courier arrived from Hayes repeating the request for aid, this time with much greater urgency. At first Hallar again said no, but after some argument Gregg persuaded him to go to Lone Jack in spite of Quantrill's orders. The guerrillas hastily saddled up and galloped off toward the battlefield, guided by the sound of the guns and the dense billows of smoke. However, before they could get there, the Union forces, their artillery captured and their ammunition exhausted, gave way before a strong Confederate assault, and the fighting, except for mopping up, was all over.[6]

Although the bushwhackers did not participate as a unit in the Lone Jack battle, several of them did as individuals on their own hook. The most notable example was Cole Younger, who gained his first fame in this engagement. During the fighting he was the only man on the field who remained mounted. In addition, he twice rode the entire length of the Confederate line under heavy fire distributing ammunition. At the end of his second such excursion Hayes personally told him to dismount or else he would shoot his horse! Cole forthwith slipped from out of the saddle onto the ground. As he did so the Federals expressed their admiration for his bravery with a rousing cheer. (Chivalry was dying but not yet dead in Missouri in 1862.) Thinking that the Bluebellies were cheering because they believed that they had shot him, Cole yelled back, "Halloo and be damned, you ain't killed nobody!" After the battle he prevented a fellow guerrilla from slaying the badly wounded Major Foster and his brother, then at their request, delivered a thousand dollars in cash to their mother in Warrensburg.[7]

The Confederates won the Battle of Lone Jack, but at a disproportionate cost: 118 men killed to only 45 on the Union side. Moreover, their ammunition was nearly exhausted at the end of the fighting. As a consequence, not only were they unable to follow up the victory, but they had no alternative except to retreat back into Arkansas when a large army of Kansans under Brigadier General James G. Blunt began pressing them on the night following the battle. Thus Confederate operations in Western Missouri, despite the spectacular successes at Independence and Lone Jack, were barren of strategically significant results. Indeed, the same could be said of the entire Confederate summer campaign in Missouri—a campaign which, as Schofield pointed out, merely demonstrated the weakness, rather than the strength, of the rebel cause in the state.[8]

Quantrill and Hayes alone remained in western Missouri to challenge the Yankee domination. With a combined force of about four hundred men, they went into camp near the headwaters of the Little Blue. Here, on August 20, a Federal cavalry regiment from Fort Leavenworth under Lieutenant Colonel John T. Burris attacked them. But after a brief skirmish they broke away, easily eluding Burris, who had to be content with plundering a few secesh barns and suppressing a rebel newspaper called *The Border Star* in Independence.[9]

Toward the end of August, Hayes also headed back for Arkansas, leaving the field again exclusively to Quantrill. But before departing he turned over to the guerrillas a Federal lieutenant named Levi Copeland who had been captured at Lone Jack. He did so at Quantrill's request. Quantrill wanted a hostage for one of his own men, Perry Hoy, who was being held at Fort Leavenworth under sentence of death.

A few days after Hayes marched away Quantrill obtained a copy of the St. Louis *Republican*. He sat down at the table in the cabin where he was staying to read it. Suddenly Gregg, who was sitting near by waiting to see the paper, saw a striking change come over his chieftain's face. Dropping the paper, Quantrill pulled a blankbook and a pencil from his pocket, scribbled a note, and handed it to Gregg with the curt order, "Give this to Andy Blunt!" Gregg was curious to know what was up, so as soon as he left the cabin he unfolded the note and read:

> Take Lieutenant Copeland out and shoot him. Go to Woodsmall's camp [?], get two prisoners from his camp, shoot them, and return as quickly as possible.

Gregg delivered the note, then returned to the cabin, where he picked up the paper and read a notice which made the reason for Quantrill's order perfectly clear: Perry Hoy had been hanged at Fort Leavenworth. After a bit several shots reverberated through the forest and Blunt sauntered in to report that the order had been carried out. Quantrill's only response was to order all the men to saddle up and get ready to march. Asked why by the always inquisitive Gregg, he replied sharply, "We are going to go to Kansas and kill ten more men for poor Perry!" [10]

The bushwhackers were soon riding toward the Kansas line. They stopped for the night near the border, then during the afternoon of the following day entered Kansas and headed for Olathe. Before reaching the town they killed ten men, most of whom, Gregg later remarked, were known to them. On the outskirts of Olathe, Quantrill divided his band. Sixty men under Gregg formed a cordon about the town to prevent anyone from escaping. The remainder, led by Quantrill himself, advanced through the streets and into the courthouse square. On the square they found 125 militiamen drawn up as if to give battle. The bushwhackers dismounted, hitched their horses to the courthouse fence, pulled out their revolvers, and called on the militiamen to surrender. The militiamen took a good look at the heavily armed raiders, remembered that they had families to support, and forthwith laid down their arms and raised their hands. Only one of them attempted to resist; a guerrilla promptly shot him dead. This made fourteen men for Perry Hoy.

With Olathe now completely at their mercy, the bushwhackers proceeded to engage in an all-night orgy of looting and murder. They took every usable horse, ransacked all the stores, robbed private homes, destroyed the presses of the local *Mirror*, stripped the male inhabitants of their money, valuables, and clothing and killed in cold blood about a dozen men—"shooting them down," reported a witness, "like so many hogs." Perry Hoy was indeed well revenged.[11]

Quantrill enjoyed himself hugely. Once again he had returned in triumph to the state which had outlawed and hunted him. Meeting with a former acquaintance, he sat down with him on a bench near the courthouse and talked for nearly an hour about old times. But when the friend called him "Bill," he politely insisted on being addressed as "Captain Quantrill," at the same time proudly displaying his Confederate commission.[12]

In the morning the guerrillas headed back to Missouri, taking along several wagons loaded with plunder and the captive militiamen, all of whom had been stripped to their underwear. The hapless Kansans thought that they were being led off to be massacred, but after marching for a few miles Quantrill released them with the admonition to return home and be good boys.[13]

News of the Olathe raid set Colonel Burris' Fourth Kansas Cavalry Regiment in hot pursuit of the bushwhackers. On the tenth it caught up with them in Cass County, but they did not attempt to make a stand. Instead they simply broke up into small groups and retreated into the timber. Burris kept after them in a long, relentless, grinding chase which lasted ten days and covered Jackson, Johnson, and Lafayette counties. Although he failed to bring them to bay, or even to kill any of them, he did manage to recover most of the Olathe loot. In addition the Kansans extracted some revenge of their own by burning farmhouses, rounding up horses, and "liberating"—to quote Colonel Burris—"upward of 60 loyal colored persons, tired of the rule of rebel masters." [14] The victims of these depredations must have ruefully concluded that Quantrill's raids on Kansas would be just fine if only they didn't make the Yankees so all-fired mean afterward!

On October 5, Quantrill reassembled his scattered band at Sibley on the Missouri River north of Independence. The following day his scouts reported that a large Union cavalry patrol was approaching. Quickly he prepared an ambush. With one-half of his men he retreated along the Independence-Lexington road, while the other half, under Dick Chiles, a new man in the gang, remained behind to waylay the oncoming Feds. Quantrill lacked confidence in Chiles and did not want to put him in charge of the ambush. He did so only at the urging of Gregg and Todd, who thought he had what it took.

Chiles posted the ambushers behind a high rail fence which fronted an old log cabin located at a point where the road took a sharp turn. The Federals, a detachment of the Fifth Missouri Cavalry, under Captain Daniel H. David, advanced warily, for they knew that Quantrill was in the vicinity. Just as the head of their column came in view, Chiles gave the word to fire. This order was premature; he should have waited until the entire patrol was in range. As a result, the guerrillas' volley hit only a few of the soldiers. Captain David quickly rallied his men, had them dismount, and led them in a charge with drawn sabers. In accordance with their now standard practice, the bushwhackers did not try to fight it out, but mounted their horses and galloped off to rejoin their comrades on down the road. As they retreated a bullet pierced Chiles' lungs, killing him. He was, somewhat ironically, the only guerrilla casualty.

David waited until reinforcements arrived from Independence, then pursued Quantrill all through the afternoon and night and well into the following day. But, as in the case of Burris, he was unable to overtake the better-mounted bushwhackers, who zigzagged through woods and hills familiar to them since boyhood, and who were dispersed into small bands which concentrated merely to scatter again. On the evening of the second day, with his troops reeling in the saddle from sheer exhaustion, David abandoned the fruitless chase. "We do not believe that guerrillas can ever be taken by pursuit, we must take them by strategy," he reported back to his superiors.[15]

Quantrill spent the next week getting ready for another Kansas raid. This took place on October 17. It was directed against Shawneetown, a settlement located just across the state line from Kansas City. As the raiders approached the village they came upon a Union wagon train escorted by an infantry detachment. The soldiers had stopped to rest, most of them were asleep, and they had posted no guards. The shooting and yelling bushwhackers pounced upon them, killed fifteen, and pillaged the wagons. They then rode unopposed into Shawneetown, which they burned to the ground after looting all the stores and houses and shooting several civilians, including a Shawnee Indian. There was no pursuit as they returned to the Sni-A-Bar with their plunder.[16]

Three times now Quantrill had struck like a deadly snake into Kansas—Aubry, Olathe, and Shawneetown—and each blow had been more vicious than the previous one. At Aubry, the emphasis had been on plunder; at Olathe mass murder was added to looting; and at Shawneetown both were climaxed by wholesale arson. Settlers living in the Kansas border counties were gripped by panic. Hundreds of them fled to the interior or left the state altogether. The few who remained cried out desperately for protection against Quantrill's raiders.

The coming of cold weather stripped the bushes and trees of their concealing leaves, making guerrilla operations unprofitable as well as uncomfortable. Therefore, only a few bushwhackers, led by Cole Younger, Joe Lea, and Dick Yeager, elected to stick it out in Missouri through the winter. All the rest assembled on November 3, at Big Creek in Cass County, under Quantrill's command and began marching for Arkansas. Accompanying them were a number of farmers, part-time guerrillas, and their families who wished to get behind Confederate lines.

As luck would have it, the march scarcely had gotten under way when the advance scouts rode back to report a Union wagon train, escorted by twenty-one soldiers, on the road ahead! Since such a tempting target could not very well be passed up, Quantrill sent Gregg with forty men to take care of it. Gregg's band swooped down on the train, killed four soldiers and six teamsters, burned the wagons, and took the escort commander, Lieutenant Newby, and several privates prisoner. The bushwhacker column then resumed its southward trek.

Meanwhile, Colonel E. C. Catherwood, Federal commander at Harrisonville, had learned that Quantrill's band was in the region. Concerned with the safety of the wagon train, he set out in its wake with 150 cavalry. He soon came upon the burned wagons and the bullet-riddled corpses of the soldiers and teamsters. At this sight he determined to get revenge. He took up the trail of the guerrillas. After a short ride he discovered them just as they were going into camp. A running battle followed, during which the Union troopers (according to Catherwood) killed six bushwhackers and wounded twenty-one. In addition they rescued Lieutenant Newby and one of the captured privates. They kept after Quantrill, who resorted to his favorite tactic of scattering into the woods, until their horses gave out.[17]

The bushwhackers regrouped as soon as they were no longer pressed by Catherwood and continued their southward movement. On November 5, they met up with three hundred Confederate cavalrymen under Colonel Warner Lewis north of Lamar in Barton County. Lewis proposed to Quantrill that they join forces and attack the Union garrison at Lamar. Quantrill readily agreed, and together they drew up a plan of battle. The bushwhackers would charge into Lamar from the south at ten o'clock that night, while at the same time Lewis would strike from the north side.

Quantrill carried out his role perfectly. His men attacked right on time, drove in the Federal pickets, and occupied the town square. But the garrison, which had been anticipating a raid, fortified itself in the brick courthouse building and poured a deadly fire into the guerrilla ranks. Moreover, Lewis failed to show up and the bushwhackers were left to fight alone. After two hours of futile fighting, during which he lost several good boys, an angry and disgusted Quantrill ordered the attack broken off. As they rode out of Lamar, the bushwhackers eased their frustrated wrath by setting fires which destroyed one-third of the town.[18] They either forgot or ignored the fact that this was a Missouri community they were burning, not a Kansas one.

Quantrill next crossed into the southeast corner of Kansas, picked up the Fort Smith road, and followed it through the Indian Territory into Arkansas. General Hindman, who had commended him in official dispatches for being "extremely zealous and useful" during the summer campaign in Missouri, assigned his company to Colonel Joe Shelby's regiment, an outfit also made up of West Missouri boys. The entry of the bushwhackers into the Confederate camp at Cross Hollows caused a great stir: everybody wanted to see these dreadful and already legendary men who fought under the black flag.[19]

chapter V The Knights of the Bush

The flames of Quantrill's ambition leaped high as bloody 1862 drew to a close. In less than a year he had rocketed from a nondescript Border Ruffian to a captain of partisan rangers in the Confederate Army and the chieftain of the largest, most formidable guerrilla band in Missouri. Was there any reason, he must have asked himself, why he should not go on to even greater things? These were revolutionary times. With a little luck, there was no telling what a man of boldness, ability, and an eye for the main chance might achieve. Already he was famous throughout the West; before long he would make the whole country take note of the name Quantrill!

Thoughts such as these no doubt were flowing through Quantrill's mind when, about the middle of December, he left his band in Arkansas and accompanied by Andy Blunt, journeyed all the way to Richmond, Virginia. On arriving in the Confederate capital he obtained an interview with Secretary of War James A. Seddon. The only source for what happened at this meeting is Edwards, who states that he obtained his information from Senator Louis T. Wigfall of Texas, who was present. Edwards' account is given here for what it may be worth, and also as a good specimen of Edwards' flamboyant literary style:

> Quantrell asked to be commissioned as a Colonel under the Partisan Ranger Act, and to be so recognized by the Department as to have accorded to him whatever protection the Confederate government might be in a condition to exercise. Never mind the question of men, he would have the complement required in a month after he reached Western Missouri. The warfare was desperate, he knew, the service

desperate, everything connected with it was a desperate fight. The Secretary suggested that war had its amenities and its refinements, and that in the nineteenth century it was simple barbarism to talk of a black flag.

"*Barbarism!*" and Quantrell's blue eyes blazed, and his whole manner and attitude underwent a transformation, "barbarism, Mr. Secretary, means war and war means barbarism. Since you have touched upon this subject, let us discuss it a little. Times have their crimes as well as men. For twenty years this cloud has been gathering; for twenty years—inch by inch and little by little those people called the Abolitionists have been on the track of slavery; for twenty years the people of the South have been robbed, here of a negro and there of a negro; for twenty years hates have been engendered and wrathful things laid up against the day of wrath. The cloud has burst. Do not condemn the thunderbolt."

The War Secretary bowed his head. Quantrell, leaving his own seat, and standing over him as it were and above him, went on.

"Who are these people you call Confederates? Rebels, unless they succeed, outcasts, traitors, food for hemp and gunpowder. There were no great statesmen in the South, or this war would have happened ten years ago; no inspired men, or it would have happened fifteen years ago. Today the odds are desperate. The world hates slavery; the world is fighting you. The ocean belongs to the Union navy. There is a recruiting officer in every foreign port. I have captured and killed many who did not know the English tongue. Mile by mile the cordon is being drawn about the granaries of the South, Missouri will go first, next Kentucky, next Tennessee, by and by Mississippi and Arkansas, and then what? That we must put gloves on our hands, and honey in our mouths, and fight this war as Christ fought the wickedness of the world? . . ."

"What would *you* do, Captain Quantrell, were yours the power and opportunity?"

"Do, Mr. Secretary? Why I would wage such a war and have such a war waged by land and sea as to make surrender forever impossible. I would cover the armies of the Confederacy all over with blood. I would break up foreign enlistments by indiscriminate massacre. I would win the independence of my people or I would find them graves."

"And our prisoners, what of them?"

"Nothing of them; there would be no prisoners. Do they take any prisoners from me? Surrounded, I do not surrender; surprised, I do not give way to panic; outnumbered, I rely upon common sense and stubborn fighting; proscribed, I answer proclamation with proclamation;

outlawed, I feel through it my power; hunted, I hunt my hunters in turn; hated and made blacker than a dozen devils, I add to my hoofs the swiftness of the horse, and to my horns the terrors of a savage following. Kansas should be laid waste at once. Meet the torch with the torch, pillage with pillage, slaughter with slaughter, subjugation with extermination. You have my ideas of war, Mr. Secretary, and I am sorry that they do not accord with your own, nor the ideas of the government you have the honor to represent so well." And Quantrell, without his commission as a Partisan Ranger, or without any authorization to raise a regiment of Partisan Rangers bowed himself away from the presence of the Secretary and away from Richmond.*

Edwards, it should be noted, states that Quantrill did not get a colonel's commission. This contradicts Quantrill's own claim upon his return from Richmond, and the belief of many of his followers.[1] Not only did he say that he was a colonel, but he began signing dispatches with that title, and sometimes even Federal commanders attributed that rank to him. Since Confederate military authorities on occasion addressed him as a colonel, perhaps he obtained such a commission (as Connelley suggests) from Sterling Price or some other Western general.[2] But there is absolutely no documentary evidence on the matter, and even supposing he indeed had the rank, it possessed no real significance, as shall be seen.

While Quantrill was gone, Bill Gregg commanded the guerrillas. Todd, who otherwise would have been in charge, returned to Jackson County late in November, along with Jim Little, Fletch Taylor, and several others. The remaining bushwhackers served with Shelby's regiment at the battles of Cane Hill, Fayetteville, and Prairie Grove in Arkansas during the months of November and December. Following Hindman's defeat at Prairie Grove, they retreated with his army south of the Arkansas River, where most of them remained through the winter, operating as scouts and harassing the local Unionists. They fought bravely in all the battles, and at Fayetteville they rescued Shelby after he had been taken prisoner by some Arkansas "Mountain Federals." [3]

Quantrill returned to Arkansas sometime in January. With the

* Edwards, *Noted Guerrillas*, pp. 156-58. A reader of Edwards' book is not surprised that Quantrill should talk in such a fancy manner. *All* of the characters in the book *always* speak in this way.

coming of spring the bushwhackers began filtering back into Missouri. Quantrill himself arrived in the Blue Springs region early in May. The Union commander at Lexington promptly reported his presence:

> Quantrill is here; he came from Price to conscript; he came with 40 men; he has joined Reid's, Jarret's, Todd's, Younger's, and Clifton's gangs to his own, which give him from 125 to 150 men; he disbanded his own force on Sunday night, with orders to rendezvous on Thursday night on the Big Sni, precise place not definitely learned; has orders from Price to stop bushwhacking and horse stealing. Price is to invade Southeast Missouri, and Quantrill is to annoy Kansas and Western Missouri; intends to conscript all of military age; has secret notice among Southern men to come to his camp and get property taken by mistake; came here to stay, not to take away any recruits; seems to be rather elevated in his purpose by his six or eight months' experience with the regular forces.[4]

Even as these lines were being written, the most spectacular and daring guerrilla raid of the war was taking place. Led by Dick Yeager, a Jackson County boy who had taken to the bush after Jennison's jayhawkers burned his family's farm, two dozen bushwhackers swept westward along the Santa Fe Trail to Council Grove, Kansas, some 130 miles from the Missouri line! They reached the outskirts of Council Grove on May 4, encountering absolutely no resistance on the way. The citizens of the town huddled helplessly in their homes, paralyzed with bewilderment and fright. But only one guerrilla—Yeager himself—rode into the town. And instead of plundering and killing, he went to a dentist's office and asked to have an aching tooth pulled!

The astonished dentist recovered his wits quickly enough to propose, "All right, but if I take care of the tooth, will you leave the town alone?" Yeager replied that he would spare the town, only get this goddamn tooth out! The dentist thereupon yanked the tooth and in turn Yeager kept his word.

The next day, however, the raiders sacked the near-by village of Diamond Springs, where they killed a man and wounded his wife—one of the few instances of the bushwhackers injuring a woman. They then swung back toward Missouri, robbing stagecoaches, burning farmhouses, and shooting settlers. Some of them, it is worth noting, were former residents of Kansas who had been forced to flee to Missouri by their Unionist neighbors early in the war. One such in particular was Bill Anderson, a black-bearded, fierce-looking fellow who was rapidly becoming notorious along the border.

The very boldness of Yeager's raid completely befuddled the Union troops in Kansas. As a result they either did nothing at all or else milled around in a frantic confusion of marches and countermarches. The only man in the state who kept his head and took effective measures to capture the raiders was James L. McDowell, U. S. Marshal at Leavenworth and Major General of the Kansas Militia. He hastily raised a posse of twenty men, then set out along the Sante Fe Trail in pursuit, picking up reinforcements as he went. At the Cottonwood River, west of Emporia, he encountered Yeager's band on its return march. He attacked immediately with overwhelming numbers, captured a dozen guerrillas, and forced the remainder, including Yeager, to scatter over the prairie. Since his horses were too exhausted for pursuit, he sent word to Emporia to intercept the raiders. Thirty men from Emporia took up a position along the Cottonwood for that purpose, but Yeager evaded them by crossing over to the Neosho River.*

As soon as they were free of pursuers, Yeager and his remaining followers resumed killing and pillaging. They shot a discharged soldier at a wayside inn, murdered another man at Willow Springs, and looted stores and houses at Rock Springs, Gardner, and Black Jack. At the latter settlement they also held up a stagecoach which contained as one of its passengers no less a personage than that redoubtable Border Ruffian of years gone by, Ex-Sheriff Sam Jones, who was now—incredible as it may seem—a Kansas Republican! Either the young raiders did not recognize Jones, or else they felt that his past virtues did not outweigh his present

* According to the *Western Journal of Commerce* the twelve raiders captured by McDowell were "placed in charge of Captain Stewart's cavalry, with directions to take them to Fort Riley. On their way to that post, the bushwhackers attempted to escape, when the guard fired upon them and the whole number were killed. A good riddance." The Captain Stewart referred to was John E. Stewart, Quantrill's former protector and fellow jayhawker. Such things could be expected of him.

sins, for they made him "shell out" along with the other passengers.

From Black Jack, Yeager's gang rode back across the border into the safety of the Jackson County bush. The Kansas City *Journal of Commerce*, describing the raid, commented acidly:

> That an insignificant band of guerrillas should have been able thus to penetrate 150 or 200 [*sic*] miles into Kansas, and make their way out again, robbing and murdering as they went, and the military authorities fully informed that they were in the State and leisurely travelling one of its great highways, is certainly not a *very* creditable state of facts.

Angry and frightened Kansans sharply criticized General Blunt, military commander of the state, and demanded increased protection against the bushwhackers.[5] The Yeager raid had convincingly demonstrated the shocking weakness of the Union border defense. What was there, many people wanted to know, to prevent the guerrillas from doing the same thing again, and on a much larger scale? Not only Kansans, but perhaps the bushwhackers themselves, began to ask this question. . . .

Blunt, a Kansas abolitionist political general with a fondness for strong whisky and weak women, tried to appease his critics by offering them blood. On May 29, he had the "somewhat notorious guerrilla" Jim Vaughn publicly hanged at Fort Leavenworth as an example to other Missouri partisans. Vaughn had been captured sometime previously when he and another bushwhacker, confident that they would not be recognized, went to Wyandotte, Kansas, entered a barbershop, carelessly removed their gun belts, and sat down for haircuts and shaves—only to have a squad of Union soldiers pounce on them. A correspondent of the Kansas City *Journal* vividly described Vaughn's execution:

> On the way to the gallows, the countenance of this somewhat notorious guerrilla, as he looked about upon the green fields and hills, so soon to be shut out of his gaze forever, wore a very saddened expression. When the wagon stopped, he evidently nerved himself for the scene. As soon as he ascended the scaffold he looked about with an unconcerned, nonchalantic air of bravado and sat down upon the rail-

ing. He was a fine looking man, about twenty-three years of age, large and powerfully built. He talked considerably with the officers on the platform, but in so low a tone that his words could not be heard. He took out some trinkets of various kinds, and some money, both Confederate scrip and U.S. notes, and gave them to the officer to forward to his sisters, who are now confined in Fort Leavenworth. He then turned and addressed the crowd in a tone of mingled defiance and bravado. He died, he said, a Southern man, and hoped he should go to a better world. Then, the fiend gleaming from his hardened face, he proceeded to threaten vengeance upon the crowd, saying some of them would suffer for his death. There was no gleam of penitence for his life of crime and sin, no relenting in the awful presence of death, but an air of bitterness and even bloodthirstiness, even while saying that he hoped to go to a better world. He desired that his friends should be told how he died, and that his body should be decently interred. When he had finished his arms were pinioned closely, the black cap was drawn over his face, and he was led upon the trap. He seemed fearful as he stepped upon it and asked somewhat sharply, "You are not going to push me off, are you?"

He stood a moment, and said, "This is my last look—let her slide!" The drop fell. Life was extinct in fifteen minutes; at the end of seventeen minutes he was cut down, and his remains placed in a plain walnut coffin, and interred about a hundred yards from the gallows.

Prior to the execution Colonel Ben Parker, a Confederate partisan leader in Northwest Missouri, sent a letter to Blunt warning him that if Vaughn were hanged, four Union prisoners would be strung up in reprisal. The letter did not reach Blunt until after the execution, but even if it had it would not have saved Vaughn. Like other Federal commanders Blunt adhered firmly to the policy of ignoring all bushwhacker communications. Parker, on learning of Vaughn's hanging, promptly carried out his threat, adding one more Union prisoner for good measure.[6]

The Federal authorities were taking an increasingly tough attitude toward rebel partisans and sympathizers in Missouri. One Union officer in particular aroused the fear and hatred of Southern elements with his harshness. This was Colonel William Penick of the Fifth Missouri State Militia Cavalry, commander at Independence after that post was re-established. Penick was a Radical Unionist who believed that the guerrillas would be cleaned out of the country "if hemp, fire, and gunpowder were freely used." During the winter his troops did so much pillaging in the pro-Southern Blue Springs neighborhood that the people there said that they were worse than Jennison's Jayhawkers. Moreover, on November 28, they hanged Sam Ramberlin from a rafter in his own barn, even though they had no specific charges against him, and on January 29, they killed John Sanders and Jeptha Crawford, two elderly neutralists. Following these outrages, the old men of Blue Springs were afraid to venture out in the daytime, and most of the boys either went into hiding, fled the country, or, if they were old enough, joined the bushwhackers.[7]

Penick's Missouri Feds were bad enough, but even worse were the Kansas Red Legs. So called because of the red leather leggings they wore, these border bandits were closely identical in personnel and character to the old jayhawker bands. Gangs of them infested both sides of the border, robbing, torturing, and killing helpless people whom they accused of being rebel sympathizers or of aiding Quantrill. "It seems impossible," declared one Missourian later, "that human beings could have been guilty of such merciless outrages as these men committed." [8]

The sufferings of pro-Southern Missourians, however, were equaled if not surpassed by those of Union supporters. In the summer of 1862, Quantrill had proclaimed his intention of driving away every Unionist living on the border; by the spring of 1863, it seemed as if he might well make good his threat. "Union men of this section of the State," wrote a Harrisonville correspondent of the Kansas City *Journal* in May,

> are very discouraged, as it is impossible for them to raise a crop this season. They dare not show their faces outside of our military lines, and . . . great suffering—yes, almost starvation, is in store for them. The bushwhackers know their men, their friends, and their enemies, and an honest Union man . . . cannot live outside of our military posts. It is a fact beyond doubt that . . . Quantrill & Co. do rule in this section of the State, and are protecting the subjects of the Jeff. Davis government. . . . Rebels and rebel sympathizers can live in the country, raise something to subsist themselves and their bushwhacker friends, and can travel wherever they please, without ever being molested, while the honest Union people have to seek refuge inside our lines.[9]

Quantrill's first act after returning to Missouri was to strike at Penick's hated troopers. Along with Todd and several others he ambushed a patrol out of Independence at the east fork of the Little Blue. Five Federals tumbled from their horses at the first fire; the survivors fled in wild disorder back toward Independence. The bushwhackers pursued and killed four more, Quantrill personally overtaking and pistoling one of them. He then had the bodies piled into a wagon and hauled into Independence by a local farmer to be turned over to Penick with the message that the same fate awaited all Bluebellies who ventured into bushwhacker country.[10]

Having thus let the Missouri Unionists know he was back in action, Quantrill next served similar notice on the Kansans. On the night of June 6 he led a second raid against Shawneetown. While one hundred of his men surrounded what was left of the little village, a small detachment went in and killed four civilians and set fire to nine houses. A resident of Shawneetown who managed to escape predicted that the raid was "only the forerunner of operations on a larger scale." [11]

Meanwhile, up in Clay County, guerrilla gangs were also bloodily active. Under the headline "Butchery at Missouri City" the Kansas City *Journal* of May 30 reported that a five-man Union militia detachment had been wiped out near there on the twenty-fifth. The bushwhackers, after decoying the militiamen into a trap, ruthlessly shot them down and then robbed and stripped their bodies. Only one soldier, Private Benjamin Rapp, survived the attack, although shot in four places. Some civilians took him to a doctor in Richfield, but the guerrillas, learning that he was still alive, rode into the town and finished him off as he lay helpless in bed. Among those taking part in the massacre was a guerrilla named "Frank Jame."

For some time now the *Journal of Commerce* had been demanding more effective countermeasures against the bushwhackers. The owner of this paper was Colonel R. T. Van Horn, the man who had saved Kansas City from the Secessionists in 1861, and its editor was Dwight T. Thacher, a Kansas Republican. Both Van Horn and Thacher were of course staunch Unionists who strongly and sincerely resented the guerrilla outrages. But more than that, they were much concerned about the effect of bushwhacking on the business prosperity of Kansas City. The guerrillas had forced hundreds of people out of the surrounding countryside, stopped or delayed work on the Missouri Pacific Railroad which was to link Kansas City with St. Louis, and, worst of all, had nearly destroyed Kansas City's great overland trade with New Mexico and the Far West, driving most of it into the hands of the rival cities of Leavenworth and Atchison.

Consequently, the *Journal* began needling the military authorities about their failure to suppress the bushwhackers. "The problem . . . of the bushwhackers," began one Thacher editorial early in May, "ought not to be a very difficult one to solve." All that was necessary was for the troops to go "into the bushes, and take the scoundrels at their own game." There were already enough troops available for the job, as the guerrillas numbered "not over one or two hundred." Sufficient soldiers should be stationed in the towns to protect them, the rest "kept in constant motion" hunting the guerrillas "in the fields where they prowl and lurk like the savage Indians." Unless this were done, and "the bushwhacker fraternity cleaned out, the border counties of Missouri and Kansas will soon be depopulated."

A few days later, Thacher took up the same theme in another editorial. "Is there not among all our Lieutenants, Captains, Majors, Colonels and Generals," he asked rhetorically, "one single man of wit, address, shrewdness, and *vim* enough to devise some means of cleaning out the miserable bushwhackers, who are keeping the border in constant turmoil? Must we give it up [*sic*] that one bushwhacker is more than a match for ten soldiers? There is a screw, and a pretty big one, loose somewhere. . . ."

Thacher's criticisms prompted a number of replies from offended army officers. They were doing everything humanly possible, they declared, to rid the country of bushwhackers, but two things made this almost an impossibility: the difficult nature of the West Missouri terrain, and the deep-seated hostility of the majority of the inhabitants. "There is no region or country better adapted to the wants of the bushwhackers than this," wrote one officer, "and the citizens, with their hypocritical professions of loyalty, are the steadfast coadjutors of the bushwhackers."

These rebuttals caused Thacher to tone down his criticism. At the same time, however, he continued to demand better protection for wagon trains and stagecoaches, to call for drastic punishment of the bushwhackers and their friends, and to feature stories of guerrilla outrages and attacks—which, as the summer progressed, increased in frequency.[12]

The difficulties experienced by the Federal troops along the border were nothing new in the history of warfare. Combating guerrillas is among the most trying of military operations, and is invariably feared and detested by the troops assigned to it. In 1863, as always, it required sharp intelligence, constant vigilance, great courage, and not a little brutality and callousness. The bushwhackers were rarely seen, were hard to track and locate, and they struck stealthily and suddenly. Capture by them meant death, sometimes, as war passions mounted, by enforced suicide or fiendish torture. And, finally, if brought to bay, the bushwhackers fought desperately because they could expect no more mercy than they gave.

The officers who answered Thacher's editorials were quite correct in stating that the bushwhackers derived enormous advantage from the character of the countryside. Most of western Missouri consisted of broad, rolling prairies which were ideal for mounted operations. Yet at the same time, its many hill and forest areas provided excellent cover and concealment. Furthermore, the guerrillas, being native to the section, had an intimate knowledge of every lane, trail, and bridle path. Federal troops, on the other hand, usually lacked such valuable information and were slow to acquire it. As a consequence, the bushwhackers were able to roam at will by little-known routes, while the Union soldiers, sticking to the main-traveled roads, searched for them in vain.

The citadel of the bushwhackers was the Sni-A-Bar country along the Jackson County-Lafayette County line. This was a wild and gloomy region of dense woods, tangled thickets, deep gorges, and narrow, twisting trails which could be defended easily by a few alert sentries. Whenever hard pressed, Quantrill's men would head for this almost impregnable refuge, and the Federals, if they followed, would do so only in great strength and with even greater caution.

More important than the terrain, however, was the other factor to which the Union officers attributed the guerrillas' success—the support they received from the civilian population. Most of the people of western Missouri looked upon the bushwhackers as their avengers and defenders. In addition, a large proportion of them had friends and relatives riding with Quantrill and the other partisan leaders. Therefore, they zealously assisted the bushwhackers in every possible way, from feeding and sheltering them, to supplying them with food and ammunition and acting as their spies. Not only did the old men and the womenfolk render this extremely valuable aid, but even the small children. Thus, Frank Smith relates that youngsters scarcely able to walk would gather up pieces of lead for use in making bullets in return for presents from George Todd, who was a great favorite with children.

The Federal commanders tried to prevent civilians from assisting the guerrillas by fining them, making them post bonds for good behavior, imprisoning them, burning their homes and crops, and even killing them. But such repressive measures proved utterly futile. In fact, if anything, they made the pro-Southern Missourians all the more defiant, and increased their determination to help the bushwhackers get back at the Yankees. Besides, a man living in "Quantrill Country" really had no choice when it came to aiding the guerrillas. Should he try to withhold food, shelter, or horses, they simply took what they wanted anyway, and maybe beat him up or killed him to boot. Consequently, the entire population assisted the bushwhackers, willingly or not. And this in turn meant that the Union troops were in effect opposed by an entire people—which made the task of suppressing the "Knights of the Bush," as the guerrillas were sometimes called, virtually impossible by ordinary military tactics.

Another important reason for the success of the bushwhackers, one which the Union officers did not mention for obvious reasons, was their superior fighting ability. The majority of Federal troops serving on the border were of the type which one might expect: second-line outfits and militia regiments, poorly trained and badly officered, lacking in *esprit de corps*, and having little stomach for the service they were called on to perform. In contrast the guerrillas were fast becoming masters of the art of partisan warfare, and they fought with the consummate fury of men who wished to avenge personal wrongs and who knew that defeat equaled death. Moreover, the guerrillas by and large were better mounted and armed than their Northern adversaries. In respect to horses, western Missouri was a region "abounding in some of the best horseflesh in the West," and the bushwhackers helped themselves to the best of this best. Union cavalrymen, on the other hand, were commonly mounted on inferior army plugs. Even worse, many Federal units sent against the guerrillas were infantry, and thus practically useless except for garrison duty.

As for arms, Quantrill's men relied almost entirely on the revolver, in particular the five- and six-shot Colt's Navy Revolver, so-called because of the picture of a naval battle engraved on the cylinder. Other types of pistols, they avowed, could not be depended on to kill a man unless the muzzle was placed against his ear! Most of the guerrillas carried two revolvers at their belt and two more in saddle holsters. However, some bedecked themselves and their horses with six, eight, and even a dozen hand guns!

They carried such a large number of weapons not out of ostentation, but because they wished to be able to maintain a high and steady fire power. Thus, during a battle, as soon as one revolver was empty they could pull out another—a tremendous advantage, especially if your opponents had to stop and reload.

Partly as a result of necessity and partly through experimentation, the bushwhackers discovered that by reducing the powder charges in their cartridges one-half they could eliminate much of the kick, thereby increasing accuracy, yet without making any notable sacrifice of carrying and striking power. The best shot in Quantrill's band, also the fastest draw, was Ol Shepherd, who had only one eye. Frank Smith states that he could "cut a one-fourth inch rope in two at twenty paces, firing just as the barrel of his pistol came out of his holster, and with his hand never raised higher than his hip." Next in shooting ability to Shepherd were Todd and Quantrill. Both were equally good shots, but Todd was faster on the draw. All the bushwhackers prided themselves on their marksmanship and practiced zealously to improve it. They were, taken as a whole, probably the most formidable bunch of "revolver fighters" the West ever knew.*

* Mr. B. James George, Sr., son of Hi George, one of Quantrill's men, informs this author that he once witnessed his father, then quite elderly, shoot and kill a chicken-destroying dog with a single bullet from a revolver fired at a range of well over one hundred feet.

The Federal cavalry, being equipped with one-shot carbines and sabers, were no match for the bushwhackers in close combat—which was about the only type of combat in western Missouri. The saber, in particular, was worse than useless. There is not a single recorded instance of a guerrilla being killed by a saber, but there *are* several cases of Federal soldiers being killed themselves while attempting to use this highly vaunted weapon. Union cavalrymen complained loudly and bitterly about their inferior arms, and asked that they be issued revolvers. Later in the war this was done, but the results were practically nil. The Federals pistols were of poor quality, and according to the bushwhackers the Yankees couldn't hit anything with them anyway.

The bushwhackers' fighting tactics were based directly on the revolver. Their favorite device was to lie in ambush beside a road along which some unwary Union patrol was approaching. When the soldiers drew close, the bushwhackers would suddenly come charging out of the brush on horseback, screaming the terrifying rebel yell and blazing away with their pistols. In a matter of seconds the whole affair would be over. The guerrillas would strip their victims' bodies, round up their horses, and disappear once more into the forests and thickets.

Another method of attack increasingly used by bushwhackers was to wear captured Northern uniforms, ride up to a detachment of unsuspecting soldiers, and shoot them down at point-blank range. After several incidents of this type, the Federals began using identification signs and passwords in order to tell their own men from the enemy. This system worked well initially, and there were even cases of the soldiers trapping the bushwhackers. But the Union officers neglected to change the signs and passwords frequently enough, with the result that the guerrillas usually caught on to them in short order and were able to perpetrate more murderous surprises.

As time went by the bushwhackers adopted a distinctive uniform of their own, which they generally wore when not disguised in Union blue. Its main ingredient was the "guerrilla shirt," a loose blouse with a low-scooped neck which was worn over the regular shirt. Usually made out of homespun and of a brownish color, it contained capacious pockets for ammunition and was gaudily decorated with beads or fancy needlework by the wives and sweethearts of the bushwhackers. A round-rimmed hat, cocked at a rakish angle and perhaps with a feather or metal star attached; baggy trousers tucked into high jack boots; and a broad leather belt bristling with revolvers completed the costume. Adequate clothing, however, was a constant problem for the partisans, and they were apt to wear whatever they could get their hands on. In fact, some of their raids were motivated, at least in part, by a desire to obtain clothes. They would always ransack the stores for men's clothing, and sometimes, as at Olathe, even strip the male inhabitants of their attire on the streets! [13]

Despite the efforts and claims of the Federal troops, the number of bushwhackers continually increased throughout 1862 and into 1863. Most of the new recruits were boys in their late teens who joined up either out of a desire for vengeance against the Bluebellies, or because of persecutions by Missouri Unionists, or simply because it seemed to be the only thing to do. An example of the first type of motivation was Ike Hall, who enlisted under Quantrill in the spring of 1862. Anthony's jayhawkers had raided the Hall farm during the preceding winter. While young Ike looked on helplessly as they made his mother set fire to her own home, then forced her to watch it burn. He already had one brother with Quantrill, and another soon followed him.[14]

Persecution, plus a desire for revenge, caused John McCorkle to become a bushwhacker. In the spring of 1861, he joined the Missouri State Guard and served under Price at the siege of Lexington. Then, like many others, he left Price's army when it began retreating, and returned to his home in Jackson County. He there tried to live peacefully, and along with his brother he took the oath of allegiance to the Federal Government. But his pro-Union neighbors regarded him with intense suspicion, the militia constantly harassed him and some Federal troops robbed him. Finally, in the summer of 1862, after being ordered to enlist in the state militia, he joined Quantrill. His book, *Three Years with Quantrill*, is one of the most valuable and interesting of the guerrilla memoirs.[15]

Frank Smith, whose account of Quantrill's band has been cited several times, typifies those who turned bushwhacker largely as a result of sheer circumstances. When the war began, Frank was only fifteen, and he continued to live with his parents on their farm near Blue Springs. But in the spring of 1863, however, conditions in the region were so hazardous and chaotic that it was impossible to plant crops. Therefore he went to Wyandotte in hopes of getting a job. But no sooner did he arrive in Kansas than the local Red Legs tried to get him to join up with them, threatening to kill him if he refused. At this point he decided there was nothing to do except "take to the bush." Accordingly in July, aged seventeen, he became a member of Quantrill's band.[16]

To the cases of Ike Hall, McCorkle, and Frank Smith, should be added one more, that of Riley Crawford. In 1862 a gang of soldiers murdered his father (Jeptha Crawford, previously mentioned). His mother thereupon took him to Quantrill and asked him to make a bushwhacker out of her fourteen-year-old son so that he might avenge her husband's death. Soon Riley was not only the youngest, but also one of the hardest fighters in Quantrill's band.

As the war moved into its third summer, the bushwhackers were never more strong, never more bold, never more dangerous. A bloodily convincing demonstration of this fact occurred on June 16 near Westport. It was evening, and the Federals, a 150-man detachment of the Ninth Kansas, were saddle-weary as they neared the end of a long day's march under the hot Western sun. They had been out since early dawn scouting for bushwhackers, but had not found a single trace of them. Now their sole thought was the cool well water up ahead in Westport. As far as they were concerned their mission was completed, and they had even strapped their carbines onto their saddles—after all, why worry about bushwhackers so close to Kansas City? Then, all at once, pistols began crackling in the surrounding underbrush, and a horde of long-haired, shouting partisans poured in from both sides. Caught completely off guard, and unable to fight back, the Federals broke into a wild, panic-stricken flight. The bushwhackers followed closely on their heels, ruthlessly killing every soldier they overhauled, right to the outskirts of Westport itself. In all, about twenty troopers were killed or wounded, but not a single guerrilla. The attackers were led by George Todd. After the slaughter was over, one of the bushwhackers, Will McGuire, stuck a note into the mouth of a dead Federal officer. "Remember the dying words of Jim Vaughn," it read.[18]

The Westport ambush was a cruel welcome to Brigadier General

Thomas Ewing, Jr., who on that very same day assumed command of the newly created District of the Border at Kansas City. This district consisted of all of Kansas north of the thirty-eighth parallel and south of the Missouri River. It had been created recently as part of a general shake-up of the Union command structure in the West, which resulted in Kansas and Missouri becoming part of the Department of the Missouri, headed by General Schofield. General Halleck, now general-in-chief of all the Northern Armies, explained that "peace cannot be restored and preserved near the border of Kansas and Missouri unless the country on both sides of the line be under the same command."

Ewing, aged thirty-four and "a very prince in appearance," was the son of a former cabinet member and the brother-in-law of General William T. Sherman. Prior to the war he had been a leader of the Kansas Free State Party, a railroad promoter in Leavenworth, and Chief Justice of the Kansas Supreme Court. In 1862 he had resigned his judgeship, raised the Eleventh Kansas Regiment, and commanded it in the Prairie Grove campaign. Personally confident that he had "few equals in mental vigor," he was by his own admission "inordinately ambitious," and hoped to secure election to the U. S. Senate. With this goal in mind he was, in the summer of 1863, stringing along with the radical Republican faction of Jim Lane, the acknowledged "king" of Kansas politics, despite the fact that he had long opposed Lane and was essentially a conservative. Thacher in the *Journal* welcomed Ewing's assumption of command and hailed him as a "man of sense and brains"—words which later were to haunt both the editor and the general.[19]

Ewing faced two main problems: the Kansas Red Legs and the Missouri bushwhackers. Shortly after taking command he moved to deal with the first one. In a speech at Olathe, Kansas, he denounced those who were "stealing themselves rich in the name of liberty," and threatened to put down the Red Legs with a rough hand if they did not cease their marauding. He backed up these words by ordering his troops to arrest all Red Legs. In addition, he placed Leavenworth under martial law, charging as he did so that the mayor—who happened to be none other than Dan Anthony —knowingly permitted the Red Legs to auction stolen horses and cattle in the town. Anthony and his close friend, editor D. W.

Wilder of the Leavenworth *Conservative*, raised a loud howl of indignation over Ewing's action and set out after his scalp.[20]

Ewing next turned his attention to the guerrilla situation. Here he adopted a two-pronged approach: suppressing the bushwhackers in Missouri and keeping them out of Kansas. In pursuit of the second objective he reorganized and strengthened the Kansas border defenses by placing permanent garrisons at Westport, Little Sante Fe, Olathe, Aubry, Coldwater Grove, Paola, and Mound City. Each post maintained a constant patrol of an assigned area so as to detect and defeat attempted guerrilla forays.

Quite correctly, however, Ewing conceived his primary task to be the suppression of bushwhacking in western Missouri. Once this was achieved, the problem of protecting Kansas would be automatically solved. His first move after taking command, therefore, was to step up the Union antiguerrilla campaign. But his efforts along this line proved no more successful than those of his predecessors. All through June, July, and into August the bushwhackers continued to run rampant. Not a day passed without its reports of fresh ambushes, raids, and outrages. Some people began to fear that Quantrill might even attack Kansas City, while over in Lafayette County, complained the Lexington *Union*, the only persons who could travel the roads safely were bushwhackers and their friends—Union men were liable to be shot down on sight.[21]

By August, Ewing concluded that unless his forces were tripled —he had only 2,500 troops for his entire district (which also included Colorado)—the guerrillas could never be suppressed by purely military means. Therefore, he adopted a plan designed to destroy the very roots of their power, the support given them by the civilian population. For some time now Union adherents had been advocating such a policy. Oaths of allegiance, they said, were meaningless—the rebels took them only to violate them. What the military authorities should do was to require every able-bodied man in western Missouri to take up arms against the bushwhackers. Those who refused would then be driven out of the state as self-revealed traitors.

Early in August, Ewing wrote Schofield outlining his new policy and asking for authority to put it into effect. Two-thirds of the families in western Missouri, he stated, were kin to the bushwhackers and were "actively and heartily engaged in feeding, clothing, and sustaining them." Hence, several hundred families of the worst guerrillas should be transported to Arkansas. This not only would deprive the guerrillas of their aid, but would cause the guerrillas whose families had been removed to follow them out of the state. Surrender terms could then be offered to the less offensive bushwhackers remaining.

On August 14, Schofield approved Ewing's plan but cautioned him to be very careful in executing it. Four days later Ewing issued General Order No. 10. It directed all company and detachment commanders in the District of the Border to arrest and send to the provost marshal in Kansas City all men and women "not heads of families" who were willfully aiding and encouraging the guerrillas. The officers were to distinguish between those who aided the bushwhackers for "disloyal motives" and those who aided them under compulsion. The wives and children of known bushwhackers, and women who were heads of families and who voluntarily assisted them, were to leave Missouri immediately. Such persons were to be permitted to take with them livestock, provisions, and household goods. Those failing to depart promptly were to be taken to Kansas City for shipment south. Guerrillas who surrendered voluntarily would be allowed to accompany their families.[22]

For some time prior to the issuance of this order Union military authorities had been arresting women suspected of aiding the bushwhackers and imprisoning them at Kansas City. Among those taken into custody were Mrs. Charity Kerr and Mrs. Nannie McCorkle, sister and sister-in-law respectively of John McCorkle; Susan Vandiver and Armenia Gilvey, cousins of Cole Younger; and Josephine, Mary, and Jennie Anderson, sisters of Bill Anderson. Ewing intended to banish them from the state in accordance with his removal policy, but before he could do so one of the worst tragedies of the entire border war occurred.

The women were confined on the second floor of a three-story brick building located between Fourteenth and Fifteenth streets on Grand Avenue. This structure was only four years old but had become vulnerable as a result of an adjoining building pressing against it. Occasionally a tremor would run through it, and chunks of plaster fall from the ceilings and walls. A Union surgeon, after visiting the prisoners, suggested to Ewing that they be removed to a safer place, but no action followed his advice. Then, on the afternoon of August 13, the building suddenly collapsed with a thunderous crash, carrying with it an adjoining structure. From the rubble rescuers pulled the crushed and mangled bodies of Josephine Anderson, Susan Vandiver, Charity Kerr, and Armenia Gilvey. One other woman died subsequently, and Mary Anderson was left a cripple for life.

As might be expected, the bushwhackers on learning of the tragedy fell into a frenzy of fury and hatred, for like other Southern partisans they were sure that the Federals had deliberately caused the collapse.[23] In particular the terrible news profoundly affected Bill Anderson, leader of an independent guerrilla gang, whose family had suffered worst of all. Already a merciless killer of men—for instance, in July he and Dave Poole led a sweep through the German settlements in Lafayette County shooting down unarmed farmers at their plows—the death and crippling of his sisters seemingly unhinged his mind and transformed him into a veritable homicidal maniac. Henceforth, his sole object was to kill as many Yankees as possible. And the more he killed, the more he wanted to kill. It is said, even, that he at times literally foamed at the mouth and would go into battle sobbing with sheer blood lust. Soon the whole border knew him by the dread name of "Bloody Bill."

In his early twenties, powerfully built, and darkly handsome, Anderson was a native Missourian who before the war lived near Council Grove, Kansas, with his father and his youngest brother, Jim. According to Kansas sources, the Andersons were even then bandits and horse thieves, and were responsible for at least one murder. After the war broke out Bill and Jim went back to Missouri, where they soon became full-time bushwhackers.

Anderson's band had a reputation for murderous ferocity which exceeded even that of Quantrill and Todd's. Among his boys two especially are worth noting. One was a tall, lanky, callow-looking youth named Frank James, who had taken to the bush in 1862 after Unionist militia tortured his foster father (at least that is what he later said).* Back home near Liberty was his fifteen-year-

* On August 7, 1863, the Liberty *Tribune* reported that "Franklin James" and two others "of the same ilk" stole $1.25 and a pocket knife from a man

old brother Jesse, who was just itching to join up with Anderson also.

The other notable member of Anderson's gang was Archie Clement, a short, slender, blond-haired eighteen-year-old. "Little Archie" was what might be termed a born killer. In fact he was, if possible, even more bloodthirsty than "Bloody Bill" himself. Eventually he became Anderson's second-in-command and trigger man. He also adopted the practice of scalping dead Union soldiers.[24]

As the war grew older, the number of psychopathic killers such as the Andersons, Todds, and Clements, kept increasing. And why not? Blood was never cheaper than it was along the border in the summer of 1863.

---

six miles west of Liberty. This is possibly the first recorded robbery of Frank James.

chapter VI Charley Hart Returns to Lawrence

"Let's go to Lawrence!"

These were the first words Quantrill addressed to a gathering of bushwhacker captains held at his camp near Blue Springs on August 10. Present were George Todd, Bill Anderson, Andy Blunt, Dick Yeager, Bill Gregg, Ol Shepherd, and several others.

"Let's go to Lawrence," said Quantrill. Then, after a short pause to let the full weight of his words sink in, he continued:

"Lawrence is the great hotbed of abolitionism in Kansas. All the plunder, or the bulk of it, stolen from Missouri, will be found stored away in Lawrence. And we can get more revenge and more money there than anywhere else."

Quantrill was not proposing anything new. Ever since the beginning of the war the Missourians had been talking about going into Kansas and "cleaning out" Lawrence.

The town represented to them all they hated and feared in Kansas. It was the citadel of abolitionism. It was the home of Jim Lane. It was the headquarters of the Red Legs. And its numerous well-stocked stores, rich banks, and fine homes offered tempting targets.

Quantrill's proposal, however, caused the other guerrilla chieftains to draw back in alarm. Talking about raiding Lawrence was one thing; doing it another. It was forty miles inside of Kansas and had almost three thousand people. Federal posts lined the border. The whole countryside would be up in arms before they could get there. The Lawrence Home Guards would be waiting for them inside the town's brick buildings. And supposing they got there and destroyed the town, they never would make it back to

Carl W. Breihan

William Clarke Quantrill, alias "Charley Hart," in Lawrence, 1860

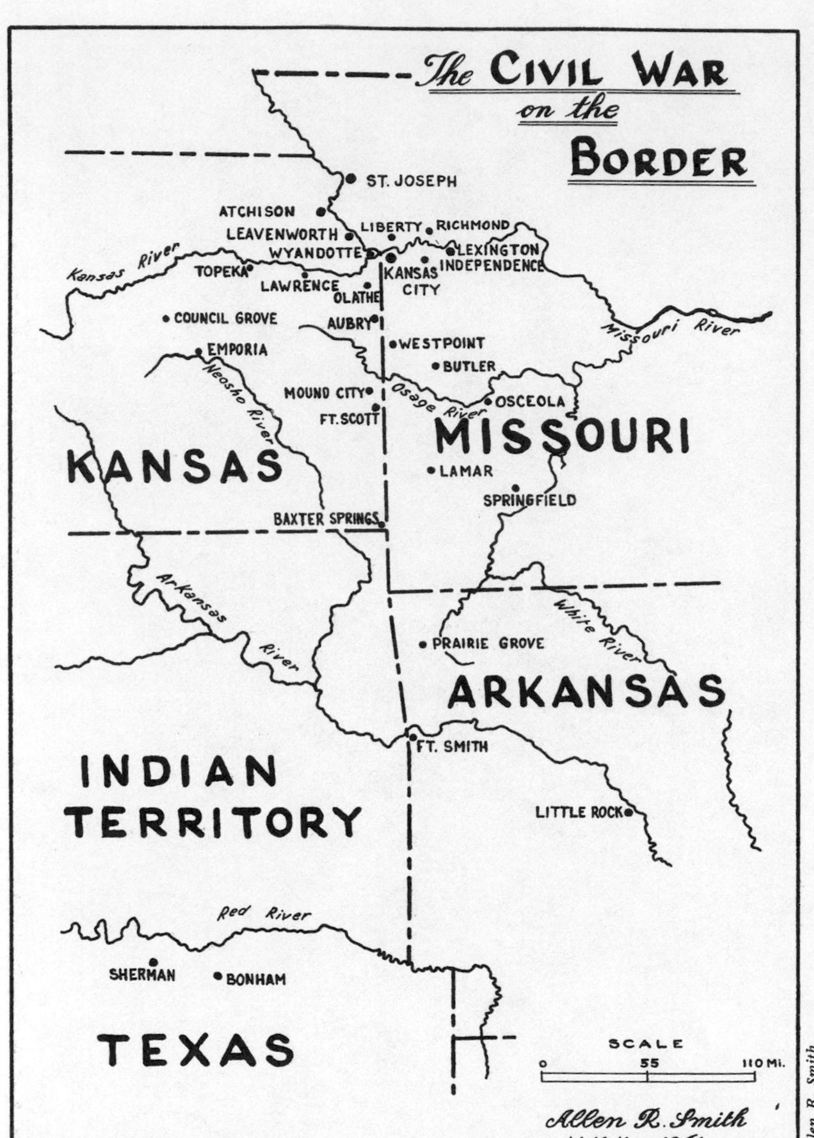

Allen R. Smith

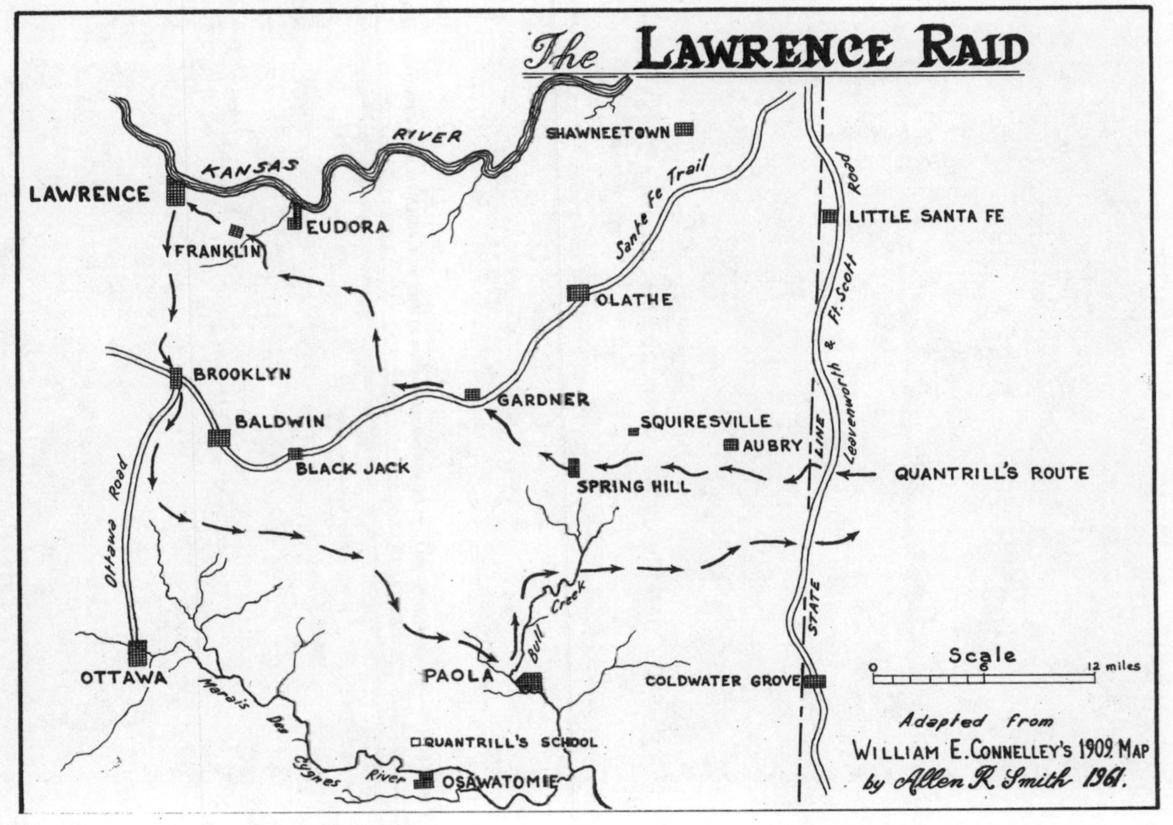
The LAWRENCE RAID
KANSAS RIVER
SHAWNEETOWN
LAWRENCE
EUDORA
FRANKLIN
Sante Fe Trail
OLATHE
LITTLE SANTA FE
Leavenworth & Ft. Scott Road
BROOKLYN
GARDNER
BALDWIN
BLACK JACK
SQUIRESVILLE
AUBRY
SPRING HILL
QUANTRILL'S ROUTE
STATE LINE
Ottawa Road
Bull Creek
OTTAWA
PAOLA
COLDWATER GROVE
Marais Des Cygnes River
QUANTRILL'S SCHOOL
OSAWATOMIE
Scale
0
6
12 miles
Adapted from
WILLIAM E. CONNELLEY'S 1909 MAP
by Allen R. Smith 1961.

Kansas State Historical Society, Topeka

Destruction of Lawrence, August 21, 1863. Sketch by Sherman Enderton.

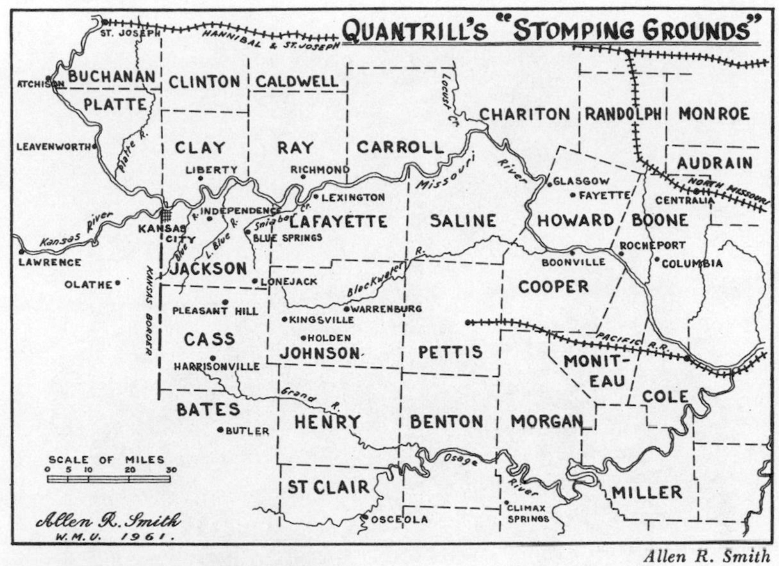

Allen R. Smith

Arch Clements

State Historical Society of Missouri

State Historical Society of Missouri

Kansas State Historical Society

Above, *Bill Anderson*. Below, *Thomas Ewing, Jr.*

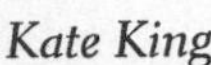

Kate King

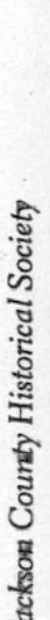

Jackson County Historical Society

State Historical Society of Missouri

George Todd

State Historical Society of Missouri

Coleman Younger

State Historical Society of Missouri

From left to right: Fletcher Taylor, Frank James and Jesse James

Missouri. No, a raid on Lawrence could not succeed. Attempting it would only result in an awful disaster.

Quantrill replied to these arguments point by point. He and two of his men recently scouted the border country, riding almost to Lawrence itself. What they saw and heard convinced him that a raid on Lawrence was feasible. The Federal border posts were weak and widely separated. The country between the state line and Lawrence was sparsely populated. By marching fast and by night they would be able to strike Lawrence without warning. Its Home Guard would not have a chance to resist. As for getting back to Missouri, if Yeager could do it from Council Grove, they could make it from Lawrence. Finally, the very fact that Lawrence was so far inside of Kansas and so large would be to their advantage. The Yankees probably figured that no one would dare attack the town. Well, let's surprise them!

The conference lasted twenty-four hours. It was, according to Gregg, very spirited. Every conceivable aspect of the raid was threshed out. In the end, all the guerrilla captains agreed to Quantrill's plan. Some of them, to be sure, still had qualms about the venture. But, as Quantrill pointed out, "If you never risk, you never gain."

Quantrill's men were already hard at work preparing for the raid. They cleaned and oiled pistols, repaired harnesses, molded bullets, and manufactured thousands of cartridges, using the powder captured at Independence and stored in Morgan Walker's house. As yet only Quantrill's closest lieutenants knew the reason for all this activity. The rank and file, however, realized that something big was up. A few guessed that it might be a raid on Lawrence, but most predicted that Kansas City was the target.[1]

While his men were making ready, Quantrill sent Fletch Taylor and a Negro named John Noland to Lawrence as spies. They spent several days there, then returned with word that the small Union garrison in the town had withdrawn to the north side of the Kansas River, that there were no pickets on the roads leading to Lawrence, and that the people of the town scoffed at any suggestion of a guerrilla attack.[2]

Early on the morning of August 18, Quantrill's band broke camp at Blue Springs and moved southward to a farm northeast of Lee's Summit. Along the way, Todd took a detachment to the house of a man named Wallace. Todd called Wallace outside and accused him of supplying information to the Federals. Wallace denied the charge, then pleaded for mercy as Todd drew a revolver. But instead of shooting Wallace, Todd leaned over his horse and struck him across the face with the barrel. As he did so, Todd growled, "If I ever hear of you talking any more we'll come back and kill you!" Todd then went inside the house, sat down at an organ, and played on it for several minutes. A man of many talents, George Todd.

Quantrill's company resumed its march after a brief rest. During the afternoon it moved eastward across the Sni to the farm of Captain Pardee on the Blackwater River, where it stopped for the night.

Here Anderson with thirty to forty and Blunt with one hundred men joined up. Quantrill brought them up to date on the situation in Lawrence and asked them if they still wanted to make the raid. The answer was yes.

In the morning the bushwhackers swung back westward. They marched slowly, surrounded by a screen of scouts on the lookout for Federal patrols. Around noon they camped at the Potter farm near Lone Jack.

Quantrill now informed his men of their objective. "Boys," he warned, "you will have to go through a lot, there is great danger ahead of us, there will be troops behind us and troops in front of us. There may be very few of us that get back alive. Now if there is any man in the outfit that don't want to go, now is your time to fall out, for after we leave here there will be no falling out or turning back."

About a dozen guerrillas decided to take advantage of Quantrill's offer. Only two of them were from his own band.

After it became dark the bushwhackers took up the march again. They continued with only a few short halts throughout the night. South of the Blue they accidentally met one hundred Confederate recruits under Colonel John Holt. Holt readily accepted an invitation to come along and have his men "christened."

The Missourians bivouacked at daylight on the middle fork of the Grand River, only four miles from the Kansas line. Here, their strength was further augmented by the arrival of fifty guerrillas from Cass and Bates counties. This addition gave Quantrill altogether approximately 450 men—the largest such force ever assembled under one command during the entire Civil War.[3]

At 3 P.M. the bushwhackers saddled up and headed for the border. Three hours later they crossed the line into Kansas. Their point of entry was about five miles south of Aubry, locale of Quantrill's first Kansas raid.

Aubry contained a garrison of one hundred Federal cavalry under the command of Captain J. A. Pike. One of Pike's scouts spotted the guerrillas and reported their presence to Pike at 7 P.M. Pike promptly forwarded the news to the other border posts. However, it did not occur to him that the raiders might be heading for Lawrence or some other interior point. Therefore, he made no attempt to check or pursue them. Even worse, he failed to send couriers to alert the towns to the west. Had he done both or either of these things, the horrible tragedy which was to come would have been averted.

Quantrill's luck was running strong on the evening of August 20. The one Federal officer who could have foiled his plan was an utter incompetent.*

The guerrilla column snaked across the prairies to a point two and one-half miles south of Squiresville, ten miles inside of Kansas, where it halted until nightfall. It then resumed the march, turning southwest to Spring Hill, then northwest to Gardner, which was reached at 11 P.M.

There were Union soldiers in Gardner. They asked Quantrill's men who they were and where they were going. The guerrillas, many of whom were wearing blue uniforms, replied that they were a Federal cavalry company on its way to Lawrence to have the horses shod.

Three miles west of Gardner the column veered northward in the direction of the small German community of Hesper. The night was moonless and very dark, the terrain difficult and treacherous. Quantrill therefore began pressing guides into service from

* According to Gregg, the bushwrackers entered Kansas only one and a half miles from Aubry, and in full view of Pike, who drew up his command on the prairie as if to give battle, but merely watched the raiders march by on their way to Lawrence. However, none of the other guerrilla accounts support Gregg's story. Either Gregg's memory over a lapse of some forty years failed him, or else he was embroidering the facts, as was his wont on occasion.

the farms along the way. Although well acquainted with the region himself, he knew that a loss of direction would be disastrous.

Whenever a guide ceased to be of any use, or in some cases was recognized as a refugee Missourian, the raiders shot him. In this way ten men soon met their death.

West of Hesper, which was passed between 2 and 3 A.M., a Missouri refugee named Joseph Stone was captured. Todd started to shoot him, but Quantrill stopped him, saying that they were now so close to Lawrence that a shot might alarm the town. Todd thereupon took a Sharps carbine and commanded Sam Clifton, a new member of the gang whose loyalty was suspected, to club Stone to death. Young Frank Smith became so sick as he watched Clifton carry out the horrible order that he nearly fell off his horse. But before the next sunset he was to regard such acts as ordinary occurrences.

The raiders reached Franklin at the first glimmer of day. The local physician, Dr. R. L. Williams, counted the mysterious horsemen as they filed through the settlement. He noted that many of them were strapped to their saddles so as to prevent falling while riding asleep. One of them, probably Quantrill, cried, "Push on, boys, it will be daylight before we get there."

Outside of Franklin, the column broke into a gallop. After a few miles it reached the crest of a summit overlooking Lawrence from the southeast. Quantrill ordered a halt and sent five men under Gregg to reconnoiter the town.

At this moment some of the guerrillas lost their nerve. "Let's give it up—it's too much!"

Quantrill's eyes flashed angrily. "You can do as you please—I am going into Lawrence!" Then, without waiting for Gregg's scouting party to return, he ordered his men to advance.[4]

The bushwhackers clattered into Lawrence at about five o'clock. The streets were deserted, most of the citizens were still asleep. They cut across vacant lots till they reached the center of town. Here Quantrill detached Holt's company to cover the east side of the town and sent Blunt's band to do the same thing on the west side. Then, at the head of his own outfit, he headed for the river.

After going a short distance, Quantrill's men came upon a tent camp occupied by twenty-two recruits of the Fourteenth Kansas

Regiment. With savage cries, they literally trampled the tents into the ground, killing seventeen of the hapless soldiers. Larkin Skaggs, one of Anderson's followers, took the U.S. flag which had been flying over the camp, tied it to the tail of his horse, and dragged it through the dust.

Next the raiders pounced on a near-by camp of colored recruits. However, most of the Negro soldiers, forewarned by the fate of the whites, managed to escape.

After disposing of the camps, Quantrill's column charged up Massachusetts Street—a yelling horde of long-haired, wild-looking men, riding with reckless skill on magnificent horses, and blazing away with their revolvers.

On reaching the river, Quantrill ordered his men to turn about and surround the Eldridge House. This famous hotel, which had been rebuilt anew after its destruction in 1856, was a formidable structure of brick, four stories high, with iron grilles on the ground windows. If there was to be any resistance in Lawrence, it would be here. The guerrillas, therefore, approached it cautiously, pistols ready.

All of a sudden, a gong began ringing inside the hotel. Startled, the raiders scurried for cover, thinking that this might be a signal for those inside to open fire. But the occupants of the hotel possessed neither the will nor the means to defend the place. After a short interval, one of the guests, Captain A. R. Banks, appeared at a window waving a white bed sheet.

"I want to talk to your commander," Banks shouted.

Quantrill rode forward. He was dressed in an elaborately ornamented guerrilla shirt, wore gray pants tucked into high cavalry boots, and had four revolvers in his belt. His face, beneath a low-crowned slouch hat, was grimy and covered by a stubble of reddish beard.

"What is your intention in coming to Lawrence?" asked Banks.

"Plunder," replied Quantrill.

"We are defenseless and at your mercy. The house is surrendered, but we demand protection for the inmates."

Quantrill promised that the residents of the hotel would not be harmed. Then, rising in his stirrups, he turned to his followers and ordered them to spread out over the town.

"Kill! Kill! and you will make no mistake!" he screamed shrilly.

"Lawrence should be thoroughly cleansed, and the only way to cleanse it is to kill! kill!"

With wild shouts of triumph and glee, the bushwhackers swarmed through the streets to carry out their chieftain's command. A large number, however, remained with Quantrill to tend to the Eldridge House. As the guests filed down to the lobby, guerrillas with drawn revolvers forced them to "shell out" their money and valuables. Other raiders went upstairs to ransack the rooms. They found the door of one chamber locked. The three Easterners inside refused to come out. Such proceedings, they declared, were simply outrageous—really, something should be done! A few shots fired through the door, wounding one of them, quickly changed their minds.

Quantrill entered the hotel to look around. One of the residents, a former Lawrence acquaintance named Arthur Spice, leaned over the banister and called to him: "Remember me, Charley? We used to have good times over on the ferry landing—you were called Charley Hart then!"

Quantrill turned a murderous gaze on Spicer. "It doesn't make any difference what I was called." Spicer hastily drew back and made no further attempt to renew old friendships.*

After thoroughly looting the hotel the raiders set fire to it. This was the second time in a little over six years that it had been burned by the Missourians. Three years later, however, it was back in existence, and to this day Lawrence's leading hotel is called the Eldridge House, occupying the same site as the original.

Quantrill left a small guard to watch the Eldridge House prisoners while he went to look after other matters. No sooner was he gone than some drunken guerrillas threatened to shoot them. Only his opportune return prevented a general massacre. As it was, a bushwhacker fired into the captives, killing one of them. Quantrill finally had George Todd take them to the Whitney House Hotel for safekeeping.

Quantrill, it will be remembered, stayed at the Whitney House when he lived in Lawrence. The owner, Nathan Stone, had be-

* Quantrill apparently had a grudge against Spicer for some reason. Later during the raid he threatened to kill him, but before he got around to doing so, Spicer escaped.

friended him, and once Stone's wife and daughter had nursed him through a long illness.

Now, out of gratitude, he ordered his men to spare the place and not molest its occupants. He also set up his headquarters there and had the Stones prepare him a breakfast. As he ate, he talked with the Stones and other former acquaintances about old times.

After finishing breakfast he took a buggy and went driving through the streets. On all sides were burning buildings, dead and dying men, grief-stricken women. Everywhere were his followers, yelling, shooting, and plundering. He drove through these scenes to the top of Mount Oread, where he stopped and looked down on the raging, flaming hell below.

This was the moment he had been waiting for—this was vengeance. Charley Hart, the man whom Lawrence had scorned and outlawed, had returned.

In essence the Lawrence Massacre consisted of many individual scenes of tragedy and horror, all combining to make it one of the most terrible events in American history. . . .

A gang of bushwhackers took all the male inhabitants of the Johnson House, hangout of the Lawrence Red Legs, lined them up in an alley, and mowed them down with fusillade of revolver shots.

Raiders shot down Dr. J. F. Griswold, State Senator S. M. Thorpe, Harlow W. Baker, a merchant, and Josiah Trask, coeditor of the Lawrence *Journal*, in a group after promising to spare their lives if they gave themselves up.

A bushwhacker pursued Judge Louis Carpenter through his house and into the back yard, shooting at him all the while. Finally Carpenter fell to the ground, wounded. His wife frantically tried to save him by shielding his body with hers. But the assailant raised her arm and pressed his pistol barrel against Carpenter's head to deliver the finishing bullet. Blood and brains splashed over the face of Mrs. Carpenter.

Guerrillas riddled Edward Fitch with bullets in his own doorway, then left his body to be consumed by the flames of his burning house while his wife and children stood by. The killers refused to allow Mrs. Fitch to remove the body, and one of them pulled

Fitch's boots off and put them on himself—"They fit good!" The presence of a toy U.S. flag on a shed in the backyard, placed there by Fitch's children, accounted for the brutal circumstances of his murder.

James Perine and James Eldridge, both eighteen and clerks in the country store on Massachusetts Street, were asleep in the back of the store when the massacre began. A party of raiders broke into the store, captured them, and ordered them to open the safe, promising them that if they did so they would not be slain. But no sooner did they comply then both were shot dead.

One man was killed while handing his slayer a cup of water. Another was killed when the crying of his child led the guerrillas to his hiding place in a cornfield. The child remained in its dead father's arms, still crying.

J. W. Thornton ran from his burning house, only to be shot three times in the hip by one of the raiders. However, he kept going until hit by another bullet. His wife ran to his side and tried to protect him, but a guerrilla pushed her aside and shot him again. Then, seeing that Thornton was still breathing, the guerrilla cried, "I can kill you!" and beat him over the head with a revolver butt until he was unconscious. Yet, despite this hideous punishment, Thornton lived for many years, although horribly crippled and disfigured.

Some bushwhackers shot and wounded D. W. Palmer and another man at the entrance of Palmer's shop. They then set fire to the shop, bound the hands of their victims, and threw them bodily into the flames. Both men burned to death, begging for mercy and screaming in horrible agony.

The death of William Laurie added irony to tragedy. During Quantrill's raid on Shawneetown the previous summer, Laurie had been captured by the guerrillas but managed to escape. He then moved to a farm near Lawrence. There he lived with his wife and his brother John. On the day before the raid the Lauries went to Lawrence, planning to return the following day. When the raiders entered Lawrence, the two brothers attempted to flee, but both were wounded. As they lay on the ground, helpless, Mrs. Laurie emplored the guerrillas to spare them. Seeing that they were ignoring her pleas, John Laurie asked that they spare his brother. But one of the guerrillas recognized William Laurie as the man who got away at Shawneetown. "We are not so particular about you, but that fellow, we will put him through." The guerrilla then killed both brothers, after which he turned to the weeping Mrs. Laurie and screamed, "We are fiends from hell! Get back into the house, or by heavens, we will serve you the same!"

Anderson's boys were the most bloodthirsty killers, with Anderson himself accounting for many victims. However, Peyton Long of Quantrill's band shot down more citizens than any other single raider. He was closely followed by three other Quantrill followers, Bill Gower, Allen Parmer, and Dick Maddox.

Colonel Holt's recruits generally abstained from the butchery. One young Missourian told a Lawrence woman that he was sorry he had come on the raid. Others showed their unfired pistols to prove that they were innocent of any killings. Sometimes the raiders even helped women remove furniture from their houses before applying the torch. They did not kill or rape any women.

The menfolk of Lawrence sought to escape death by hiding in cellars and attics, in cornfields and underbrush, and even under the board sidewalks. Some preserved their lives by claiming they were Southerners, by advancing the claims of Masonic brotherhood, by aiding the raiders in various ways, or by offering them large sums of money. However, one man who gave a guerrilla a thousand dollars to spare his life was killed immediately afterward by another bushwhacker!

One of the most amazing escapes was that of the Reverend H. D. Fisher. He had been a chaplain in Lane's Kansas Brigade and was high on the bushwhackers' wanted list. As soon as he heard the raiders enter the town he started for a place of safety. But after going a short distance he decided that he could not escape by flight, so returned to his house and hid in the cellar. A few minutes later the guerrillas came tramping into the house and demanded that Mrs. Fisher reveal her husband's whereabouts. When she refused, they began searching for him. Deciding that he was in the cellar, they took a lantern and went down to investigate. Fisher had climbed upon a bank of dirt and was lying by a drain. Even though one of the searchers held the lantern right up to his face he was not discovered, and they went back upstairs. However, they were positive that the "damned abolitionist preacher" was somewhere in the house and so attempted to smoke him out by setting it on fire. Mrs. Fisher held the flames in check for a while, but finally had to give up. She told her husband that he must get out of the house somehow or burn to death. Fisher thereupon crawled out through a small window in the cellar. His wife then rolled him up in a rug and dragged him over to a tree in the backyard. Next she brought out various pieces of furniture and piled them on top of the rug. The guerrillas in the meantime stood around the burning house waiting for Fisher to emerge. They did not leave until the house was in ashes.

Henry S. Clarke, a Lawrence furniture dealer, had a much less dramatic experience than Fisher, but in a way a more interesting one. When the guerrillas came charging into town, Clarke's first impulse was to grab his gun and join the Home Guard company. Luckily, however, his wife persuaded him to remain inside the house.

Soon two young bushwhackers came up on the porch and pounded at the front door. When Clarke opened it they shoved carbines into his stomach. Clarke calmly said that he knew what they wanted and was prepared for them. "Shell out, then, God-damn you," one of the guerrillas yelled. Clarke gave them seventy-nine dollars. "Is this all you got?" demanded the raiders. "That's all," lied Clarke, who had given two hundred dollars to his wife to hide. "Every damned cent?" they insisted. Clarke thereupon turned over some small coins he had in his pocket. This satisfied the robbers, who left after telling Clarke to get his things out of the house, as they would return shortly to burn it—a threat, however, they failed to carry out.

Clarke went outside. He saw the brutal slaying of Judge Carpenter. This convinced him that it would only be a matter of time before he was killed also.

After a while a guerrilla approached, riding a horse which Clarke recognized as having belonged to James Eldridge, one of the clerks murdered at the country store. Clarke decided to try to make friends with the rider, and so hailed him. A conversation followed, in which the man on the horse stated that he was Colonel Holt, that he had originally been a Union man, but that he had joined up with Price after Jennison burned his hardware store in Vernon County, Missouri. Holt also declared that "Union men have not only robbed and burned houses, and killed defenseless men, but they have shot down women and burned the houses of widows over their heads."

Clarke asked Holt if he would care for some breakfast. Holt accepted the offer, but had the food brought to the front gate, where he ate it sitting on his horse. Moreover, he first had Clarke taste it in order to make sure it had not been poisoned. Other bushwhackers came along, and Clarke fed them as well. One, who arrived after all the food was gone, begged Mrs. Clarke to get him something—anything—to eat. She brought out a dish of cold potatoes, which he gulped down saying, "Oh, how good they are!"

Holt's presence eventually paid off for Clarke. A swarthy bushwhacker with a gray beard down to his belt rode up and aimed his revolver at Clarke, who thought that his moment had come. But Holt ordered the ruffian away, saying as he did so that Clarke was a friend and must not be harmed.

Still another passer-by was Todd. He was wearing a Federal uniform taken from Captain Banks at the Eldridge House. With a big smile on his face, he called out, "How do you like my new uniform, Holt?"

Holt stayed with Clarke until the raiders began assembling for their departure. As he rode away he advised Clarke's wife and sister to get him into the house or otherwise he would be killed. But Clarke remained standing by his front gate until all the raiders were gone—perhaps the only man in Lawrence to save his life through friendliness.

The most famous citizen of Lawrence to escape the bushwhackers was Senator Jim Lane. Quantrill originally planned to capture Lane and take him back to Missouri and burn him at the stake! But John Noland, the Negro spy, had reported that Lane was out of town.* So, instead of making straight for Lane's house in the northwest part of Lawrence, Quantrill did not go there until after the fall of the Eldridge House. This gave Lane, who knew what to expect if he fell into the hands of the bushwhackers, time to scamper to the shelter of a near-by cornfield, where he huddled clad only in his nightshirt.

Mrs. Lane met Quantrill and a squad of guerrillas at the front

* Noland's information was correct: Lane was not in Lawrence when Noland was there. But he returned a day or two before the raid to attend a railroad meeting.

door. With mock politeness Quantrill asked to see her distinguished husband. In the same manner she replied that the Senator was not a home to receive visitors. Since this squared with Noland's information, Quantrill did not bother to make a search. Instead he set fire to Lane's fine new home, in the parlor of which, according to John McCorkle, there were two pianos formerly belonging to Southern people in Jackson County.

The only organized resistance encountered by the raiders came from a number of soldiers and surveyors stationed on the opposite bank of the Kansas River. They fired across the river and wounded three men—Jim Bledsoe, a member of Quantrill's band, and two of Holt's recruits.

The guerrillas as a rule steered clear of stone and brick buildings, also of cornfields and thickets. This cautious conduct caused some Kansans to stigmatize them as cowards. However, they were merely avoiding unnecessary risks. They knew that getting wounded would greatly reduce their chances of making it back alive to Missouri.

The bushwhackers looted all the stores and robbed all the banks (early training for Frank James and Cole Younger, who were on the raid). They also pillaged the hotels and most of the private houses, forcing the occupants to turn over money, watches, and jewelry. In several instances they even snatched wedding rings off the fingers of women.

Shouting "Whisky! Whisky!" they also smashed into the saloons where they proceeded to get savage-drunk. Even Quantrill had trouble controlling some of his followers as a result.

Small squads moved systematically from building to building on Massachusetts Street, setting fire to each. Thick billows of smoke swirled up into the sky and stood like giant columns along the street. Overhead a cloud of smoke and ashes darkened the entire town, blotting out the bright summer sun.

Shortly before nine o'clock, a lookout atop Mount Oread reported to Quantrill that the dust of approaching troops could be seen off to the east. Quantrill at once gave the order to reassemble. The guerrillas formed into a column of fours in the south end of town. Then, almost as suddenly as they came, they departed.

However, a few drunken stragglers remained behind. Among them was Larkin Skaggs. A former Baptist preacher, he had marched with the Border Ruffians and taken part in the first sacking of Lawrence. Now he was literally insane with whisky and blood lust.

Earlier in the morning he had stolen a diamond ring from Lydia Stone, Nathan Stone's daughter. Quantrill had given her this ring in 1860. She complained to Quantrill, who made Skaggs return it. As he did so, he muttered that she would be "damned sorry for it."

Now he proceeded to carry out his threat. With another guerrilla he rode up to the Whitney House and ordered everyone to come out. As they started to do so, Skaggs and his companion opened fire. Nathan Stone was killed and another man wounded. To cries of "They are killing the prisoners!" the others ran back inside or dashed for the cover of the river bank.

Skaggs, content with this vengeance, galloped off alone to the home of Fred Read. He tried to set fire to the house, but was frustrated by Mrs. Read. Every time he lit a match she calmly blew it out. "You are the queerest woman I ever saw!" he exclaimed in exasperation.

At this moment James Faxon, a neighbor, came to the door. Mrs. Read shouted, "Run for your life!" Skaggs chased him, but was unable to kill him. He returned in a fury and threatened to kill Mrs. Read. Then, all of a sudden, he realized that the other raiders had left and he was alone in Lawrence. "I shall be killed!" he cried, and hastily mounted his horse.

But he was so befuddled with drink and fear that he went in the wrong direction. A clamoring mob pursued, cornered, and finally killed him. Some Negroes took his body, stripped it naked, and dragged it through the streets tied to a horse in exactly the same fashion he had dishonored the U.S. flag. Later, they tried to burn it but failed, and it lay exposed in a ravine all winter. Skaggs was the only bushwhacker killed in Lawrence, and not even his comrades expressed any regret over his death.

Lawrence was almost totally destroyed. The business center along Massachusetts Street was a pile of smoking rubble. One hundred houses had been burned, another hundred damaged by fire, and practically every house pillaged. Bodies littered the sidewalks, streets, yards, and gardens. Bones were visible among the embers, and "the sickening odor of burning flesh was oppressive." Some of the corpses were so charred that they could not be recognized, nor "scarcely be taken up." The exact number of dead is unknown, but it was at least 150 and probably more than 200.[5]

The bushwhackers retreated southward from Lawrence. Along the way they continued to kill, loot, and burn. They shot one man simply because he was a preacher— "Oh, we intend to kill all the damned preachers," the slayer explained to the victim's wife.

After crossing the Wakarusa they stopped to burn the bridge. Frank James rode up to Quantrill and, pointing off toward Lawrence, said: "There's about sixty Red Legs come into Lawrence. Hadn't some of us boys better go back and clean them up?"

Quantrill shook his head. "No—look to the east, look to the north. Boys, you'll get all you want of it before the day is over. It's going to be a running fight all the way back and I'm going to need every one of you."

Quantrill was right. Sizable Union forces were straining to catch up with the Missourians. Heading the pursuers was Major Preston B. Plumb, Ewing's youthful chief of staff. He had received word in Kansas City of Quantrill's invasion at half-past midnight. He passed the news on to Ewing, who was at Fort Leavenworth, then set out with fifty men, all he could raise on short notice. Since he did not know Quantrill's objective, he headed for Olathe as the most likely danger spot.

He reached Olathe at daylight, learned that the raiders had gone toward Lawrence, and so turned in that direction. Six miles from Lawrence he overtook 180 cavalry under Captain Charles F. Coleman, commander of the post at Little Santa Fe. He added this force to his own and pushed on. Soon he saw smoke south of Lawrence and realized that Quantrill was retreating. Therefore, he swung toward Baldwin in hopes of intercepting him.

Near Baldwin he met up with several dozen armed citizens from Lawrence, headed by Jim Lane. Following his escape Lane went to a farmhouse, where he obtained a pair of trousers and a plow horse. Soon after the raiders left he galloped theatrically into Lawrence shouting, "Let's follow them, boys, let's follow them!"

Quantrill's column picked up the Santa Fe Trail and headed

east. Then, at the small settlement of Brooklyn, it turned off the trail and took the Fort Scott road toward Ottawa. South of Brooklyn Plumb's pursuit began to close the gap. A number of shots were exchanged without loss to either side.

At this juncture the guerrillas came to a narrow lane running south through a large cornfield. Bunching up, they galloped through the lane, then began scattering in all directions over the prairie. An unreasoning panic stirred in their ranks. "This was," Frank Smith later commented, "the most excited I ever saw Quantrill's outfit."

Todd, who was riding in the rear of the column, realized that something had to be done, and done fast. Quickly, he dismounted at the exit of the lane and, swearing at the top of his voice, stopped the remaining bushwhackers as they came out. As soon as he had collected twenty men he shouted, "Boys, let down those rail fences, part of you go up one side through the corn and part of you follow me right up the lane and by God we'll charge them! We've got to check them or the whole outfit is lost!"

Todd led his men in a furious assault against the oncoming Federals. At point-blank range they emptied their revolvers into the enemy's front ranks. It went down in a tangle of whinnying horses and cursing men. The following ranks piled on top of it, so that it seemed to the bushwhackers that the Yankees were heaped as "high as a house." Its mission accomplished, Todd's force fell back down the lane.

During the charge, Todd's horse, a magnificent steed named Sam Gaty, was shot from under him. He sprang clear and ran back to the end of the lane. As he did so, he hastily doffed the Federal uniform coat taken from Captain Banks—no doubt fearful that his own men might mistake him for a Yankee. Not until later did he remember that the coat contained four thousand dollars in U.S. greenbacks!

Todd obtained another horse, then with his twenty followers rejoined Quantrill, who had rallied the rest of the command a short distance further south.

"George," said Quantrill, after thanking Todd for repelling the Union attack, "if there is a man that can hold that rear, you can. Cut out fifty or sixty of the best men for a rear guard and throw out a skirmish line. I know the country and will take the main body and lead the outfit out. If I run into any Federals in front of me I'm going to cut right through them."

Todd at once set about organizing the rear guard. For it he picked the steadiest men and the best shots out of Anderson's, Blunt's, and Yeager's bands, as well as Quantrill's own company.

While this was taking place, many of the bushwhackers began disgorging surplus plunder. Soon the prairie grass was littered with bolts of cloth, women's dresses, hats, saddle gear, furniture, and even children's toys.

The retreat was resumed. It continued without pause through the morning and into the afternoon. The sweating bodies of the raiders ached with fatigue, their faces were grimy with dirt and smoke. An intense physical and emotional letdown had set in after the wild excitement of the massacre. The only thing that kept many of them going was fear of capture and desire to reach Missouri and safety.

The rear guard had little trouble holding Plumb's pursuers at a distance. Todd divided his force into two lines of skirmishers. The first line fired away at the Federals for a while, then fell back behind the second, which in its turn withdrew back of the first line. In this way the Federals were always faced with a row of blazing revolvers.

Plumb could not concentrate enough strength for an all-out attack on the raiders. His saddle-weary troopers straggled haphazardly across the prairie. Their horses were so jaded by constant marching and the intense August heat that they were able to move only at a slow walk.

The guerrillas, on the other hand, had obtained hundreds of fresh horses at Lawrence, both to carry plunder and provide extra mounts. Although these steeds were mostly too fat to bear up long under hard going, they enabled Quantrill's men to conserve the strength of their own horses. Whenever one of the Lawrence horses gave out, they would shoot it and mount another one.

Late in the afternoon, Quantrill again swerved eastward. So far he had lost only five men during the retreat—two killed outright and three slain by vengeful Federals while lying wounded.

Now, all of a sudden, another man, Joab Perry, broke from the ranks and galloped off to the northwest. Gregg wanted to catch and kill him, but John Jarrette held him back—"No, let him go. He will get it soon enough."

However, Perry later turned up alive in Missouri, but horseless, barefooted, with only one pistol, his clothes in tatters, and his body a weltering mass of bruises, sores, and scratches. His was the sole case of desertion during the retreat. The bushwhackers knew that their best chance of staying alive was staying together.

Just before sunset the raiders came in sight of Paola. Quantrill called a halt and pulled out his spyglass to survey the town. There, waiting to oppose him if he came that way, he saw about a hundred troops.

At this moment a determined charge by a fresh company of Kansas Militia which had reinforced Plumb drove the rear guard back onto the main body. Quantrill hastily turned his entire force about and deployed it in line of battle.

The advancing militia, seeing that they were up against vastly superior numbers, drew rein. For a while both sides faced one another, each waiting for the other to make the first move. Finally the bushwhackers formed back into a column and resumed their retreat. But instead of marching east, they turned north, thus bypassing Paola.

Plumb did not attempt to follow, but went on to Paola, where he turned over command of the pursuit to Lieutenant Colonel C. S. Clark. Most of the Union horses were by now completely broken down. Several soldiers had died of sunstroke.

The bushwhackers halted five miles north of Paola for some badly needed rest. Quantrill and Gregg, going a little off to one side, rode their horses flank-deep into a pond and greedily gulped water from their cupped hands. But in less than an hour scouts reported the approach of Union troops. Groaning, the guerrillas hauled their stiffened bodies back into the saddle. Some of the men were so groggy that Quantrill and the other chieftains literally had to kick them to their feet.

Shortly after midnight the bushwhacker column crossed back into Missouri, doing so only a few miles south of where it entered Kansas. And at dawn it reached a line of timber along the Grand River.

"Boys, we are back home!" announced Quantrill happily. "Not all the troops in Kansas can catch us now."

The guerrillas unsaddled and sent details to fetch food from the neighboring farmhouses. While waiting to eat, they divided their loot. Each private received twenty dollars, the leaders kept the rest. Watches, rugs, clothing, and other such items of plunder were also portioned out.

But no sooner had this been done, and just as the food details returned, Quantrill through his spyglass spotted enemy troops crossing the Kansas line. At the same time a farmer informed him that a large force of Missouri State Militia was present just over the next hill.

Quantrill mounted his horse and rode among the men. "Boys, saddle up, we got to get going again."

"What!" exclaimed his followers indignantly. "We haven't had a chance to eat yet."

"See those Kansans coming across the line?"

"Damn the Kansans! We whipped them yesterday and can whip them today!"

"Yes, I know you can whip the Kansans, but what will you do with the twelve hundred Missouri troops just over the divide?"

"Well, that is a horse of another color! We will saddle up!"

Many of the mounts were now totally played out, others were sick from drinking too much water while hot. Since there was a five-mile gap of open country before the next timber belt Quantrill ordered all the men with bad horses to hide amidst the brush in small groups of two and three until nightfall. Then, with their horses rested and well, they could slip across the gap under the cover of darkness. Meanwhile, the Federals would be following the main body.

So far during the retreat Jim Bledsoe and the two recruits from Holt's company wounded at Lawrence had been carried along in a wagon. Now their comrades were forced to leave them at a farmhouse, where it was hoped they would be safe from enemy pursuers. However, a Kansas search party soon found them. Bledsoe's companions started pleading for mercy, but Bledsoe cried: "Stop it! We are not entitled to mercy! We spare none and do not expect to be spared!" The Kansans killed all three; then an Indian who was with them scalped the corpses.

Vengeance-seeking Kansans, headed by a gang of Red Legs under George Hoyt, tracked down a number of the dismounted guerrillas, always killing them ruthlessly, along with any farmer found sheltering them. In several instances the Red Legs "strung up" their victims on tree branches so high that the bodies could not be cut down, and so remained hanging there, slowly rotting, month after month.

The main bushwhacker force under Quantrill brushed aside the Missouri troops (who actually numbered only 150) and reached the safety of the brush and timber. Here, on Quantrill's command, they scattered into small bands so as to elude further pursuit.[6]

The great Lawrence Raid was over.

"Quantrill and his men," confessed Bill Gregg years later, "went to Lawrence with hell in their necks, and raised hell after they got there." The Lawrence Massacre was the bloody climax of the Kansas-Missouri border conflict dating back to 1854. It was also the most atrocious single event of the entire Civil War. Nothing else quite matched it in stark melodramatic horror.

Immediately after the massacre General Schofield wrote that the bushwhackers raided Lawrence in retaliation for Ewing's removal policy, as set forth in Order No. 10. On the other hand, several historians have expressed the opinion that the guerrillas destroyed Lawrence in revenge of the women killed and injured in the collapse of the Kansas City prison.[7]

Both of these views are plausible, especially the latter, which can be bolstered by the testimony of John McCorkle, who declared that "this foul murder [the collapse of the prison which he believed was deliberately engineered by Ewing] was the direct cause of the famous raid on Lawrence, Kansas." [8]

However, almost all the other available evidence clearly indicates that Quantrill was planning and preparing for the raid not only prior to the tragic prison collapse, but long before Ewing's removal policy was announced. Therefore, at most, these two events merely intensified the desire of the bushwhackers to "get back" at their enemies by raiding Lawrence, and increased their fury and blood lust when they attacked the town. As mentioned previously, the collapse of the prison in particular affected Anderson, who during the massacre declared to a citizen of Lawrence, "I had two sisters arrested in Kansas City by Union men, for entertaining Southern sentiments. They were imprisoned in a dilapidated building used as a guard house. The building was known to be unsafe, and besides it was undermined. One night that building fell, and my two sisters, with three other ladies, were crushed to death." [9]

The bushwhackers raided Lawrence in quest of revenge and out of a desire for plunder. Of these two closely allied motives, the former was probably the uppermost in the minds and emotions of most of them. Thus, during the massacre, they yelled, "Jennison!" "Osceola!" and "Butler!" as they rode about shooting, pillaging, and burning. And one of the Lawrence "sufferers" testified that "these demons claimed they were here to revenge the wrongs done their families by our men under Lane, Jennison, Anthony and Co. They said they would be more merciful than were these men when they went into Missouri." And "Bloody Bill" Anderson announced: "I am here for revenge—and I have got it!" And Quantrill himself, when asked by a citizen why he had come to Lawrence, replied, "To plunder, and destroy the town in retaliation for Osceola." [10]

But if the bushwhackers' desire for vengeance explains the Lawrence Massacre, it does not excuse it. The vast majority of the people murdered and burned out in Lawrence had not marched with Lane and Jennison and were not jayhawkers or Red Legs. At most they should be blamed for countenancing this element and their deeds. Very few, if any, of the really guilty were killed. Lane escaped, Anthony and Jennison were in Leavenworth, and Hoyt and his Red Legs were not even in town. On the other hand, some of the victims, such as Mayor Collamore, had opposed the Red Legs and denounced their activities.

The ruthless slayings and shocking atrocities committed by Quantrill's followers at Lawrence plainly reveal the personal degeneration produced by two years of lawless guerrilla warfare. The bushwhackers were no longer simply angry young farm lads defending their homes against Yankee invaders. They had now become, or were fast becoming, professional killers—desperate, half-savage men accustomed to a life of wild violence, men who would keep on killing until killed themselves.

Most of the personal odium for the massacre justly falls on Quantrill. By the same token, however, he rightly deserves most of the credit for the raid's success. He conceived it, planned it, and led it. From a purely military standpoint it was a brilliant feat. Especially worthy of admiration are the courage and determination he displayed in carrying it out, and the magnificent timing which enabled him to strike at Lawrence just at dawn and to retreat back to Missouri before the enemy forces could concentrate against him. Lloyd Lewis, author of one of the greatest Civil War biographies, *Sherman, the Fighting Prophet*, was not totally unjustified in saying that "Quantrill, if viewed objectively, was a great cavalry man, probably as skillful as General Nathan Bedford Forrest." [11]

Quantrill, we can imagine, was very happy and very proud as he scurried into hiding after disbanding his forces. Very happy because he had gotten back at the detested Kansans and hated Lawrence. Very proud because he had demonstrated for all to see his great power and superior ability. This last no one could now deny or doubt. Was it not proved by the smoldering ruins of Lawrence and the bullet-mangled corpses sprawled in their midst?

He had shown them—he had shown them all!

chapter VII "Brought None of Them Through"

Jim Lane was mad—hopping mad. And who could blame him? Not only had he barely escaped with his life and had his home burned down, but to cap it all, the villains responsible for these outrages to Senatorial dignity had gotten away practically scot-free.

Lane vented his wrath on General Ewing. He met the general on the evening of August 22, at a point near the Kansas-Missouri border. Ewing, after an arduous forced march from Leavenworth, during which several of his soldiers died of sunstroke, had just joined the forces pursuing the Lawrence raiders.

Mincing no words, Lane accused the general of following a milk-and-water policy along the border. "Unless you do something, and do it fast," he threatened, "to clean out Quantrill and his murdering thieves, you will be a dead dog, Ewing!"

Ewing detested Lane personally. But Lane was the king of Kansas politics, and Ewing had political ambitions. Therefore, he sought to appease the irate Senator. Taking him aside to a log cabin, he wrote out in his presence the rough draft of a military proclamation which, he vowed, would take care of the bushwhackers once and for all. Lane read it, said this was more like it, and promised not to make trouble for Ewing.

Three days later, on August 25, Ewing's Kansas City headquarters published General Order No. 11. In brief, it announced that all persons living in Jackson, Cass, and Bates counties, with the exception of those residing within one mile of Independence, Hickman Mills, Pleasant Hill, Harrisonville, and Kansas City, were to leave their homes by September 9. Those who, by that date, established their loyalty with the commanding officer of the military station nearest their place of residence would be permitted to remove to any military station in the district, or to any part of Kansas other than the eastern border counties. Persons failing to establish their loyalty were to move outside the District of the Border—an order which would be enforced by military action if disobeyed.[1]

Ewing's Order No. 11 was the harshest military measure directed against civilians during the Civil War, or for that matter in American history up to the herding of thousands of Japanese-Americans into concentration camps in 1941-42. In essence, it was a drastic extension of the removal policy already in effect under Order No. 10. Like that order, it was based on the theory that the only way to destroy the guerrillas was to deprive them of their civilian support. By issuing it Ewing hoped not only to placate Lane, but to restore a feeling of confidence and security among the people of Kansas, who had been greatly alarmed by the Lawrence Massacre and were demanding more effective action against the bushwhackers.

During the next two weeks a mass exodus took place from the border counties. Federal officers permitted only a small number to remain. The rest, numbering in the thousands, loaded their household goods onto wagons, gathered up their stock, and either crossed into northern Missouri or began trekking southward. In Clay County the Federal authorities, faced with a serious guerrilla problem of their own, forced all refugees to move along further north.

Much suffering attended the evacuation. H. B. Bouton, a Unionist living near Kansas City, told of seeing large numbers of "poor people, widows and children, who, with little bundles of clothing, are crossing the river to be subsisted by the charities of the people amongst whom they might find shelter." Jo Shelby's regiment, on the way from Huntsville, Arkansas, to raid Missouri, encountered "hundreds of fleeing families . . . toiling slowly and painfully southward. Tender and gentle women, barefooted and shivering in the cold, were driving oxen and riding upon miserable broken-down horses without saddles." Colonel Bazel Lazear, Union commander at Lexington, wrote his wife: "It is heartsickening to see what I have seen. . . . A desolated country and men & women and children, some of them all most [*sic*] naked. Some on foot and some in old wagons. Oh God."

Marauding by Union troops increased the misery of the refugees. Most of the soldiers enforcing the order were vengeance-minded Kansans who welcomed such a splendid opportunity to punish the Missourians. In addition, gangs of Red Legs swarmed into the depopulated area, looting, burning, and murdering indiscriminately. Ewing repeatedly ordered his troops not to engage in wanton plundering, and he continued his campaign against the Red Legs. However, his efforts were largely in vain.[2]

The bushwhackers had destroyed a town. The jayhawkers were now completing the ruin of an entire region. The people of West Missouri, as they trudged wearily along the roads or saw their homes go up in smoke, must have asked themselves whether Quantrill's raid was worth the cost. But even so, they did not slacken in their hatred of the North or in their devotion to the South. If anything, and if possible, Order No. 11 merely intensified these feelings all the more.

Pro-Southern and Conservative Union Missourians angrily denounced Order No. 11 as "inhuman, unmanly, and barbarous." Its most vehement critic was George Caleb Bingham, the artist. Bingham hated all Kansans in general and Ewing in particular.* After Order No. 11 was announced he went to Ewing's headquarters and demanded that it be rescinded. Ewing refused, and the interview became highly acrimonious. Finally, as he departed, Bingham warned: "If you persist in executing that order, I will make you infamous with pen and brush as far as I am able." [3]

Bingham carried out his threat with a painting entitled "Order No. 11," the original of which hangs today in the Missouri State Historical Society Library in Columbia. It shows Ewing astride a horse complacently supervising his troops as they expel a Missouri family from its home. A Red Leg has just shot down a young man, and another is about to shoot the elderly head of the family, oblivious to the pleas of a beautiful young woman kneeling at his feet with clasped hands. The house is being pillaged by Union soldiers, one of whom, also on horseback, bears a likeness to

* Bingham, it will be recalled, owned the building in which the female prisoners had been confined. Ewing refused to compensate him for its collapse, which he believed had been deliberately caused by Ewing's soldiers.

Jennison. In the background columns of smoke rise from burning fields, and a long, funereal line of refugees winds its way along the road. The painting was mediocre art but superb propaganda, and it did more than anything else to create the popular conception of Order No. 11.*

Ewing defended his order by arguing that it was necessary to suppress bushwhacking and prevent another Lawrence Massacre. In any case, he added, "It cannot work much hardship upon the truly loyal men, for there are now very few such outside the towns in the counties of the border; and those who are loyal are at the mercy of the bushwhackers. At the worst, it can make matters no worse than they are now, and have been for the last two years." [4]

Meanwhile, Lane disregarded his promise not to cause trouble and called on the men of Kansas to assemble at Paola on September 8 for the purpose of "exterminating" the Missouri border counties. Ewing decided that this was going too far, and he warned Lane that his troops would oppose any mob invasion of Missouri. At the same time he notified Brigadier General Odon Guitar, commander of the Missouri State Militia along the border, of the danger. Guitar quickly mobilized his forces, commenting as he did so that "If our Kansas friends come over on their *mission of love* I shall endeavor to give them such a reception as becomes a *brave* and *hospitable* people."

Both Ewing and General Schofield, who came to investigate the situation along the border for himself, tried without success to dissuade Lane from going ahead with his "Paola Expedition." For a time it seemed as if a clash between Kansas and Missouri Unionists was inevitable. But when September 8 arrived, only a few hundred men turned up at Paola. And instead of marching into Missouri, they merely listened to Lane make a speech. Ewing heaved a deep sigh of relief on learning that Lane's "Paola camp meeting" had been, as one caustic observer put it, a "fizzle." [5]

By the September 9 deadline, over two-thirds of the population of Jackson, Cass, and Bates counties had evacuated the area. Most of the remainder huddled in the towns or near military posts. Vast stretches of territory were completely uninhabited.

* Bingham exhibited the painting in Ohio in 1877 to help defeat Ewing in a campaign for the governorship.

Stark chimneys, standing above charred ruins, dotted the silent countryside. Gloom and desolation reigned supreme.

Ewing had created a desert—but he could not call it peace. Those whom his order was designed to destroy, the bushwhackers, were least injured of all by it. In fact, its immediate effect on them was practically nil. To quote one of Ewing's Missouri critics, they "laughed at it."

Although the farmhouses had been vacated, in nearly every smokehouse bacon and ham still hung from the rafters. Moreover, the country was full of stray horses, cattle, and chickens which their owners had been forced to leave behind. Thus the bushwhackers had little trouble finding plenty to eat. They simply went out at night and obtained all they needed. Likewise, ample forage for their horses was available.

Federal patrols, with orders from Ewing not to take prisoners, scoured the countryside in the weeks following Lawrence. But, as usual, they kept to the main roads and trails, and the guerrillas easily evaded them. Union officers claimed the deaths of over 150 partisans by early September, but this figure was undoubtedly a gross exaggeration. Besides, most of the "bushwhackers" actually slain were farmers or part-time guerrillas. Very few of Quantrill's "old men" were killed.

Quantrill's followers established camps at various places in the Blue Springs region. Jackson County swarmed with so many Federals that they dared not leave their hiding places except at night. On September 15, a scouting party of the Ninth Kansas, under Captain Coleman, stumbled onto Quantrill's own camp, killed two of his men, captured forty horses, seized a large quantity of food, bedding, clothing, and ammunition, and forced the bushwhackers to flee into the impenetrable thickets of the Sni-A-Bar. Following this affair, Quantrill led his band to the hills south of Wellington, then back again to the Blue Springs neighborhood.

A Federal patrol discovered the trail, but trotted right by the guerrilla camp without seeing it. Quantrill got forty men together and started out to bushwhack the unwary soldiers. But suddenly he changed his mind and decided to break camp again. He explained that he did not want the Yankees to know that he was in Jackson County.[6]

The new camp was located at the Stanley farm, also in the vicinity of Blue Springs. Quantrill now had his mistress with him. Her name was Kate King, the daughter of a farmer who lived near Bone Hill. She "took up" with Quantrill earlier that summer, and rejoined him while the guerrillas were near Wellington. Sometimes, dressed in men's clothes, she rode with his band as it roamed the hills and brush.[7]

Quantrill and Todd were in a one-room log house with Kate and Todd's mistress when a picket reported that Federal troops were approaching. They hastily put the two women on good horses and sent them out of the camp well ahead of the soldiers. The guerrillas then collected their gear, saddled up, and rode off deeper into the timber without attempting a stand.

Quantrill established the next bivouac at Joe Dillingham's farm southwest of Blue Springs. This was the very best of all his hide-outs, as it could be approached by only one route, which was easily guarded.

The Federals never discovered the Dillingham camp, with the result that the guerrillas remained in it several days. Every night details went out to bring in supplies. They became very skilled at covering their trail so that the soldiers could not track them back to the camp.

Late in September the bushwhackers began preparing to march south for the winter. Order No. 11 and pressure from Union troops had little or nothing to do with their decision to leave Missouri. Cold weather had set in unusually early, and Quantrill and the other leaders felt that the season for profitable operation was at an end.[8]

All of Quantrill's men gathered at their old rendezvous on the Blackwater, Captain Perdee's. Here they were joined by Anderson's gang and Holt's company. These outfits had some new recruits, but many old faces were missing—an indication that they had not fared as well as Quantrill's own band. Andy Blunt and a number of other veterans elected to stay in Missouri for the winter. Kate King went back to her father's home to wait for her lover to return in the spring.

On October 1, about four hundred guerrillas, all under Quantrill's command, began marching southward. Moving by way of

Lone Jack and Harrisonville, they turned west in the vicinity of Carthage, then picked up the Fort Scott road leading down into Indian Territory.

The advance guard was under Dave Poole. On the morning of October 6, it captured two Federal teamsters driving a wagon loaded with lumber. The prisoners said that they were on the way to the Union fort at Baxter Springs, Kansas, a few miles to the south. This was the first the guerrillas had heard of this post. Poole's men killed the two teamsters and went on to investigate, leaving behind a picket to tell Quantrill about the fort.

Quantrill, on hearing the picket's message, sent a detachment under Gregg to reinforce Poole. Then with the main body he left the road and headed into some timber north of the reported site of the fort, planning to attack it from that direction.

The Union garrison at Baxter Springs consisted of 150 Negro and white troops, 60 of whom were away on a foraging expedition. Its commander was Lieutenant James B. Pond of the Third Wisconsin Cavalry, "a brave and gallant officer with six months' experience fighting guerrillas in their own style." The fort itself was a mere dirt and log embankment four feet high and open at one end.

Gregg and Poole attacked just as the garrison was assembled for its noon meal in a cooking camp some two hundred feet south of the fort. The soldiers, taken completely by surprise, and without their arms, ran pell-mell for the fort. The guerrillas, shooting and yelling, followed close at their heels, cutting off and killing some of the fugitives, and charging right into the fort itself.

Only prompt and brave action by Lieutenant Pond saved the garrison from being wiped out to the last man. Although unfamiliar with artillery, he singlehandedly manned a small howitzer and fired three salvos from it. These, while doing no damage, startled the bushwhackers and caused them to fall back in disorder. This gave the garrison a chance to rally, and Poole decided to break off the attack until Quantrill arrived.

About thirty minutes later, Quantrill emerged from the timber several hundred yards north of the fort. Instantly he drew rein. Drawn up on the Fort Scott road was a column of wagons accompanied by a company of Federal cavalry.

Quantrill did not know it yet, but what he saw before him was the personal escort and headquarters train of Major General James G. Blunt, the rough-and-ready abolitionist commander of the District of the Frontier. Blunt was on his way from Fort Scott to Fort Smith, and by fantastic coincidence had arrived at Baxter Springs just as the guerrillas attacked. No one in his party, however, could hear the firing at Baxter Springs, or see the fort itself, because of an intervening ridge.

Blunt at first thought that Quantrill's men, many of whom were wearing Federal uniforms, were Pond's cavalry out drilling. Then, becoming suspicious, he ordered his bodyguards to form a line of battle while two officers went forward to investigate. They returned soon with word that the strange horsemen were bushwhackers. On hearing this, Blunt laughed and said, "Oh, it is just a few of Jackman's guerrillas from South Missouri. Give them a few rounds and they will run off to cover."

Meanwhile, Quantrill, after seeing that the Federals numbered only about a hundred, commanded his men to fan out for an attack. But before all of them got into line, Todd, on his own initiative, ordered a charge. Immediately two hundred screaming bushwhackers thundered across the prairie, a revolver in each hand.

This fearful sight was too much for Blunt's soldiers, most of whom were raw recruits. They fired a few scattering shots, then broke into a wild, panic-stricken rout. Blunt, almost beside himself with astonishment and anger, cursed them as cowards, but had no choice except to join the flight. John Jarrette, Dick Yeager, and Frank Smith, sensing that he must be an important Federal officer, signaled him out and gave chase. But his magnificent horse quickly outdistanced them and he escaped by leaping a deep gorge.

Most of his troops, however, were not so fortunate. The better-mounted bushwhackers overtook them one by one, and in every case, ruthlessly killed them. Nearly all their victims were later found shot through the head, stripped, beaten, and mutilated.

Among the slain was Major Henry Z. Curtis, Blunt's chief-of-staff and the son of General Samuel Ryan Curtis. Ironically, the Baxter Springs post had been established by him only a month previously. Thus in a sense, he had set the stage for his own death.

Quantrill's men also murdered James O'Neal, artist-correspondent of *Leslie's Weekly*, who was accompanying Blunt with the intention of covering the little-known war in the West. They remarked contemptuously that his career of drawing pictures of masses of frightened Confederates being routed by a few "noble lads in Blue" was over. As far as is known, O'Neal was the only newspaperman killed in actual battle on either side during the Civil War.

The members of Blunt's headquarters band suffered a particularly grisly fate. As they attempted to escape in their wagon, Bill Bledsoe called on them to surrender. Instead, they shot and killed him. In savage retaliation the guerrillas wiped out the entire band, including a twelve-year-old drummer boy, then set fire to the wagon and burned all the bodies.

When the shooting stopped, seventy-eight Union soldiers had been slain and another eleven so badly mangled that they were no longer recognizable. The few lucky enough to escape did not stop running until they reached Fort Scott, thirty-eight miles away.

The bushwhackers lost only two men besides Bledsoe, both killed in the attack on the garrison. In addition, John Koger was wounded by a soldier who suddenly sallied out from the fort, shot him, and dashed back before the surprised guerrillas could fire a single bullet at him.

Quantrill's men took only two prisoners, both Negroes. One was a barber named Zack who had formerly lived in Kansas City and was well known to the guerrillas. The other, Jack Mann by name, had committed criminal acts in Jackson County before fleeing to Kansas. Todd ordered that both be brought along, Zack to serve as an orderly, Mann to perform another sort of job.

Anderson's men did not get into the fight, but consoled themselves by gathering up most of the plunder while Quantrill's and Todd's followers were busy chasing the Federals—an act which produced some strained feelings between the two bands.

Most of Blunt's troops had carried canteens full of whisky. Therefore, it was not long before many of the bushwhackers were reeling drunk. Quantrill personally helped himself to a five-gallon demijohn found in Blunt's buggy and proceeded to get drunk also—the first time any of his followers had seen him in that condition. He rode about the battlefield cradling the huge jug in his arms and boasting, "By God, Shelby could not whip Blunt, neither could Marmaduke, but I whipped him."

Quantrill was still carrying the jug when he spotted John McCorkle riding toward him. Since McCorkle was a member of the scouting party which had discovered the existence of the Baxter Springs post and thus brought about all the fighting and killing, Quantrill decided to have some fun with him. "John," he shouted in a very gruff manner, "I thought you knew that whenever a pilot led me into trouble, I always shoot him!"

McCorkle thought his leader was serious—whenever Quantrill talked of killing, he usually meant it. Therefore, he grabbed a revolver, at the same time yelling, "If you think you can shoot quicker than I can, shoot!"

Quantrill laughed and said, "Put that thing up, you damned fool; I'm going to shoot you in the neck." He then handed the jug to McCorkle, who, quite relieved, proceeded to "shoot himself in the neck" with whisky.

Around two o'clock, Quantrill sent Todd forward with a white flag to demand the garrison's surrender. Pond refused, and Quantrill, overruling Anderson and Todd, decided that it would be useless as well as foolhardy to attack the fort. The liquor had made him drunk but not reckless.

Late in the afternoon, the bushwhackers marched away to the south. They carried Koger and Bledsoe's body in an ambulance taken from Blunt's wagon train. After a while Koger complained that the corpse was beginning to smell. The column thereupon halted and the Negro Jack Mann was ordered to dig two graves. When he finished, the guerrillas placed Bledsoe's body in one, then shot Mann and dumped him into the other. They also killed a stranger who had joined them on the march to Baxter Springs and who was suspected of being a spy from Lawrence.[9]

After marching fifteen miles Quantrill bivouacked for the night. During the ensuing days he continued to move through the Indian Territory toward Texas. On October 12 he reached the camp of Confederate General Douglas G. Cooper on the Canadian River. There, on the following day, he sat down and wrote the only known official military report of his career.

In it he gave a vague account of the Baxter Springs battle and claimed to have killed Blunt. He also described the march through the Indian Territory, stating that his men captured "about 150 Federal Indians and Negroes in the [Cherokee]

Nation," but "brought none of them through." He concluded by promising to write at some future date a complete report on his "summer's campaign on the Missouri River." He signed the report "W. C. Quantrill, Colonel, Commanding, &c.," and sent it to General Sterling Price, along with Blunt's sword and general's commission.[10]

Quantrill had reached the pinnacle of his career, carried there on a wave of blood. What, now, lay ahead?

chapter VIII **Bushwhacker Against Bushwhacker**

The bushwhackers remained at General Cooper's camp several days, then crossed the Red River into Texas. At Mineral Creek, about twelve miles northwest of Sherman, they constructed a number of log shacks and went into winter quarters. Deer abounded in the region, so they had no difficulty securing plenty of fresh meat. In addition, Quantrill sold a six-mule team and the ambulance captured at Baxter Springs, then used the proceeds to buy four hundred-pound sacks of coffee—a rare luxury in the South late in 1863.[1]

On November 2, General Price replied to Quantrill's report. Addressing him as "Colonel," Price congratulated Quantrill on the Baxter Springs victory and thanked him and his men for their "gallant struggle" against Northern oppression in Missouri. However, he stated that he was anxious to have a report on the Lawrence raid, so that "your acts should appear in their true light before the world." Also, he desired information on the treatment accorded captured guerrillas, in order that "the Confederacy and the world may learn [of] the murderous and uncivilized warfare" inaugurated by the Federals, and "thus be able to appreciate their cowardly shrieks and howls when with a just retaliation the same 'measure is meted out to them.' "

Price, as did most Southerners, discounted Northern stories of wholesale massacre at Lawrence. Probably, like the Richmond *Examiner*, he believed that "the expedition to Lawrence was a gallant and perfectly fair blow at the enemy," one which served the "malignant and scoundrely people of Kansas right." Nevertheless, he was obviously disturbed by the charges against the guerrillas, and also uneasy over their reputed "no quarter" policy.

Quantrill doubtlessly was flattered by Price's letter, just as he must have felt great pride on learning that Major General John B. Magruder, commander of the District of Texas, had published a general order congratulating "Colonel Quantrill" for his victory over Blunt.[2]

But had he been able to see the letters being written about him by Brigadier General Henry McCulloch, commander of the Sub-District of North Texas, his reaction would have been less joyful. McCulloch, whose headquarters were at Bonham, only a few miles from Sherman, had a close view of the guerrillas, and he did not like what he saw. Shortly after they arrived in his area, he wrote as follows to General Kirby-Smith, commander of the Trans-Mississippi Department:

> A good many of Colonel Quantrill's command have come into this sub-district, and it is said he is now within it. He has not reported here, and I do not know what his military status is. I do not know as much about his mode of warfare as others seem to know; but, from all I can learn, it is but little, if at all, removed from that of the wildest savage; so much so that I do not for a moment believe that our Government can sanction it in one of her officers. Hence, it seems to me if he be an officer of our army, his conduct should be officially noticed, and if he be not an officer of our army, his acts should be disavowed by our Government, and, as far as practicable, he be made to understand that we would greatly prefer his remaining away from our army or its vicinity.
>
> I appreciate his services, and am anxious to have them; but certainly we cannot, as a Christian people, sanction a savage, inhuman warfare, in which men are to be shot down like dogs, after throwing down their arms and holding up their hands supplicating for mercy.

Ten days later, McCulloch again expressed a low opinion of the bushwhackers to Kirby-Smith, this time stating: "It may be said that Quantrill will help you, but I have little confidence in men who fight for booty and whose mode of warfare is like that of the savages."

McCulloch's views, however, failed to make much of an impression on Kirby-Smith. The Confederate Trans-Mississippi needed fighting men—and the bushwhackers, whatever else they might be, were certainly that—and they could, therefore, be of use. So in November, Kirby-Smith wrote McCulloch suggesting that he employ "Colonel Quantrill and his men" to round up deserters. The guerrillas, he stated, "are bold, fearless men, and moreover, from all representations, are under very fair discipline. They are composed, I understand, in a measure of the very best class of Missourians. They have suffered every outrage in their person and families at the hands of the Federals, and, being outlawed and their lives forfeited, have waged a war of no quarter whenever they have come into contact with the enemy." Kirby-Smith added that in case McCulloch had no immediate need of Quantrill's services, he was to have him report in person to departmental headquarters at Shreveport.

Apparently McCulloch did not have any such need, for soon afterward Quantrill did travel to Shreveport, where he conferred with Kirby-Smith. The Confederate commander must have been favorably impressed by the lean young guerrilla leader, for on November 19 he again wrote McCulloch urging him to employ "Captain Quantrill's company" against deserters.[3]

Meanwhile, things had not been going well at the Mineral Creek camp. A subtle, yet significant, change was taking place in the band. The process set in after the Lawrence Massacre. From that time on, according to Gregg, the unity of purpose and enthusiastic initiative which had distinguished Quantrill's following seemed to vanish. To be sure, the men continued to fight hard and to obey orders promptly. But they increasingly lacked "individual devotion and mutual trust," and they were oppressed by a feeling that there was no real future or valid purpose to the war.

A number of factors produced this degeneration of morale and cohesiveness. First of all was the fading prospects of Southern victory after Gettysburg and Vicksburg. Secondly, there was a sense of revulsion on the part of at least a minority of the guerrillas over the excesses committed at Lawrence. Such deeds, they declared, were not only wrong in themselves, but would eventually lead to disaster for all concerned. And lastly, there was resentment and friction over the manner in which the spoils from Lawrence had been divided. If we are to credit Gregg, Quantrill prior to the raid promised to distribute the plunder among the needy inhabitants of Jackson County, à la Robin Hood. But following the raid he failed to do this; instead he arranged matters so that Todd and a few others close to him got the lion's share.

Early in November, Gregg, Jarrette, Cole Younger, and about forty other men, most of them "old, tried, and true," quit Quantrill. Jarrette's and Younger's motives are not known, but Gregg left because he resented Quantrill's constant favoritism of Todd, of whose power and popularity he was jealous.

During the summer, some time before the Lawrence expedition, Gregg led an independent raid on Plattsburg, Missouri. With him were Jim Little and Fletch Taylor, both close friends of Todd. Prior to the raid they agreed that all money obtained on it would be divided equally. But during the raid Little and Taylor got hold of six thousand dollars which they subsequently refused to share as promised. Gregg complained to Quantrill and Todd, but Todd said that Taylor and Little had a right to keep all they got, and Quantrill backed him up.

This, at least, is Gregg's version of what happened. Doubtlessly Taylor, Little, and Todd would have told a different story. But they never did.

Gregg was staying with some Missouri friends in Sherman when he decided to quit. He rode out to the Mineral Creek camp to get a leave of absence from Quantrill. On the way he met Poole and Jarrette. They told him that he had better go back, as Todd would probably try to kill him. But Gregg shrugged off the warning and went on to the camp.

Quantrill's first words were to urge him to go away: "You have some enemies in camp."

"Who are these enemies?"

"Why, there are Taylor and Little, whom you denounced as thieves, and Barker* don't like you first-rate."

"Well, are not these men thieves?"

"Yes, they are."

"Now, you say that I have been a good soldier and officer and an honest man. Why do you want me to leave and the thieves to stay?"

* The Barker referred to is probably John Barker, a veteran bushwhacker and a very tough character.

Quantrill replied only that the men had such a strong devotion to Todd that he could not risk offending him.

Gregg then asked for a leave of absence so that he might go to Shreveport and get assigned to another command. Quantrill gave him one and bade him good-by. Gregg never saw him again.

As Gregg rode back to Sherman, he was passed on the road by Todd, Little, Taylor, and Barker. Suspecting that they might try to bushwhack him, he stopped for the night at an inn. The following morning he went on into Sherman.

There he again saw Todd, Taylor, and Barker. They were standing on the opposite side of the street, talking and looking very nervous. He passed by them, alert for any hostile move.

Todd turned to Barker and Taylor and said: "There goes that damned son-of-a-bitch—now kill him!"

But Taylor answered, "I will not kill Gregg. He is a Southern man, and he has been a good soldier and officer. If you want him killed you will have to kill him yourself."

Todd did not try anything, and Gregg rode on to Shreveport. There Kirby-Smith assigned him to Shelby's Missouri Brigade. He remained in the regular service until the end of the war, in time becoming captain of Company H, Shank's Regiment.[4]

Jarrette and Younger soon followed Gregg's example and likewise joined the regular army. McCulloch assigned Younger to an expedition which went to New Mexico in the spring of 1864 to recruit a regiment for the Confederate Army. The mission failed, and Younger went to Arizona, then down into Mexico, from whence he sailed to San Francisco in the fall of 1864. He remained in California, living with an uncle, until after the end of the war.*

Eventually, General McCulloch found some work for the bushwhackers. First he sent them in pursuit of a party of marauding

* Bronough, pp. 59-60. Many years later, in a book entitled *The Story of Cole Younger, by Himself*, written to publicize a "wild west" show with which he was connected, Younger related that after leaving Quantrill he carried out a series of spectacular special missions for the Confederacy in Louisiana, Texas, Arkansas, Colorado, Mexico, and California. Although these yarns are obviously and even absurdly fantastic, they are sometimes presented as fact. Cf. Homer Croy, *Last of the Great Outlaws* (New York, New American Library, 1958).

Comanches. They chased the Indians for a week, but never came close to catching them. In this case they were up against enemies more experienced than themselves in the techniques of guerrilla warfare.

On their return from this mission McCulloch ordered them to destroy all the whisky stills in the Red River Valley. It seemed that the Indians in Cooper's army were getting drunk so often that they were worse than useless. However, since the guerrillas also were obtaining "firewater" from these stills, Quantrill instructed them, with a wink of the eye, to carry out McCulloch's order only "somewhat." As a result, they wrecked just one still, killing its operators, and it can be presumed that they did this only because the still was producing a bad brand of whisky!

Next they went after a Union raiding party in the Indian Territory. They pursued the Federals as far as present-day Coffeyville, Kansas, where they killed six of them in a skirmish. After a couple of days' rest, they returned to Mineral Creek, having been gone two weeks altogether.

Eventually McCulloch got around to using the guerrillas, as Kirby-Smith had suggested, to round up deserters, of which there were a great many in North Texas. In giving them this assignment he instructed Quantrill not to do any killing, as dead deserters would be of no use in bolstering the thin ranks of the Confederate armies in the West. Quantrill replied that he would try to take prisoners, although not exactly accustomed to doing so, but that he reserved the right to kill the deserters if they attempted to resist his men. As it turned out, the bushwhackers shot down more than they brought back, and McCulloch was confirmed in his low opinion of their military value.

When not out chasing Federals, Indians, deserters, and moonshiners, Quantrill's men took life easy in their winter quarters. Every day some of them rode to Sherman, where they held horse races or engaged in horse-trading at the local race track. Sometimes Quantrill himself participated in the races with Old Charley. This horse originally belonged to a Union officer and was captured at Independence. It became very attached to its master and would not permit anyone else to ride it. Should another person so much as come near, it would begin to kick, rear, and bite. But with Quantrill it was very gentle. Since no other guerrilla's horse matched Old Charley's speed, Quantrill invariably won the races he entered.

The best rider among the bushwhackers, who were all excellent horsemen, was Dick Maddox. Every time he got drunk—which was often—he would put on an amazing exhibition of bronco-busting and also of rope-throwing, another art at which he excelled.

On Christmas Day several dozen bushwhackers, yelling and firing their revolvers in the air, galloped into Sherman for a spree. Some eggnogs at a friend's gave them a good start; then Maddox, always on the outlook for such things, discovered a barrel of whisky in a cellar. In no time at all they were running amuck. Some of them shot the church steeples full of holes. A couple of others rode their horses into the lobby of the town hotel, shooting out the gaslights and the knobs off the doors. And another bunch had a photographer take their pictures, then, apparently displeased with the results, destroyed his camera and ransacked the studio.

The terrified citizens of Sherman were helpless to stop the rampaging Missourians. However, Ben Christian, proprietor of the hotel, sent word to Quantrill as to what his drunken young followers were doing. Quantrill hastily summoned all of his available men and rode to town. He rounded up the celebrants, apologized to the townspeople, and promised that full restitution would be made. The next day the guilty men, now sobered and chastened, returned on Quantrill's orders and paid Christian and the photographer for the damage they had committed.

On New Year's Eve about twenty of Quantrill's boys went to Sherman to attend a dance at Jim Crow Chiles' house, a place described as having been a "gambling house and hangout for loose women." They had arranged the affair themselves, and had not invited any of the other men. As a consequence, there was much resentment, and a couple dozen of those left out decided to go to Sherman and break up the dance. Their attempt to do so resulted in a large-scale fist fight. Once again Quantrill had to hasten into town to restore order.

During January and February the unruliness and demoralization of the bushwhackers increased. Not only were they guilty of acts of rowdyism in Sherman, but some of them robbed and murdered citizens in the region. One bunch killed a local farmer after taking three hundred dollars from him. Another farmer was found dead on a roadside following a poker game with Jim Crow Chiles, Andy McGuire, John Ross, and Fletch Taylor at Chiles' place. And at about the same time Fletch Taylor murdered and robbed a prominent citizen named Major Butts.[5]

General McCulloch was outraged on learning of these and other crimes committed by, or attributed to, the bushwhackers. In a letter of February 3, to Magruder, he wrote that:

> Quantrill will not obey orders and so much mischief is charged to his command here that I have determined to disarm, arrest, and send his entire command to you or General Smith. This is the only chance to get them out of this section of the country, which they have nearly ruined, and I have never yet got them to do any service.
>
> They regard the life of a man less than you would of a sheep-killing dog. Quantrill and his men are determined never to go into the army or fight in any general battle, first, because many of them are deserters from our Confederate ranks, and next, because they are afraid of being captured, and then because it won't pay men who fight for plunder. They will only fight when they have all the advantage and when they can run away whenever they find things too hot for them. I regard them as but one shade better than highwaymen, and the community believe that they have committed all the robberies that have been committed about here for some time, and every man that has any money about his house is scared to death, nearly, and several moneyed men have taken their money and gone where they feel more secure.

McCulloch, however, made no move to implement his threat to disarm and arrest the guerrillas. Instead he tried to get them off his hands by transferring them to the command of Brigadier General H. P. Bee on the Texas coast. In a letter of February 6 to Bee, he stated:

> There is no doubt about [the bushwhackers] being true Southern men, and, no odds what happens, will fight only on our side. They have been bad behaved [*sic*] in some instances, but have not been guilty of a fourth of what has been charged against them. They are in a country filled with the very worst character of men, numbers of whom are hid in the bush and come out at night and rob and steal; and there are plenty of enemies to the country who would have been glad to get up a conflict by telling bad tales upon them besides those that were true,

and I really think the people are to a great extent unnecessarily uneasy about them. If these men are not kept on partisan service they will disband and scatter through the country, where, if bad men, they will do us great harm; if kept together under Quantrill they can be controlled. . . .

They are superbly armed and well mounted, and there is no reason that they should not do good service. They have not been paid for months [!], this should be done immediately, and let them see that they are to be treated properly, and required to behave themselves.[6]

In view of what he had written to Magruder only three days before about the guerrillas, McCulloch was being less than candid with Bee—no doubt he wished to forestall any objections on that general's part to having the tumultuous Missourians placed under his command. But McCulloch could have spared himself the trouble. Quantrill defied his order to report to Magruder, stating that he had an independent partisan commission from Jefferson Davis and therefore was not subject to McCulloch's command. Since McCulloch could not prove otherwise, the bushwhackers remained at Mineral Creek.

From the moment Quantrill entered Texas the Confederate authorities placed pressure on him to enter the regular service. Price and Kirby-Smith believed that on the whole bushwhacking resulted in more harm than good, and that the guerrillas would be of greater value in the army. The unwillingness of Quantrill's men to join the army stemmed from the fact that many of them were deserters, and from fear that they might be executed by the Federal Army in case they became prisoners as the consequence of a mass surrender by one of the weak and incompetent Confederate Trans-Mississippi generals. Also, most of them were interested mainly in fighting in Missouri, avenging personal wrongs, and obtaining plunder, rather than in serving the Confederate cause as such.

Ultimately, Quantrill bowed partially to official wishes. Early in March, after conferring with Price, he returned to the Mineral Creek camp with orders to reduce the band to eighty-four men and to send the remainder into the regular service. In the reorganization which followed, Anderson's gang was absorbed into Quantrill's command. Quantrill, Todd, and Anderson personally selected the men they wanted to keep, after which an election of officers was held. Todd became captain, Anderson first lieutenant, Fletch Taylor second lieutenant, Jim Little third lieutenant, and Ike Berry orderly sergeant. Quantrill as "Colonel" was to exercise a general command over all the West Missouri bushwhacker bands.*

This was the second time that the bushwhackers were organized in a regular manner. But scarcely had the new organization been set up than it fell apart.

A man from Anderson's old gang named Morgan stole a bolt of cloth from one of Quantrill's men and had a pair of pants made out of it. Quantrill, on learning of the theft, had Morgan taken across the Red River, disarmed, and then turned loose with the warning that if he ever returned to the other side he would be shot. But, disregarding the warning, Morgan came back and robbed and murdered an old farmer. Quantrill thereupon had a squad go out and kill Morgan.

Anderson roared with anger when he heard of Morgan's death. His first impulse was to go shoot Quantrill, but on second thought he abandoned the idea—Quantrill had too many friends on hand, and was no slouch with a pistol himself. Instead, he rode out of the camp, vowing that he would not serve any longer in "such a damn outfit." He went to Jim Crow Chiles' place, where his newly acquired wife, a "saloon girl" named Bushiba "Bush" Smith, lived.† About twenty men left with him, among them Fletch Taylor and Ike Berry, whom Quantrill had threatened to punish for having robbed civilians.

Quantrill maintained his usual calm in face of this defection.

† According to some accounts (cf. McCorkle, *Three Years With Quantrill*, p. 97), in marrying Bush Smith, Anderson went against Quantrill's will, thereby causing the break between the two. However, it seems unlikely that Quantrill would have cared one way or the other whether Anderson got married or to whom. That Anderson indeed married her is confirmed by a letter from her found on his dead body in October 1864 and by a marriage license discovered many years later in a Texas courthouse. According to Frank Smith, another bushwhacker named Andy Walker married while in Texas during the winter of 1863–64—and he already had a wife in Missouri!

Stating that he did not care if Anderson left, but that he was not going to let him take part of his men, he assembled the remaining bushwhackers and headed into Sherman. His force surrounded Chiles' house, but found it empty except for Bush Smith and several other prostitutes. Someone had warned Anderson that Quantrill was coming after him, with the result that the deserters had hightailed it for Bonham.

On returning to the camp Quantrill's party captured Fletch Taylor, who was found lurking in the vicinity. Quantrill promptly ordered him disarmed and placed under guard; at the same time he threatened to have him court-martialed for the murder of Major Butts and other crimes. But Taylor, who was highly popular with the men, escaped during the night with the connivance of his guards.

Anderson, when he arrived in Bonham, went to McCulloch and told him that Quantrill was responsible for the lawless deeds of the guerrillas around Sherman. Taylor, on rejoining Anderson, backed up this charge, also declared that Quantrill had ordered him to rob Butts.

These accusations delighted McCulloch. Here at last was a good excuse to crack down on Quantrill and his Missouri troublemakers! Accordingly, he sent an order to Quantrill to report at once to headquarters in Bonham.

Quantrill fully realized that Anderson and Taylor had probably been giving McCulloch an earful, and that the general was out to get him. Nevertheless he obeyed the summons. Taking all of his men except twelve under Todd, who remained behind to guard the camp, he set out for Bonham.

Quantrill reached the town at noon (there is no record of the exact date). He went to the City Hotel, where McCulloch's headquarters were located, dismounted, tied his horse to the hitch rail, and told his men to remain mounted and on the alert for trouble. Then he went inside the building and up the stairs to the general's office.

McCulloch, as soon as he saw the guerrilla chieftain, got up from his desk and snapped: "Quantrill, you are under arrest! Remove your side arms and throw them on the bed."

Quantrill did as he was ordered, but protested, "What's the meaning of this?"

"Well," answered McCulloch evasively, "it is dinnertime—come and go down and have dinner with me and I will discuss it with you after dinner."

"No, sir," replied Quantrill angrily, "I will not go to dinner." Then, stamping his boot on the floor, he shouted in utter exasperation, "By God! I don't care a goddamn if I never eat another bite in Texas!"

McCulloch shrugged his shoulders and went off to his dinner, leaving two soldiers to guard Quantrill until he returned.

Quantrill sat in sullen silence on a chair in the office. After a while he stood up, asked, "Mind if I get a drink of water?" and sauntered casually across the room to a water cooler in the corner. He filled a cup and raised it to his lips—then, suddenly, he dashed it to the floor, sprang to the bed, grabbed his revolvers, and covered the two astonished guards before they could make a move!

He ordered the guards to lay down their guns. He then backed out through the door and locked it after him. Next he ran down the stairs and got the drop on two sentinels stationed at the bottom. Pushing them ahead of him at pistol point, he went through the lobby and out onto the street.

"Boys!" he shouted. "The outfit is under arrest! Let's get out of here!"

His men waited just long enough for him to unhitch and mount Old Charley, then they all galloped out of Bonham on the road back to Mineral Creek.[7]

McCulloch had not yet finished his dinner when he received word of Quantrill's spectacular escape. Immediately he issued peremptory orders to Colonel J. Martin of the Texas Militia to go after the bushwhacker and bring him back dead or alive.

Anderson's gang joined the militia and together with them pursued Quantrill all afternoon. Several times the two guerrilla forces fired at each other, but no one on either side was hit. With the coming of darkness Martin abandoned the chase and Quantrill made it back safely to camp.

Quantrill quickly told Todd what had happened. Todd at once took nine of the men who had remained behind and went out on a scout. Two miles from the camp he saw some fires and came upon a party of horsemen in a small clearing.

"Who are you?" he demanded, at the same time signaling his followers to draw their pistols.

"We are Confederate militia," came the reply.

But before anything more could be said, the revolver of one of Todd's men went off accidentally and the bullet struck the left arm of Jim Little. The sound of the shot panicked the militia. They wheeled their horses about and fled pell-mell into the timber!

Deciding that there was little to fear from the militia, Todd turned back toward camp. Suddenly, out of the shadow, loomed another body of horsemen—Anderson's gang!

Todd's party quickly took shelter in a near-by wood. Anderson shouted, "If you are not a damn set of cowards, come on out in the open and fight!"

Todd scornfully yelled back, "You have the most men with you—if you are not a set of damn cowards, come on in and take us out!"

Both sides then began firing at each other. But neither was really out for blood, with the result that although over fifty shots were exchanged, no one was hurt. Finally Anderson's band rode away, and Todd returned to camp.

Later on during the night some of Anderson's men managed to slip into the camp, where they captured Andy Walker and tried to take Old Charley. But the wild kicking and rearing of the horse frustrated them, as well as arousing the whole camp and forcing them to flee.

In the morning Todd, with a small force, again went out to reconnoiter. Before long he encountered Colonel Martin at the head of his regiment.

"What in the hell are you doing?" Todd demanded.

"We have been sent down by General McCulloch's orders to get Quantrill."

"Well, don't you know that you're not going to get him? Now you listen to me—you had better get your men together and go back to Bonham and tell General McCulloch that Quantrill said that if he was molested any further he would turn his bushwhackers loose in Texas and he would not be responsible for anything that might happen or what his men did!"

Todd then turned about and rode away, leaving Colonel Martin sitting on his horse in dumb-struck amazement.

Apparently the warning had the effect desired—the militia were not seen again in the vicinity of Mineral Creek. A disgusted McCulloch wrote Magruder that he was unable to do anything about the depredations of the "Captain Quantrill command" because he lacked troops with the "physical and moral courage to arrest and disarm them." [8]

Quantrill remained at Mineral Creek several days, then crossed to the north bank of the Red River, where he established a new camp beyond McCulloch's jurisdiction—no doubt much to that general's great relief.

The grass was turning green and the leaves appearing; it was time now to return to Missouri. Around the tenth of April the bushwhackers started northward. It rained all the way, and the going was slow and tough. While passing through the Cherokee Nation they stopped at the site of the graves of Bledsoe and Jack Mann. They found both their skeletons lying on the ground, the flesh eaten away by vultures and "varmints."

In Missouri, practically every river had to be forded by swimming the horses. At the Osage, Quantrill and Todd went over first, then lit fires on the bank to guide the others. On further, they found the Grand River so swollen by rains that they would not have been able to get across at all had it not been for a rickety bridge.

From the Grand, they moved through the Dayton region into Johnson County. They stopped at a farmhouse near Chapel Hill, where a woman fixed them a good, hot breakfast of bacon and biscuits. Here Quantrill ordered the band to scatter into groups of three and four while he and Todd sniffed out the situation in Jackson County.[9]

During the winter a complete reorganization of the Union command structure in the West had taken place. Kansas and Missouri were again divided into separate departments, the first under General Samuel R. Curtis, the second headed by General William S. Rosecrans. The District of the Border disappeared and Ewing was transferred to the St. Louis area. Jackson County and the rest of the region affected by Order No. 11 became part of the District of Central Missouri, commanded by Brigadier General Egbert B.

Brown of the Missouri State Militia. Brown, after he took over, relaxed the terms of the order and permitted a great many refugees to return to their homes. However, he was determined to stamp out bushwhacking, and he had his troops on the alert for Quantrill's return. In Jackson County itself there was a new regiment, the Second Colorado Cavalry, under the command of Colonel James H. Ford. It was made up of twelve hundred "hardy mountaineer boys" and had been brought in for the express purpose of dealing with Quantrill's bushwhackers.[10]

Quantrill and Todd did not have to look around long before they concluded that conditions were "too squally" in Jackson County for profitable operations. Therefore, they sent word to the men to rendezvous in Lafayette County, where things looked much more promising.

At this juncture the most mysterious event in the annals of the bushwhackers occurred: a quarrel between Quantrill and Todd which resulted in Quantrill leaving the band and Todd becoming its sole leader.

For some time conflict between the two chieftains had been brewing. Todd was the idol of the men, especially the younger, wilder ones. Increasingly he had acted independently of Quantrill, or even violated his instruction—as witness his order to charge at Baxter Springs. Quantrill, for his part, realized Todd's popularity and appreciated his services. Also, he knew that the enmity of such a man would be deadly. Therefore, he sought to conciliate him by giving him greater authority and by favoring him in the division of the spoils. But the more power Todd got, the more he wanted, and by the summer of 1863 he, not Quantrill, was in many ways the actual chieftain of the band. Todd's position was further enhanced, moreover, by the fact that Quantrill acted more and more as a sort of general commander of all the West Missouri partisans and so ceased to exercise direct authority over the band, which, significantly enough, began to be called "Todd's gang."

In Texas, the first signs of an open break appeared. One day in the camp Todd began to brag about his superior courage. "I am not afraid of any man on the planet!" he crowed.

Quantrill looked over at him and quietly said, "How about me?"

"Oh, well," laughed Todd, who was not yet ready for a showdown, "you're the only damned man that I ever was afraid of."

Later, soon after the reorganization of the band, and just before Anderson's defection, a much more serious incident took place. Todd became drunk and boisterous in camp, and when Quantrill ordered him to shut up, he told Quantrill to go to hell. Enraged by this defiance, Quantrill grabbed a revolver and shot at Todd, but missed. He then ordered his men to shoot Todd, but they all ran off to the creek bottom except John Barker. Quantrill and Barker both fired at Todd but again missed him, and Todd fired back, also missing. Some of the men then intervened and stopped the fight. After cooling off, Quantrill declared that he had not shot to kill, and the two men shook hands and agreed to let bygones be bygones.

The final split came during a game of cards at a hideout in Missouri. Quantrill and Todd were sitting at a table playing seven-up, a hundred dollars a game. Quantrill suddenly threw his cards down and heatedly accused Todd of cheating—a charge that was true. Todd made a threatening remark, and Quantrill replied that he was not afraid of any man. Instantly Todd whipped out a pistol and shoved it into Quantrill's face.

"You are afraid of me, aren't you, Bill?" he snarled, his face twisted with demonic fury.

Quantrill knew that there was only one answer he could make —any other, and Todd would kill him on the spot.

So he choked out the words: "Yes—I'm afraid of you."

This was what Todd wanted—to humiliate Quantrill before the other men. He withdrew his pistol and leaned back, a sardonic, mocking smile of triumph on his lips. The other bushwhackers present looked on in silence. Not one moved to support Quantrill.

Quantrill got up and without saying a word he walked outside, saddled Old Charley, and rode away. A few of the older men followed him, but all the rest stayed. Todd's victory was complete.[11]

All the known facts of Quantrill's fall from power have been described. Yet in themselves they fail to provide an adequate explanation. One still wonders why he should suddenly and totally lose out. He had won spectacular victories and was at the peak of his renown. No one denied his courage, all admitted his skill.

And he was obviously more steady and intelligent than the illiterate, vicious, semi-insane Todd.

Although this is sheer speculation, the underlying causes of Quantrill's downfall were probably threefold.

First, the degeneration in the character of the bushwhackers. As stated before, they had ceased to be merely tough young farm boys defending their homes and revenging wrongs. They were now prairie freebooters who, in fact, did regard, to paraphrase McCulloch, the life of a man as less than that of a sheep-killing dog. Quantrill, although a murderer and bandit himself, had tried, as the evidence demonstrates, to maintain at least a modicum of discipline and order, and to restrain the worst tendencies of the guerrillas. Todd, on the other hand, did not stand in their way—instead, he led the way!

Secondly, by 1864 Quantrill had lost faith in the future of the Southern cause. While in Texas, he told one of his men that the Confederacy was a failure and the war lost.[12] The rank-and-file bushwhackers, at least those who had not given up, probably sensed his defeatism and hence, quite understandably, were more than willing to abandon his leadership in favor of the fanatical Todd. This is all the more likely in view of the fact that some of the Missourians still suspected Quantrill, despite his exploits, as an outsider and opportunist.

And, finally, there can be little doubt that Quantrill was sorely disappointed at the failure of the Confederate authorities to give him higher rank and a larger command. Far from promoting him, they had first taken most of his men away, then tried to court-martial him! If this was to be all the thanks he got for Lawrence and Baxter Springs—the only victories won by the Confederacy in the West in 1863—and for the pinning down of thousands of Union troops along the border, then why should he continue to fight and suffer for the South in Missouri? So if Todd wanted the band, let him have it—and all the "glory" that went with it. Sooner or later he would get a lot of the boys killed, and himself with them. The survivors then would realize their error and come back and ask him to take over again. Meanwhile he would lay low and wait. . . .

Early in June Quantrill rode to Bone Hill and picked up Kate. Then with a few followers, he crossed the Missouri and went into hiding in the rugged Perche Hills of Howard County.[13] Although his name continued to figure prominently in Union reports and the newspapers, he ceased to play an important part in the Missouri guerrilla warfare.

chapter IX "Now You Are Skelpt"

Quantrill had quit. But Todd, Anderson, Poole, Yeager, Taylor, Clement, and a half-dozen other chieftains remained in the field. Only Andy Blunt was missing. The First Missouri Cavalry had killed him on March 7 in Lafayette County. They left his body to rot where it fell, a grim warning to other bushwhackers.[1]

The summer of 1864 saw partisan warfare reach new heights of ferocity. The guerrillas, along with other Southern adherents in Missouri, expected Price's army to invade the state in a last desperate bid to conquer it for the Confederacy. Consequently, they went all-out to prepare the way by terrorizing Unionists, disrupting communications, and wearing down Federal troops. They knew it was now or never, and so stopped at nothing. All of central Missouri was engulfed in a tidal wave of blood.

To combat bushwhacking and withstand Price, General Rosecrans, Union commander in Missouri, had less than fifteen thousand troops, and most of these were poorly equipped, ill-trained, and badly led "Paw-Paw" militia. In addition, he had to worry about the Order of American Knights (OAK), a secret organization of Confederate sympathizers who planned to spring to arms the instant Price entered the state. Finally, as if all this were not enough, the Conservative and Radical Unionists were at each other's throats. The Radicals advocated immediate abolition of slavery in Missouri, the Conservatives (who were very conservative indeed) wanted to postpone emancipation until 1876. The Conservatives denounced the Radicals as "Nigger-lovers," the Radicals accused the Conservatives of being "copperheads." So bitter was their struggle that a civil war within a civil war threatened to break out in Missouri!

From the Federal standpoint, the worst conditions continued to prevail in Quantrill's old stamping grounds in western Missouri. Every day brought news of fresh guerrilla outrages, and practically every day the Kansas City *Journal* bewailed the failure of the troops to suppress bushwhacking. "For all practical purposes," it declared in mixed despair and disgust,

> the rebels control the countryside. No loyal man can till a farm or raise a crop . . . or safely travel the highways. Should he venture to run the gauntlet from one military post to the next, he does so at the risk, the imminent risk, of assassination. . . . In a word, the rebels hold the country, while the loyal people are besieged in the towns.

Editor Thacher blamed this sad state of affairs on General Brown's relaxation of Order No. 11, which allowed large numbers of people to resettle in the depopulated district. Although these people were required to furnish evidence of loyalty, a great many of them were Southern sympathizers who willingly aided the bushwhackers. In fact, even the "veriest bushwhackers" were able in some cases to get persons to vouch for their loyalty and thus obtain settlement permits.[2]

On June 11, the guerrillas provided terrifying proof of their unabated power. A Union detachment of thirteen men headed by a sergeant was on patrol near Warrensburg. Suddenly they were confronted by a large body of horsemen dressed in blue uniforms. Thinking that they were friends, the soldiers allowed them to approach. At point-blank range the disguised bushwhackers pulled out their revolvers and opened fire. Twelve soldiers were killed, and only the sergeant, badly wounded, managed to escape to tell the tale. After robbing a stagecoach, which happened along, the attackers disappeared into the brush. The bodies of the murdered soldiers were later found stripped and mutilated—the mark of Anderson's gang.*

* According to Edwards (*Noted Guerrillas, pp. 207-8*), the scalping of Jim Bledsoe by the Indian during the retreat from Lawrence caused the bushwhackers to retaliate in kind. Andy Blunt found Bledsoe's body soon after it had been mutilated and declared: "We have something to learn yet, boys, and we have learned it. Scalp for scalp hereafter." Blunt, Anderson, Clement, Peyton Long, and Bill McGuire were the first guerrillas to engage in the practice.

Two days later the bushwhackers waylaid a supply train south of Lexington, killed eight soldiers, burned two wagons, and shot fifteen mules. They also robbed another stagecoach and cut the telegraph wire between Independence and Lexington.

At the same time other guerrilla bands began attacking river boats near Waverly on the Missouri. Usually, they stood on the bank and peppered the boats with revolver and rifle bullets as they chugged by, sometimes with women standing in front of them so as to forestall any return fire. However, on one occasion twenty bushwhackers dashed down to the river on horseback, seized the ropes of the steamer *Live Oak* as it hastily backed off from the Waverly landing, and tried to haul it back to shore. Ultimately, steam power prevailed over horse power, but not before the crew of the *Live Oak* passed through some anxious moments, and had their boat riddled with over two hundred bullets.[3]

The Warrensburg ambush and other bushwhacker successes caused Thacher to take up his pen again in wrathful indignation:

> It is no longer to be disputed that this state is overrun with guerrillas and bushwhackers more completely than at any time for the last two years. . . . You cannot pick up a paper from any county in the western part of the State, north or south of the Missouri river, without finding a long catalogue of bushwhacking orgies. . . . The bushwhackers have shown their capacity for hazardous and unlooked-for enterprises. Their uniform success—unbroken as yet by a single failure, has emboldened them to make desperate ventures. . . . This bushwhacking question is assuming an importance which threatens the utter ruin of Western Missouri and Kansas. . . . It does seem to us that the civil and military authorities of the State are either ignorant of the condition affairs are assuming, or else are powerless to devise and apply a remedy.[4]

Goaded by criticism of this type, the Federal troops did their best to put down the guerrillas. During the middle part of June a column from Kansas and Ford's Colorado regiment joined in scouring the hills and forests of the border counties. The Kansans failed to kill or capture a single bushwhacker, but the hard-riding Coloradans claimed that they "mustered out" thirteen partisans, among them Dick Yeager. Some of Ford's troops acted as "foot-scouts" during the operation, "lying in wait of the guerrillas and meeting them at their own game." [5]

Ford's sweep caused Todd's gang to scatter into small bands of three and four once again. Then, early in July, Todd sent out word to assemble at Bone Hill. About sixty men answered the call. They asked Todd what was up, but he merely replied, "It's time to go out and bushwhack a few Feds."

A swift night march brought them to the Ginter farm south of Independence on the morning of July 6. They concealed themselves in the brush near the Independence-Glasgow road and waited for a Union patrol to come along. But the morning and early afternoon passed without a sign of the enemy. The only thing to appear was the Glasgow stage, which they stopped and robbed.

At five o'clock Todd decided that there was no sense in waiting any longer. Accompanied by Lee McMurty, he quit his hiding place and started for the Ginter house to tell the prisoners from the stage that he and his men were leaving and that they were free to do the same. But just at this instant a twenty-six-man detachment of the Second Colorado under Captain Seymour W. Wagner came trotting down the road. The troopers saw Todd and McMurty and immediately spurred their horses in pursuit—thus plunging straight into the bushwhacker ambush.

Wagner toppled from his horse at the first fire. However, he staggered to his feet and advanced toward the bushwhackers, banging away with a revolver in each hand. Then several more bullets tore into him and he fell to the ground, where the howling guerrillas finished him off.

Wagner's men fought with equal valor and determination. But, according to Frank Smith, "they couldn't hit a thing." They were armed with inferior Savage pistols which tended to fire into the ground. In the end, most of them broke through and escaped back to Independence. They left behind, however, seven dead besides Wagner. The bushwhackers had only one man wounded. This was their first real encounter with the Coloradans, and they were impressed by their fine horses and the "sand" they showed fighting.[6]

North of the Missouri things were popping also. Bands led by "Coon" Thornton, Clif Holtzclaw, and John Thrailkill ran amuck, murdering Radicals, attacking Federal posts, burning bridges. In Clay County guerrillas shot down a Union man in front of his wife and children, whom they then stripped of all their clothing, "even the frocks from the little girls." Over in Platte County the St. Joseph *Herald* reported that hundreds of loyalists had been driven from their homes and were "wandering in the jungle." The bushwhackers warned the families of these men that if they returned they would be killed without mercy.

Brigadier General Clinton Fisk, commander of Northwest Missouri, tried desperately to suppress the guerrillas in his district. However, most of his troops were Paw-Paw militia, large numbers of whom were either secretly or openly pro-Southern. In response to his pleas for help, Rosecrans commissioned an individual named Harry Truman to conduct an independent antiguerrilla campaign. But Truman, instead of fighting the bushwhackers, turned out to be one himself! Riding in an open carriage with a drunken prostitute on either side, he led a column of ruffians from town to town, robbing and murdering Unionists and Secessionists alike. His glowing telegraphic reports of victories over the guerrillas at first deceived Rosecrans and Fisk, but on learning of the true nature of his activities they had him arrested. He was subsequently court-martialed and sentenced to prison—the only known case of a Missouri Unionist guerrilla.[7]

Rumors of imminent bushwhacker raids and Confederate invasions swept the border country. Westport, Wyandotte, and Kansas City all formed Home Guard units to defend against attack, the one in Kansas City numbering five hundred men. In Kansas, towns as far west as Emporia and Topeka clamored for military protection. A false report that the garrison at Lawrence was going to be moved out caused the people of that community to howl with panic.

Quantrill's name continued to be mentioned more than that of any other guerrilla leader, and it was a name that inspired terror. Julia Lovejoy of Baldwin City, Kansas, wrote to her family in Massachusetts that she lay awake nights fearful that Quantrill might at any hour "silently issue from the woods." Late in June a rumor that Quantrill with seven hundred men was marching on Leavenworth resulted in troops from the near-by fort rushing to the defense of the town. And in July, "Doc" Jennison, back again in the Union Army as colonel of the Fifteenth Kansas Regiment, informed General Curtis that he had it on "good authority" that

Quantrill was in western Kansas organizing the Indians for a raid on the frontier settlements! [8]

The wild rumors of Confederate invasions, and the exaggerated reports of Confederate strength, so disgusted the level-headed editor of the Liberty *Tribune* that he published the following summary of the "news":

> Shelby with 3,000 in Lafayette. Marmaduke coming up line between Missouri and Kansas with 8,000.
>
> Quantrill in Jackson with 3,500. Col. Thos. McCarty on Hannibal R.R. with 26,000.
>
> 20,000 troops on way from Illinois to join Quantrill.
>
> The main column, 240,000 strong, on way to capture St. Louis.[9]

The real news for Union adherents early in July was bad enough. On the tenth, "Coon" Thornton's band, several hundred strong, captured Platte City without firing a shot. Not only did the Paw-Paw militia garrison fail to put up a fight, but most of it gleefully joined the guerrillas! Thornton was accompanied by Fletch Taylor, who made a speech in the town calling for the extermination of all "Radical Unionists," at the same time flourishing a bloody knife which he said was fresh from the bosom of a Radical!

The fall of Platte City, and the manifest inability of Fisk's Paw-Paws to cope with the guerrillas, resulted in Ford crossing into North Missouri with most of the Second Colorado. On July 14, near Camden Point, he caught Thornton in the open, defeated him, and scattered his band. The Coloradans pursued the bushwhackers into the brush, and soon were claiming to have slain thirty to forty of them—doubtlessly an exaggeration.

Three days later, however, some of Ford's troopers were not so fortunate. Seven miles northeast of Liberty a forty-seven-man detachment under Captain Thomas Moses encountered a much larger force of guerrillas. Once more the partisans wore Federal uniforms, and they were even able to reply correctly to Moses' challenge. As soon as they were at close pistol range they charged and routed the Coloradans, killing eight and wounding four of them.[10]

Todd took advantage of Ford's absence north of the river. After first feinting at Independence, he raided Arrow Rock. Accompanied by Poole and Yeager (who was not at all dead), he dashed into Arrow Rock on the night of July 20 and took forty horses and twenty thousand dollars' worth of property, then hustled back to the safety of the Sni-A-Bar. However, during the foray Yeager received a serious wound. The guerrillas carried him to Ike Flannery's father's house, where two weeks later a Federal patrol found and killed him—this time for real.

Todd's band remained in its Sni fortress the better part of the next two months. It sallied forth only occasionally to rob stagecoaches, cut telegraph wires, and harass the workers on the Missouri Pacific Railroad, which was under construction from Warrensburg to Kansas City.[11]

It was now that "Bloody Bill" Anderson took the center of the bushwhacking stage. The year of 1864 was to be particularly his. To it he imparted his own frightful character of unrestrained violence and sheer viciousness. Between July and October he made more raids, rode more miles, and killed more men than any other guerrilla chieftain, including Quantrill, ever did.

The early part of July found Anderson near Lexington. Made cocky by recent easy victories over Federal patrols, he wrote—or had someone write for him—a letter to the Union commander at Lexington, Colonel James McFerran:

I have seen your official report to General Brown of two fights that have taken place in Johnson and LaFayette Counties with your men. You have been wrongfully informed, or you have wilfully misrepresented the matter to your superior officer. I had the honor, sir, of being in command at both of those engagements. To enlighten you on the subject and to warn you against making future exaggerations I will say to you in the future to let me know in time, and when I fight your men I will make the proper report. As to the skirmish I had with your men in Johnson, I started to Kingsville with fifty men to take the place, but before I arrived there I discovered a scout, fourteen or fifteen of your men, on the prairie some half a mile distant to my left. I immediately gave chase. They fled. There were not over eight of my men ever got near them. They did not surrender or I would not have killed them, for I understood that Company M were Southern men; they sent me that word. I ordered them to halt and surrender. I was astonished to see them refuse after sending me such word. One of their lieutenants even planned the assassination of General Brown and the taking of his headquarters, but I refused to commit so foul a deed. But they refused a surrender and I had them to kill. I regret having to kill such good Southern men, but they are fit for no service but yours, for they were very cowardly. Myself and two men killed nine of them when there were no other men in sight of us. They are such poor shots it is strange you don't have them practice more. Send them out and I will train them for you. After that I came down near Burris' camp with twenty-five regulars, all told, belonging to the Kansas First [Guerrillas], some of my first men. I understood that Burris was anxious to give me a thrashing. Not wishing to lose more than twenty-five men at one time, I thought I would try him with the aforesaid number, but while I was waiting for him to come out from camp, that I might devour him or be devoured, forty-eight of your men coming from Lexington with three wagons had the audacity to fire on my pickets, and very imprudently asked me to come out of the bush and fight them. I obeyed reluctantly. They dismounted and formed on a hill. I formed under their fire under the hill and charged. They fled and I pursued. You know the rest. If you do not, I can inform you we killed ten on the ground and wounded as many more. Had all my men done their duty we would have killed thirty of them. Farewell, friend.

A short postscript was attached:

TO BURRIS:

Burris, I love you; come and see me. Good-by, boy; don't get discouraged. I glory in your spunk, but damn your judgment.

Anderson also wrote letters in a similar vein to the Lexington newspapers and to General Egbert Brown. He signed them, "Yours, respectfully, W. Anderson, Commanding Kansas First Guerrillas." McFerran sent them to Brown, who in turn forwarded them to Rosecrans, "as a curiosity and specimen of a guerrilla chief's correspondence." [12]

On July 11, Anderson crossed the Missouri and went on the warpath in Carroll County. In short order he and his twenty men, all of whom were wearing Federal uniforms, murdered nine Unionists. Clement cut the throat of one of the victims.

Four days later, with thirty-five men, he raided Huntsville, his home town. His gang killed only one man, but pillaged all the stores and took $45,000 from the bank.

On July 17 he appeared at Rocheport. Its pro-Southern inhabitants welcomed him with open arms, and he called the place his "capital."

Next he swung back into Randolph County. On the twenty-third, his force swollen to one hundred men, he burned the railroad depot at Renick, destroyed several miles of telegraph wire, and made an unsuccessful attack on a Federal post at Allen.

The following day he ambushed a Union detachment near Huntsville, killed two soldiers, and routed the remainder. The sadistic Clement scalped both the dead men, then cut a circle of skin the size of a dollar from the forehead of one, and a strip of skin from the forehead of the other. So that nobody would be left in doubt as to who committed these atrocities, Anderson pinned this note on one of the bodies:

You come to hunt bush whackers. Now you are skelpt. Clemyent Skelpt you. Wm. Anderson.

He next galloped into Shelby County, where he destroyed the Hannibal and St. Joseph Railroad bridges at Salt River and burned two depots. Following this raid, he reversed his course once more and by the second week of August was in Clay County. There, on August 12, near Fredericksburg, he bushwhacked a Union patrol, killing five.

The latter part of August brought him into Boone County, where he linked up with Holtzclaw's gang. On the twenty-eighth he and Holtzclaw ambushed a Federal detachment from Rocheport and killed seven out of its total force of forty-four. His men scalped one captive, and cut the throats of three others.

Two days later he occupied Rocheport, and his followers proceeded to engage in an orgy of drinking and looting. He remained in the town for nearly a week, unmolested by Union forces in the area, before riding off northward to make further attacks on the Hannibal and St. Joseph.

Editor Thacher, as he read the daily reports of the raids and atrocities committed by Anderson, Thornton, Todd, Holtzclaw, Poole, Thrailkill, Taylor, and the rest, became oppressed with gloom and near-despair.

"The very air," he wrote, "seems charged with blood and death.

East of us, west of us, north of us, south of us, comes the same harrowing story. Pandemonium itself seems to have broken loose, and robbery, murder and rapine, and death run riot over the country."[13]

Thacher had no way of knowing that the worst was yet to come.

chapter X **All Shot to Hell**

"Pap" Price's long-expected invasion was under way. On September 19 he led twelve thousand cavalrymen, including Shelby's brigade, northward out of Arkansas. It was to be, as John N. Edwards later wrote, "the stupidest, wildest, wantonest, wickedest march ever made by a general who had a voice like a lion and a spring like a guinea pig."

Price sent advance word of his coming to the guerrillas by means of Captain John Chestnut, who contacted Todd at Bone Hill on September 8. Chestnut asked Todd to do everything possible to disorganize the Union defenses and communications, paying special attention to the railroads, so as to smooth the way for Price's thrust.

Todd promptly called in his scattered followers, and on September 14 crossed the Missouri River at Sibley. He then linked up with Thrailkill's band, and with it swept through Ray and Carroll counties, murdering seven militiamen along the way.

Early in the morning of September 20, Todd and Thrailkill clattered into Keytesville, Price's home town, and surrounded the courthouse, which was held by a thirty-five-man Paw-Paw garrison under Lieutenant Anthony Pleyer. Thrailkill, who had the "physique of a Cossack and the bearing of a Comanche," rode forward under a white flag and shouted to Pleyer that he had 250 fighting men, and that if Pleyer did not surrender within fifteen minutes, he would burn the entire town and kill all the garrison. Pleyer, who was subsequently described by one of his superior officers as a "poor, miserable poltroon," asked the Carroll County sheriff what he should do. The sheriff answered, "We can do nothing with these men," meaning the guerrillas. Pleyer thereupon marched his men out of the courthouse and surrendered them to Thrailkill. Seven of the Paw-Paws promptly joined the bushwhackers, the rest received paroles from Thrailkill, who signed himself, "Major, Commanding Recruits."

As he scrawled out Pleyer's parole, Thrailkill complimented him on his decision to surrender, declaring that if the Federals had fired a single shot he could not have kept his men from "burning the last house in town and killing every man at the same time." He then backed up these words by pointing to Todd, who was standing near by. Todd sauntered over and said to Pleyer, "I'm the bushwhacker Todd. You need not consider me a Confederate officer. I intend to follow bushwhacking as long as I live."

The bushwhackers burned the courthouse, robbed the citizens of horses and guns, and marched the sheriff and another prominent Unionist outside the town and shot them. Before leaving, Thrailkill made a speech extolling the Confederacy which the townspeople greeted with cheers and cries of "Bully!" [1]

From Keytesville, Todd and Thrailkill marched southeastward into Howard County. During the night of September 23, near Fayette, they were joined by bands under Poole and Quantrill, the latter's consisting of only six or seven men. And in the morning, Anderson's gang came riding in also. All of its members, noted Frank Smith, wore squirrel tails in their hats, and some of them had human scalps dangling from their bridles. Smith also saw for the first time Frank James' kid brother, Jesse, who had joined up with Bloody Bill early that summer. He was a tough-looking youngster of seventeen with tow hair and cold blue eyes.

Anderson's boys were in a fighting mood. Just the day before they had ambushed a Union supply train in the Perche Hills, killed twelve soldiers and three Negro teamsters, and burned most of the wagons. However, pursuing Federal cavalry had overtaken seven of their comrades, killed six of them, and then scalped the corpses. They didn't like being paid back in their own coin, and were boiling for revenge.

For the first time since Texas the bushwhackers were assembled in full force. The only important figure missing was Fletch Taylor. On the night of August 8, he had been ambushed by the "Bush Bottom militia" near Wellington and his left arm mangled by a buckshot charge. His men "kidnaped" a doctor, who amputated the arm and saved his life, but for the time being he was out of action.

Anderson's and Todd's men tacitly agreed to forget about their troubles in Texas. Quantrill likewise buried his resentments, and indicated that he was willing to co-operate with his former lieutenants.

The guerrilla chieftains engaged in what one eyewitness described subsequently as "an animated and heated argument." Anderson, seconded by Todd, wanted to attack Fayette. Quantrill opposed the idea. He declared that the place was too heavily garrisoned, that nothing would be gained, and that a lot of lives would be lost.

Anderson and Todd, secure in the knowledge that they controlled most of the men, replied contemptuously: "We are going into Fayette no matter what! If you want to come along, all right. If not then you can go back into the woods with the rest of the cowards!"

At this deliberate insult, Quantrill moved away, leaving Anderson and Todd to plan the attack. Anderson claimed that the town would be easy prey, and stated that his gang would take the lead, clear out the troops, and that all Todd would have to do was take possession and sack the place. Todd agreed to this scheme.

At 10:30 A.M. Anderson's men galloped into Fayette. They were attired in Federal uniforms and the townspeople, thinking that they were a Union patrol, paid them little heed. Probably they would have been able to surprise and overwhelm the garrison had not a trigger-happy bushwhacker started shooting at a Negro dressed in a blue uniform standing on the sidewalk. This gave the alarm, and while noncombatants scurried to places of safety, the garrison took up battle stations in the brick courthouse and in a blockhouse atop a hill outside of the town. The defenders numbered only thirty men, not counting a few armed civilians who joined them, but they were determined to fight rather than be butchered by the guerrillas.

Anderson dashed straight through the town, killing two soldiers but doing no other damage. Todd followed him in, as planned, and was immediately greeted by a fusilade of musket balls from the courthouse. His men returned the fire with their revolvers, but merely shot out the windows. Cursing, they retreated outside the town, where they soon received word from Anderson to come and help him take the blockhouse.

On arriving they found that Anderson had attacked the blockhouse and been repulsed, with several dead and wounded. Nothing was going right! Todd became enraged, as only he could, and ordered his band to charge the blockhouse.

Riding far in advance, he led them in a headlong assault. But the defenders did not waver at the fearsome sight of the dread bushwhackers, who came on screaming and shooting. Secure behind the thick log walls of the blockhouse, they poured forth a withering fire through its narrow loopholes. Guerrilla after guerrilla toppled to the ground or swayed in his saddle, and finally Todd and his followers fell back to regroup.

Todd's second charge was no more successful than the first. Again he was beaten back with heavy losses. Strangely enough, although the main target of the garrison's rifles, he himself did not receive a single scratch. His life continued to be a charmed one.

Anderson and Todd decided that there was no point in trying another attack. Without artillery they could not hope to dislodge the defenders, and frontal assaults with revolvers were obviously suicidal. Thirteen dead bushwhackers, all good men, proved that fact. Therefore they loaded the wounded, some thirty in number, into wagons and carriages, and marched away. It had been the worst defeat they had ever suffered, and it had been at the hands of a vastly inferior force to boot.

Among the wounded was Jim Little. One of his fingers had been shot off, he had been hit in the left hip, and he was covered with blood. On seeing him, Quantrill, who had not taken part in the attack, cried, "Boys, I will take Jimmie to cover—he is all shot to hell." He then rode off with Little into the brush. This was the last most of the bushwhackers ever saw of their former captain.

Todd, who was "raving like a madman," wanted to kill Quantrill. Completely ignoring the facts, he blamed Quantrill for the setback, and ordered his men to go get him. They replied, however, that Quantrill was not responsible, that he had always treated them well, and that rather than kill him they would leave the outfit.

Todd then declared that he would go shoot Quantrill himself, and started off to do so. But the men gathered around him and finally talked him out of going. They pointed out that killing Quantrill would not accomplish anything and that he would probably lose his life also, thus leaving them without a leader.

The bushwhackers retreated from fatal Fayette along the Glasgow road. On the way they left their seriously wounded to be tended by sympathetic farmers. They camped for the night nine miles from Fayette.[2]

In the morning they headed due northward, crossing into Randolph County. Late in the afternoon they approached Anderson's home town of Huntsville. Here they halted while Anderson sent a farmer into the town with a demand that the garrison surrender or be massacred. The demand was made in the name of Colonel Caleb Perkins, a Confederate recruiting officer who was accompanying the guerrillas. A half-hour later the farmer returned with the post commander's reply: "Tell them if they want us to come in and get us."

The bushwhackers were in no mood, so soon after the Fayette fiasco, to attack another fortified town. Therefore, they moved on, doubling back in the direction of Renick, and tearing down miles of telegraph wires and skirmishing with Union patrols as they marched.

On the twenty-sixth they crossed the North Missouri Railroad and passed into Monroe County, where they threatened Paris. But on learning that the town contained a large militia force, they turned southward into Boone County. That night they camped three miles southeast of Centralia, a whistle stop on the North Missouri Railroad.

In the morning Anderson went into Centralia to get news about Price's movements. His men pillaged all the stores and houses after forcing the terrified inhabitants to fix them breakfasts. At the depot they found a barrel of whisky and several cases of new boots, and proceeded to help themselves to both. In some instances they filled the boots with whisky and used them as giant leather drinking cups! In short order many of them were reeling drunk and in a murderous mood.

At 11 A.M. the Columbia stage rolled into town and was promptly robbed by the bushwhackers. One of the passengers happened to be U. S. Representative James S. Rollins, a good friend of Bingham, the artist. Rollins realized that if the raiders discovered his identity he would either be killed or held for ransom. Therefore, he pretended that he was a farmer and a fervent Confederate sympathizer. This dodge succeeded, and eventually he was able to slip away to a place of safety. However, he had a very anxious moment when one of the robbers rifled through his luggage and donned a silk shirt inscribed with the initials, "JSR."

Shortly before Anderson's gang entered Centralia the local telegraph operator sent word up the line that bushwhackers were in the vicinity and that it would be dangerous for trains to come through without guards. The warning reached the conductor of the westbound St. Louis train, but he decided to disregard it. After all, he reasoned, if you get excited over every such report, all train travel would come to a standstill. Besides, he had twenty-five uniformed soldiers on board. Although they were unarmed, the sight of them would be enough to scare off any roving guerrillas.

At noon, right on schedule, the train approached Centralia. The crew and passengers saw smoke arising from the town and a large number of armed men standing about the station. They all knew at once what this meant—the bushwhackers were there!

At first the passengers thought—and hoped—that the train, which was moving at a fast clip, would race right through Centralia. But instead, much to their horror, it began slowing down. Its boilers, unfortunately, were nearly empty, and the engineer felt he had no other choice except to stop. Moreover, the bushwhackers had piled ties across the tracks and set them afire.

As the train puffed into Centralia, Anderson's men, who were screaming and capering about like devils, fired volley after volley into it. When it finally ground to a halt, they burst into the cars brandishing their revolvers and shouting, "Surrender! Surrender!" To the soldiers they said, "Do as we tell you, and you'll be treated as prisoners of war."

Prodded by guns in the hands of dirty, unshaven, long-haired guerrillas, all the passengers left the train. Two soldiers who held back were immediately shot by Anderson personally, their bodies tumbling down between two of the cars. The bushwhackers divided the prisoners into two groups—the civilians, whom they marched off to one side, and the soldiers, whom they lined up on the platform.

All of the soldiers were on furlough, most of them were from regiments in Sherman's army. Some were sick and wounded, and one was on crutches.

Anderson, a smoking revolver in each hand, stood looking at them for a moment, a fiendish expression contorting his handsome face. Then, in a sharp, cracked voice, he shouted: "You Federals have just killed six of my men, scalped them, and left them on the prairie. . . . I will show you that I can kill men with as much skill and rapidity as anybody. From this time on I ask no quarter and give none. Every Federal soldier on whom I put my finger shall die like a dog. If I get into your clutches I expect death. You are all to be killed and sent to hell. That is the way every damned soldier who falls into my hands shall be served."

Several of the soldiers began protesting that they were from Sherman's army and so had nothing to do with killing and scalping Anderson's men. But Anderson yelled them down: "I treat you all as one. You are Federals, and Federals scalped my men, and carry their scalps at their saddle bows."

Anderson then told the soldiers to take off their uniforms. In mute misery they did so. Next he ordered Sergeant Thomas Goodman to step forward. Goodman obeyed, expecting to be shot down immediately. Instead, Anderson turned him over to a couple of his men, whom he instructed to guard the sergeant from harm, as he had special plans for him.

A large number of bushwhackers lined up facing the soldiers. As Anderson raised his revolvers and cocked them, they followed suit. The soldiers turned instinctively away, their arms half-raised. Some fell to their knees, others cried "No! No!" Anderson and his men stepped forward and, placing the muzzles of their pistols right up to the heads of the soldiers, opened fire.

Every one of the soldiers was shot at least three times, all in the head. One victim, a Sergeant Peters, broke away, although badly wounded, and took refuge under the platform. The howling guerrillas set fire to the station and forced him out. Grabbing a club, he sprang forward and knocked several of his assailants down before falling, riddled by twenty bullets.

The bushwhackers, who now "were in a condition bordering on insanity," then proceeded to club the still living victims to death with rifle butts. In addition, they scalped two of the corpses.

While this orgy of murder and mutilation took place, other bushwhackers robbed the civilian captives of their money, watches, jewelry, and other valuables. One young man, who was traveling with his mother, slipped a hundred-dollar bill into his boot leg before surrendering the rest of his cash. A guerrilla then told him that he would be searched, and that if any money was found on him, he would be killed. On hearing this, the young man admitted he had money hidden in his boot. The guerrilla pulled it out, then shot him dead before his horrified mother. A German who tried to conceal a gold watch in his boot suffered the same fate. Otherwise, the bushwhackers did not harm any of the civilians, except to rough them up a little. Some of the raiders ill-treated women, but Anderson quickly put a stop to that.

After looting the train, the bushwhackers set it afire and sent it rolling down the tracks toward Sturgeon, its whistle screaming loudly. As it left the station, its wheels ran over the bodies of some of the soldiers sprawled across the tracks, mangling them horribly. After going about two miles, the boilers emptied and the train came to a halt on the open prairie. There it continued to burn, wreathed in flames, until it was nothing but a smoking pile of charred wood and twisted metal.

Soon after the passenger train had been disposed of, a freight train pulled into Centralia. Either its engineer also found it impossible to back up, or else he mistook Anderson's blue-uniformed followers for Federal troops. In any case, the bushwhackers killed the crew and plundered the cars.

Wild with whisky and blood, yelling and laughing, Anderson's men now mounted their horses and galloped back to camp to show off their plunder to Todd's boys and tell them about the big time they had been having in Centralia.

A half-hour later Major A. V. E. Johnston led a 147-man detachment of the Thirty-ninth Missouri State Militia mounted infantry regiment into Centralia. Johnston was tracking the guerrillas, and had been attracted by smoke. When he saw and heard what Anderson's bushwhackers had done, he vowed to attack them at once and secure vengeance. The townspeople pleaded with him to wait for reinforcements, telling him that the bushwhackers were numerous and heavily armed. But he refused to be dissuaded: "I will fight them anyhow!" Leaving thirty-six soldiers under Captain Adam Theis to guard the town, he set off in the direction of the guerrilla camp.

Some bushwhackers riding near Centralia spotted Johnston's column approaching and hurried back to the camp to sound the alarm. Anderson and Todd ordered their men to saddle up and get ready for a big battle. At the same time a small squad under Clement went out in advance to try to lure the Federals into an ambush.

The bushwhackers formed in a long curving line. In their rear were scattered clusters of trees and bush; in front, an open field sloping upward. Anderson's gang occupied the center, with Poole's behind it. Todd was on the left, partially concealed by the timber, and Thrailkill took up the right. They advanced at a slow, steady trot, silent, their pistols ready.

Johnston followed Clement's decoy straight into the trap. On seeing the guerrilla array, he halted and ordered his men to form a skirmish line. They were riding plow horses, brood mares, and mules pressed into service from the countryside, and in addition were armed with long-barreled, muzzle-loading Enfield rifles with fixed bayonets. For these reasons, and because his men had been trained as infantry, Johnston felt that his best chance of victory would be to fight on foot. One out of every four of the militiamen remained behind to hold the mounts while the others moved forward.

A bushwhacker riding near Frank Smith exclaimed, "My God, the Lord have mercy on them, they're dismounting to fight!"

At two hundred yards distance Anderson shouted "Charge!" and the guerrillas, with a savage yell, broke into a thundering gallop. Johnston's men fired one volley, which killed three bushwhackers and wounded ten others, then turned and fled in wild panic, many of them throwing away their now empty and useless rifles.

Hardly had they run a few steps than the bushwhackers, screaming and firing, were on top of them. Some of the hapless soldiers stopped and threw up their hands in surrender—only to be shot down or trampled underfoot by horses. One desperate militiaman slashed at Todd with a bayonet, missed, and was killed by Frank Smith. Jesse James (according to highly unreliable brother Frank) shot Major Johnston. The soldiers who had been left behind to hold the horses mounted them and tried to escape. But the better-mounted guerrillas quickly overtook and killed most of them also.

The pursuit of Union fugitives carried many of the bushwhackers back into Centralia. Theis' detachment, on seeing them approach, fled toward Sturgeon. The guerrillas gave chase and killed fifteen more militiamen before drawing to a halt in front of the Sturgeon blockhouse.

During the remainder of the afternoon part of the bushwhackers completed the job of ransacking Centralia, while the others roamed over the battlefield. Here certain sadistic fiends among them committed sickening atrocities:

Stripped most of the bodies, including Johnston's.

Cut off the heads of dead soldiers and switched them to different bodies, or labeled them with obscene epitaphs and inscriptions, or stuck them on the barrels of rifles, or tied them to saddles, or placed them grinning hideously at each other atop fence posts and tree stumps.

Stuck the fallen with bayonets, and sliced away their ears and noses.

Scalped Major Johnston and a dozen other corpses.

Cut off the genitals of a still living Federal and thrust them into his mouth.

In all, 124 of Johnston's command had been killed. The dead lay so thick that cocky little Dave Poole, a cigar stuck in the corner of his mouth, amused himself by hopping from one body to another. This, he declared was the best way to count them. "If they are dead I can't hurt them. I cannot count them good without stepping on 'em. When I got my foot on one this way I know I've got him."

In the evening the bushwhackers straggled drunkenly back to their camp. Not since Baxter Springs had there been such a day! In fact, in some ways it even beat the Lawrence raid. Not only had they taken in a great haul of plunder, but they had sent 150 Bluebellies to hell. Who said they needed Quantrill to lead them! [3]

The bushwhackers were correct in regarding the Centralia Massacre, as it soon became known, as an "extra occasion." But on the other hand it marked their final and complete degeneration into a group of vicious, almost subhuman bandits and murderers. Deeds which most of them would have recoiled from in disgust as late as the spring of 1863 were now accepted as a matter of course.

What special circumstances or reasons, if any, account for the utter viciousness, the nauseating barbarity, of the guerrillas at Centralia?

According to Hamp Watts, one of Anderson's men, the Union garrison at Fayette, following the futile attack on that town, placed the bodies of five bushwhackers on the street, then rode their horses roughshod over them. This he indicates, was the immediate motivation of the massacre.* And we have already noted that Anderson's followers were aroused over the slaying and scalping of six comrades by Federal troops near Rocheport, and that Anderson himself was quoted by an eyewitness as giving this as a reason for shooting the soldiers from the train.

But although these incidents partially explain the conduct of the guerrillas at Centralia, they do not and cannot excuse it. The bushwhackers were guilty, at Centralia, of the most foul and fiendish atrocities of the entire Civil War. As Watts himself admitted, what they did there "was without palliation or excuse." [4]

During the night the bushwhackers began retreating in the direction of Howard County. Sergeant Goodman, still alive and still in his underwear, rode with them. They had, he noted, a "fair amount of military deportment," and from their conversation he gathered that their leaders possessed official Confederate commissions. He was especially impressed by Anderson, whom he described as being about five foot ten, slender and compact of build, very quick in his movements, with dark brown hair hanging in a thick mass about his head and neck, and having cold, expressionless eyes of a strange blue-gray color. Like nearly all the

* Watts, who was a postwar resident of Fayette, stated that the trampling of the dead bushwhackers was witnessed by Dr. I. J. Bailey and Joseph Megrow of Fayette, both of whom were still alive at the time Watts wrote his account.

other partisans, he wore a Federal uniform jacket, black pants tucked into high cavalry boots, and a slouch hat. He seemed to have no trouble controlling his wild young followers, treated them well, and appeared to be on easy, familiar terms with them.

In the morning a large Federal force, with two cannons, began to press the fleeing raiders. At one point it got close enough to open up with the cannons. But their salvos went high, showering leaves and branches on the guerrillas, who forthwith scattered into small bands.

When it became dark the Federals broke off the pursuit and the partisans reassembled at a predesignated spot. Their camp was one which they had used before, and there was a large supply of "grub and whisky" on hand. Before long practically all of them, including Anderson and Todd, were drunk—"even to madness." They shouted, ran, and jumped about like savages. Once Anderson leaped on a horse and galloped wildly through the camp firing his revolvers and yelling like one possessed. Finally, one by one, the guerrillas dropped off into sleeps of drunken stupor.

In the morning, the leaders held a council and decided to split up for a while, then later regroup and cross the Missouri. They had "stirred up a hornet's nest" as a result of Centralia and could not hope to accomplish anything for some time north of the river. Besides, it was risky for such a large force to be together, and they could not hope to cope with the artillery.

Leaving the wounded at the camp, the bushwhackers accordingly broke up into small parties. Goodman went with Anderson, and during the next week moved about from one hiding place to another in Howard and Boone counties. Anderson never got around to dealing with him, and Goodman of course took care not to remind him of the matter. His captors did not molest him; they eventually provided him with some clothes, and even became rather friendly.

However, Goodman knew that sooner or later Anderson would kill him and so was constantly on the alert for a chance to escape. The opportunity finally came on October 6 near Rocheport. Anderson's band had assembled there and was in the process of crossing the river. Left temporarily unguarded, Goodman simply walked away. Several guerrillas saw him but did not recognize him, and since he was wearing civilian clothes they either assumed that he was a local farmer or a fellow bushwhacker. Ultimately he made it to a Union post and lived to relate his experience to his children.[5]

The Centralia Massacre shocked, enraged, and frightened the Unionists. General Fisk raised the battle cry, "Remember Centralia," and ordered his troops to make an all-out effort to destroy the bushwhackers. At the same time he wrote Rosecrans explaining why such horrible outrages as Centralia could occur, and why it was so difficult to stamp out bushwhacking:

> . . . I am aware that it may seem to yourself and the impatient public remote from this section that we ought to accomplish more than we do; that the guerrillas ought to be exterminated from the country, and such disasters as those at Centralia prevented, but could you see this section of the State and study not only the topography of the country but the hearts and consciences of the people you would readily discover the great difficulties in the way of finding and exterminating bushwhackers. . . . Boone and Howard are now our two worst localities. In one of them I have General Douglass, who is a native of the country, has been its sheriff, and knows intimately the character of the country and the hearts of its citizens; and in Howard is Major Leonard, whose advantages for operating in his county are equal to those of General Douglass for Boone. . . . Yet with all their knowledge, industry, and perseverance the guerrillas thus far scatter and concentrate so as to elude our forces. Our movements, though made as secretly as possible, are discovered by the bushwhackers' friends and revealed from one to another. The citizens at home are our secret and most dangerous foes, and in no spot of all our disturbed territory has the rebellion more earnest friends than in the Missouri River counties of this district. . . . We have in these counties not only the resident rebels, but in addition a large proportion of those, who, by General Ewing's order, were last year expelled from Johnson, Jackson, and other border counties. Depopulation and devastation are extreme measures, but if this infernal warfare continues it will be humane and economic of human life to adopt and vigorously enforce such measures.[6]

Fisk's troops failed to bring the bushwhackers to bay after Centralia, and were unable to prevent Anderson crossing the Missouri at Rocheport, despite having ample advance intelligence that he would pass over at that point. Early in October Fisk had to suspend all antibushwhacker operations and hurry to the defense of Jefferson City, which was being threatened by Price's army.[7]

Todd's band crossed the Missouri at about the same time as Anderson's. On October 9 it raided the Missouri Pacific Railroad town of Otterville in Cooper County, then swung back into Johnson and Lafayette counties.[8]

Anderson, after crossing, marched to Boonville, where, on October 11, he met Price's army, which had failed to take Jefferson City and was now heading westward along the south bank of the Missouri.

Price, on first seeing "Bloody Bill's" boys, was shocked and revolted by the scalps dangling from their bridles, and angrily ordered them to throw the ghastly trophies away. As soon as they did so, he became more friendly, accepted a gift of two silver-mounted revolvers from Anderson, and declared that if he had fifty thousand such men he could hold the state permanently. As a matter of fact, he welcomed the bushwhackers as valuable reinforcements. His invasion, after initial successes, was not going well, and he was being pressed by a large cavalry force under Major General Alfred Pleasonton.

Price decided that the most useful work Anderson's band could perform would be to destroy the Federal railroad communications. Therefore he issued this order to Anderson:

SPECIAL ORDER) HEADQUARTERS ARMY OF MISSOURI
BOONVILLE, October 11, 1864

Captain Anderson with his command, will at once proceed to the north side of the Missouri River and permanently destroy the North Missouri Railroad, going as far east as practicable. He will report his operations at least every two days.

By order of Major-General Price:

MCCLEAN
Lieutenant-Colonel and
Assistant Adjutant General

Price also dispatched orders to "Colonel" Quantrill to wreck the Hannibal and St. Joseph Railroad. Obviously he did not know that Quantrill had fallen from power. Quantrill never received this order, and he did not take an active part in the campaign.

Anderson's gang, or at least part of it, recrossed the river and raided as far east as Montgomery County, where on October 15 it sacked Danville and burned the depots at Florence and High Hill. But it failed, complained Price subsequently, to do any "material damage" or to "destroy the large railroad bridge that was in the end of Saint Charles County," which "was the main object proposed."

In justice to Anderson, however, it should be observed that his raids, especially the one on Centralia, had already stopped all ordinary traffic on the North Missouri, as well as the Hannibal and St. Joseph. And in any case, these lines played no part in Federal operations against Price. Therefore, Price assigned the bushwhackers a mission which had slight military value or purpose.[9]

Perhaps for this reason Anderson did not personally lead the raid on the North Missouri Railroad. Instead he followed Shelby's brigade to Glasgow on October 14. After Shelby captured the town, he beat and robbed a citizen, and his men killed a number of paroled Union prisoners. Also Quantrill, with several followers, briefly emerged from the Perche Hills hideout to rob $21,000 from a Glasgow bank—perhaps the richest single haul any of the guerrillas ever made.[10]

Price remained in Boonville two days, then marched toward Kansas City. Pleasonton's Union cavalry followed close on his heels, and Curtis and Blunt moved out from Kansas to intercept him. On the eighteenth, he entered Lafayette County, where he was joined by Todd's band, which had been awaiting his arrival.

The following day, the Confederates encountered Blunt east of Lexington. From that point on they were engaged in almost constant fighting as they pushed their way westward, first through Lexington, then to the Little Blue.

At noon on the twenty-first Price forced Blunt to retreat to the other side of Independence. Todd, with about a half-dozen men, scouted the Confederate advance. Riding to the crest of a hill, he stopped to survey the countryside, his finely proportioned figure outlined against the autumn sky. Suddenly there was a sharp crack, and a Spencer rifle ball tore through his neck. He slid from his saddle and thudded to the ground, unconscious and choking with blood. The man who had charged again and again through storms of bullets absolutely unscathed had been hit by a single shot fired by an unseen sniper.

Todd's comrades carried him to a house in Independence. Efforts to stop his bleeding failed, and in an hour or so he died. That night his men buried him in the town cemetery. As they did so, tears of grief coursed down the cheeks of the hard-bitten young bushwhackers. "I loved Todd," wrote McCorkle many years later, "more than a brother."

Union newspapers cheered the death of the "notorious Todd." [11] Soon they had equally good news to report: "Bloody Bill" Anderson also had been killed!

Anderson, following the raids on the North Missouri and Glasgow, made no attempt to rejoin Price's army, but instead marched westward through Howard, Chariton, and Carroll counties. His trail, as always, was marked by pillaged houses and mutilated corpses.

The morning of October 27 found him in southwest Ray County, a short distance from Albany. He took breakfast at a farmhouse near his camp, and while waiting for it to be prepared, washed his hands and face, and combed his hair. Regarding himself in the mirror, he bowed and said, "Good morning, Captain Anderson, how are you this morning? Damn well, thank you." [12]

Later in the morning a force of 150 militia under Major Samuel P. Cox attacked Anderson's pickets. Cox had been tipped off to the bushwhacker's whereabouts by a local woman (no man would have dared). After driving the pickets through Albany, Cox dismounted most of his men and advanced cautiously into the woods where Anderson's camp was located. At the same time he sent a cavalry squad ahead to flush out any concealed guerrillas.

Anderson readily accepted Cox's challenge to a fight. Why, it would be another Centralia! He led his band in a column down a narrow road through the woods. The Federal cavalry withdrew before his advance. As soon as they saw the dismounted militia, the bushwhackers raised a savage yell and charged, shooting as they came. Anderson, astride a magnificent horse, rode far in front, his long hair streaming wildly in the wind.

Cox's troopers did not waver. Their steady, accurate fire caused the attackers to draw rein and fall back in confusion. But Anderson himself, and another guerrilla, kept on coming. On and on they rushed, bullets whizzing about them, right into the Union lines and beyond! Then two balls smashed into the back of Anderson's head. His arms flew up, he fell backward from his horse, and plunged to the leaf-strewn ground, some fifty yards behind Cox's position. The other guerrilla rode on, but later his dead body was found in a cornfield.

Anderson's followers saw their chieftain go down. Desperately they fought to recover the body. One of them, the giant, red-bearded John Pringle, died attempting to drag his body away with a lariat. In the end they had to leave him in the hands of the enemy.

Cox's troops put the famous bushwhacker's body in a wagon and hauled it triumphantly to Richmond. There the local photographer took some pictures of it, after which it was placed on public display, the long dark hair matted with leaves, dirt, and blood, in the courthouse. Later the militiamen cut off the head, stuck it atop a telegraph pole, and dragged the decapitated corpse through the dusty streets behind a horse. Finally, their vengeance glutted, they buried the remains in the town cemetery in an unmarked grave.[13]

These items were found on Anderson's body: six revolvers; a photograph of himself and another of his wife; a letter signed "Bush Anderson" and a lock of her hair; a mirror and a pocketbook containing six hundred dollars in gold and greenbacks; some Confederate money and a couple of orders from Price; and a small Confederate flag inscribed with the words: "Presented to W. L. Anderson by his friend, F. M. R. Let it not be contaminated by Fed. hands." In addition, a number of human scalps dangled from the bridle of his horse.[14]

Thus, in the space of less than a week, both Todd and Anderson had been killed. Each died as he probably would have wanted to—fighting—and as he inevitably had to—violently.

Two days after Todd's death and four days before Anderson's, the Union armies routed Price at Westport and sent him hurtling down the Kansas line. During the fighting before Westport the bushwhackers, now led by Poole, murdered several captured Kansas militiamen—an act which only gave Jennison's Fifteenth Kansas an excuse for doing the same to Confederate prisoners. In fact, the presence of the partisans proved such an embarrassment to Price on this account that on the night prior to the Westport battle, he ordered them to leave his army. This they promptly did, swinging back eastward to the Johnson County border. When Price's shattered army began retreating, most of them headed south in its wake.

The pursuing Federals defeated Price again at Mine Creek, Marmiton, and Newtonia. Only a shattered, starving remnant of his army made it across the Arkansas River. Then, as it staggered through the Indian Territory, bitter cold and a smallpox epidemic completed the debacle. It was not until December, when he reached Texas, that Price's long flight finally came to an end.[15]

Price's invasion had been the last, gasping effort of the Southern cause in Missouri. The bushwhackers, as they constructed their winter quarters, must have known that the war was lost and the Confederacy doomed. And they must have also realized that bushwhacking itself was just about played out.

chapter XI "Here's a Heart for Every Fate"

Quantrill must have experienced a feeling of grim satisfaction on learning that Todd and Anderson had been killed. They had defied him, taken away his men, insulted and humiliated him. Now they were rotting in their graves, and it served them right.

He wasted no time in staging a comeback as a partisan leader. Only instead of Missouri, it was to be in Kentucky. Price's debacle obviously meant that bushwhacking was about done for in Missouri, along with the Confederate cause. Kentucky, on the other hand, offered a promising field for new ventures. Political conditions there were disturbed, many of the people were pro-Southern, and numerous guerrilla bands already prowled the state. Moreover, should it become necessary to surrender, the chances of being treated as a prisoner of war and not as an outlaw were far better in Kentucky, where he was not known, than in Missouri, where he was known only too well.*

Late in October he shipped Kate King to St. Louis, quit his hideout in Howard County, and went into the Sni Hills, from where he sent word that all bushwhackers who wanted to go with him to Kentucky were to gather at the Dupee farm. A large number of guerrillas still remained in West Missouri, so that over thirty of them responded to their old chieftain's call. They also realized that the bushwhacking game was up in the state, and that it was high time to move on if disaster was to be

* Some of Quantrill's men later claimed that he intended to march through Kentucky and Virginia to Washington, D.C., and there assassinate President Lincoln. But other ex-guerrillas laughed at this story, and in view of Quantrill's conduct in Kentucky, it is most likely without any real foundation in fact.

avoided. Most of them were hardened veterans of the partisan war, some original members of Quantrill's gang—Jim Little, John Koger, John McCorkle, Ol Shepherd, "Babe" Hudspeth, Frank and Jesse James, Jim Younger, John Barker, Clark Hockensmith, Allen Parmer, and the murderous Peyton Long, to name the more outstanding.

Quantrill and his followers spent all of November preparing for the Kentucky expedition. Early in December they began marching eastward through Saline County. They all wore Federal uniforms, Quantrill that of a captain.

From Saline they cut southward, and about December 15 reached the Osage River at Tuscumbia, the seat of Miller County. A small Federal garrison, quartered in a hotel, occupied the town. Quantrill informed a sentinel that he was Captain Clarke of the Fourth Missouri Cavalry and would like to talk to the post commander. The soldier directed him to a house on a near-by hill.

Accompanied by "Babe" Hudspeth, Quantrill went to the house and talked a while with the commander, pumping him for information about Union troop dispositions in the area. As soon as he learned what he wanted to know, Quantrill whipped out a revolver and ordered the astonished commander to surrender the garrison. He did so, and the guerrillas proceeded to take over the town and eat a hearty breakfast at the hotel. After finishing, they released all the prisoners, except one, whom they kept to serve as a guide, dumped the garrison's rifles and ammunition into the river, and then crossed to the south bank on a ferry boat, which they then sank. It was Quantrill's last raid in Missouri.[1]

The guerrillas continued to push on, in bitterly cold weather, through southeastern Missouri and down into Arkansas. Near Pocahontas six of them abandoned the expedition and headed for Texas. They included Koger, Jesse James, Shepherd, and "Babe" and Rufus Hudspeth. Vess Akers also started to leave, but Quantrill persuaded him to remain. "I got you into this war," Quantrill declared, "and I want to get you out of it."

On the night of January 1, 1865, Quantrill and forty-six other bushwhackers crossed the Mississippi in a yawl at Devil's Elbow, fifteen miles above Memphis. The moment they did so whatever tenuous claim they had to fighting for the Confederacy and in defense of their homeland disappeared completely. From now on they were nothing more nor less than bandits.

Quantrill led his gang northward through Tennessee. All along the way he obtained food and forage from Union military posts by representing himself as Captain Clarke, in command of a detachment of the (nonexistent) Fourth Missouri Cavalry.

About the middle of January the bushwhackers crossed into Kentucky near the little town of Canton. Old Charley had developed a loose shoe, so Quantrill went to the local blacksmith shop to have it tightened. But when Quantrill attempted to raise the horse's hoof, it jerked away and in some manner severed a tendon just below the hock joint. The accident completely ruined Old Charley and there was nothing to do except destroy him. Quantrill was badly shaken by the loss of his magnificent steed, to whom he was as devoted as it was to him. He had ridden Old Charley through most of the war, the horse had saved his life on numerous occasions, and he had gained his greatest successes after acquiring him at Independence. He felt, therefore, that now that Old Charley was gone, so was his luck. "My career is run," he murmured gloomily to his men, and began talking of surrendering.

Two days later Quantrill suffered another deep personal loss. The bushwhackers had encountered a small force of Union cavalry and had promptly given chase. However, all the Federals had gotten away except six, who were holed up in a house. John McCorkle and Jim Little crawled along behind the fence, hoping to slip up on the house. Just as they reached a corner of the fence, the Federals spotted them and fired. One of the bullets hit the luckless Little, who cried, "John, I am shot; my leg is shattered."

McCorkle and three other guerrillas placed Little on a blanket and carried him off under the fire of the soldiers; a bullet tore the heel off of one of McCorkle's boots. Then, "mad and desperate," McCorkle started back toward the house to avenge Little. But Quantrill yelled, "John, you damned fool, come back from there!" and stopped him from going ahead with his suicidal venture.

Quantrill then ordered the house set on fire. Immediately the soldiers offered to surrender if they would be treated as prisoners of war. Quantrill promised not to harm them, and they came out with their hands up. Since Little was too badly wounded to ride or be moved, the bushwhackers left him at the house with the Federals, who said they would take good care of him. However, he soon died of his wound, as the guerrillas learned later.

Thus in a space of two days Quantrill lost his favorite horse and closest friend. From the very beginning the Kentucky expedition was proving ill-starred.

The guerrillas continued on to Houstonville, where they stole a number of horses. One of the horses belonged to a militia lieutenant, who came running up just as Allen Parmer started to ride the steed out of a stable. Grabbing hold of the bridle, the lieutenant cried, "If this horse leaves here, it will be over my dead body."

"That is a damned easy job!" sneered Parmer, who then drew a revolver and shot the lieutenant dead.

The Missourians next made their presence felt at Hartford, the seat of Ohio County, on January 22. Quantrill, claiming as usual that he was Captain Clarke of the Fourth Missouri, told the post commander that he was on his way to the Ohio River to search for guerrillas and asked for a guide. A Lieutenant Barnett volunteered to act in that capacity, and two other Federals, a discharged veteran and a soldier on furlough, asked to go along also. Three miles from Hartford, Quantrill's men hanged the discharged veteran in the timber, nine miles further they shot the furloughed soldier, and fourteen miles away they killed the lieutenant.[2]

A week after this atrocity the bushwhackers raided Danville in the eastern part of the state, plundering a boot store, gutting the telegraph office, and robbing the citizens. They then rode on to a point five miles west of Harrodsburg, where they decided to stop for the night. Dividing into three groups, they went to three different houses in the vicinity to get supper and find places to sleep. But while they were still eating, a company of Kentucky Militia under Captain J. H. Bridgewater, which had pursued them from Danville, surrounded the house containing John Barker and eleven other guerrillas, and called on them to surrender.

The trapped bushwhackers tried to break out, but Barker,

Henry Noland, and Foss Key were killed, and the survivors captured. Also slain was Chad Renick, who came over from a near-by house to see what all the shooting was about, and found out the hard way. Quantrill and the other Missourians, warned by the firing, escaped by scattering into the woods.

This was a terrible setback for Quantrill, in fact one of the worse he had ever suffered. Not only had he lost close to a third of his command, but some of his oldest and toughest followers. Among the guerrillas taken prisoner were such men as Jim Younger, Andy McGuire, Bill Gaugh, Tom Evans, and Vess Akers (whom Quantrill had promised to get out of the war). The Federals placed the captives in a prison at Lexington, and on three different occasions took them out into the yard as if to hang them. Each time, however, they came out cheering for Jeff Davis and daring the Bluebellies to hang them, at the same time warning that their deaths would be avenged. Eventually in April eight of them were taken to a Louisville jail, from which they soon escaped with the aid of friendly civilians. The one who remained at Lexington, Tom Evans, was kept there because the Federals believed that he had killed the lieutenant at Houstonville. He did not secure his release until after the war was over, when John McCorkle made out an affidavit declaring that Allen Parmer was the person guilty of the murder.

Following the Harrodsburg fiasco, Quantrill went into Nelson County, where he joined forces with the Kentucky guerrilla chieftain, Sue Mundy. Together they burned a railroad depot at Midway, northwest of Lexington, on the night of February 2. Six days later they captured a wagon train at New Market, killing three of the guards and capturing four others, whom they subsequently murdered also.

Meanwhile, Bridgewater's company doggedly pursued the guerrillas. The night after the New Market raid he overtook them west of Houstonville, killed four of them, captured four more, and ran the remainder, mostly barefooted, into the woods. According to his report, Quantrill, who had been identified by the Federals in Kentucky, was among those forced to flee horseless and bootless.[3]

This was the second severe, even humiliating, blow administered the bushwhackers by Bridgewater's company. Either the

Kentucky Militia were more formidable than their Missouri counterparts, or else Quantrill's followers had lost their zest for fighting, now that the war was lost and they were operating on alien soil.

During the next several weeks the bushwhackers kept low while obtaining fresh horses and new equipment. Many Kentuckians proved as willing to aid them as did the pro-Southern people of Missouri. Part of the time Quantrill stayed at the home of one such friend, a man named Jim Dawson. He became friendly with Dawson's daughter, Nannie, and at her request wrote a poem for her autograph album:

My horse is at the door,
And the enemy I soon may see.
But before I go Miss Nannie
Here's a double health to thee.

Here's a sigh to those who love me
And a smile to those who hate.
And whatever sky's above me,
Here's a heart for every fate.

Though the cannons roar around me,
Yet it still shall bear me on.
Though dark clouds are above me
It hath springs which may be won.

In this verse as with the wine
The libation I would pour
Should be peace with thine and mine
And a health to thee and all *in door*.

Feb. 26, 1865 Very respectfully
your friend
W. C. Q.

Quantrill adapted the verse from Byron, and he had used it before with Anna Walker. But Nannie did not know this, and it was this sort of thing which was well calculated to impress a young lady in 1865. We can be fairly certain that Quantrill cut a romantic and dashing figure in the eyes of Miss Dawson and other Bluegrass belles. She kept the poem until 1892, when she turned it over to Quantrill's mother, who was traveling through Kentucky in quest of information about her son. Aside from the report to Price on Baxter Springs, it is the only known piece of writing by Quantrill during the Civil War. In a way it was rather appropriate.[4]

February went by and so did March. The Missourians confined their activities to petty raids and robberies, plus an occasional skirmish with the militia. Their "stamping ground" was now Spencer County, south of Louisville, a region predominantly pro-Southern. On April 15, the day after Lincoln's assassination, they turned up, drunk and merry, at Judge Jonathan Davis' house in Spencer County. "Excuse us, ladies," said Quantrill, grinning. "We are a little in our cups today. The granddaddy of all greenbacks, Abraham Lincoln, was shot in a theater at Washington last night."

The continued and constant depredations of Quantrill's gang ultimately stirred Major General John M. Palmer, Union commander in Kentucky, to take special action. Because pro-Southern civilians always kept the guerrillas posted on Federal movements, regular troops had proved incapable of catching and destroying them. Therefore, he decided to fight fire with fire. He commissioned a young Kentuckian named Edwin Terrill, leader of a band of "Federal guerrillas" in Spencer County, to pursue Quantrill until he got him, dead or alive.

Terrill, who had served in the Confederate Army earlier in the war, had his first brush with Quantrill on April 13. In conjunction with some militia his gang attacked the bushwhackers near Bloomfield, killed two of them, and wounded three others. Thereafter, throughout the rest of April and into May, he chased and harassed the bushwhackers, but could never quite catch them.

Quantrill's main hideout in Spencer County was the farm of James H. Wakefield near Bloomfield. Wakefield was a Confederate sympathizer, and he gladly provided the Missouri guerrillas with food and shelter. In addition, a number of Kentucky youths joined Quantrill, attracted by his fame and the prospect of high adventure and easy plunder.

On the morning of May 10, Quantrill and about twenty followers rode into Wakefield's farmyard.* They hitched their horses under a shed and took shelter from the drizzling spring rain inside the barn. Quantrill and several others climbed up into the hayloft and went to sleep. The rest sat around talking and amusing themselves by flinging corncobs at each other.

Farmer Wakefield stood in the horse shed talking with Dick Glassock and watching the rain. Suddenly a large body of horsemen crested a slope to the east and charged full tilt toward the barn, yelling and firing carbines. It was Terrill's outfit!

"Here they come," cried Clark Hockensmith, sounding the alarm. The bushwhackers, caught completely by surprise, made no attempt to resist; this was 1865 and Kentucky, not 1862 and Missouri. Instead, they ran to their horses. Most of them quickly mounted and galloped off down a bridle path. Others, however, were not so fortunate. Their horses, frightened by firing and tumult, broke loose and they were forced to flee on foot.

Quantrill was one of those unable to mount his horse. He had obtained the steed only a few days previously from a Miss Betty Russell, and it was not accustomed either to war or to its new master. It bucked and reared wildly, and finally broke away from Quantrill and galloped about the shed snorting with terror.

Abandoning his futile attempts to mount, Quantrill ran after his men, frantically calling on them to wait up. Glassock and Hockensmith heard him, halted their horses, and opened fire with their revolvers to hold back Terrill's men, who were now swarming through the farmyard. Quantrill soon caught up with them and started to climb on behind Glassock. But just at that moment Glassock's horse was struck by a bullet and it became unmanageable. Quantrill then ran alongside Hockensmith, desperately trying to mount his horse. As he did so a bullet pierced his back and he pitched forward into the mud on his face.

The pursuers came pounding by, nearly trampling the prostrate body. One of them fired at Quantrill again and by some freakish chance shot off his right index finger—his trigger finger.

* According to McCorkle and other guerrilla sources, the bushwhackers on this day were planning to surrender in the near future. This may have been the case, but since they actually didn't surrender until late in July, it is rather doubtful.

They soon overtook and killed Glassock and Hockensmith. Had these two not tried to save their leader, they both would have escaped easily.

Quantrill was still conscious, but unable to move. The bullet had lodged against his spine and he was paralyzed from the chest down. He lay in the rain, covered with mud and blood. It was the end of the trail. Quantrill, the Northern renegade, had met his nemesis in Terrill, the Southern turncoat.

Terrill's men came back after a while, took Quantrill's revolvers, and yanked off his boots. They then rolled him onto a blanket and carried him inside Wakefield's house, where they placed him on a couch. Since Wakefield was obviously guilty of harboring and aiding guerrillas, he was legitimate prey and they started to ransack his house. But Wakefield was a shrewd man. He slipped Terrill twenty dollars and a jug of whisky, and the grateful captain forthwith ordered his followers to desist.

Terrill walked over to where Quantrill lay. He asked the wounded man who he was. Quantrill replied, automatically perhaps, that he was Captain Clarke of the Fourth Missouri Cavalry. He then asked Terrill to let him remain at Wakefield's. Terrill at first refused, but noting that Quantrill was paralyzed and could not escape, finally consented. However, he warned Wakefield that he would be held accountable if "Clarke" was not there when his company returned. Quantrill thereupon gave Wakefield his word that he would not let his men take him away.

Terrill then departed. Although he perhaps did not realize it yet, he had accomplished with thirty men in one month what ten thousand Union troops in Missouri and Kansas had failed to do in four years: captured the dread William Clarke Quantrill.

Wakefield sent for a local doctor to look after Quantrill's back wound. After examining it, the doctor shook his head sadly and said that it was fatal.

That night some of the bushwhackers returned to the Wakefield farm. They wanted to carry Quantrill to a place where he would be safe and his wounds tended. Quantrill, however, refused to let them move him. He had given Wakefield his word, he said, and if they took him away, Wakefield's property would be burned. Besides, he was going to die anyway, and he did not care to be dragged around in the brush. Terrill had promised to let him remain at Wakefield's, and that was what he wanted to do.

Southern sympathizers in the neighborhood came to see Quantrill, whose true identity was known to them, when they learned he was lying wounded at Wakefield's. Two girls brought him a beautiful bouquet, to which was attached a card bearing the inscription, "Compliments of Miss Maggie Frederick and Sallie Lovell to Mr. Quantrill." He talked with his visitors about his past exploits in Kansas and Missouri. The Northern accounts of the Lawrence raid, he asserted, were substantially correct except for one thing—had he captured Jim Lane, he would have taken him to Jackson County and, instead of hanging him, burned him at the stake!

During the second night at Wakefield's some more guerrillas visited Quantrill for the purpose of carrying him away. But again he refused to be moved.

On the morning of May 12, Terrill returned. He had learned "Captain Clarke's" true name and hence ignored his promise to let him remain at Wakefield's. His men placed Quantrill in a farm wagon, stuck some pillows and straw under him, and then headed for Louisville. Before leaving, Quantrill thanked Wakefield for his help, and told him that he would write to him from Louisville concerning some money he wished his mother and sister in Ohio to have. Wakefield, however, never heard from him. The fact that Quantrill referred to his sister at this time indicates that he did not know that she had died in 1863.

Terrill stopped for the night at Jeffersontown, where they had a couple of physicians treat Quantrill's wounds. One of them, a Dr. Marshall, had lived formerly in Shelby County and had tended Quantrill on a previous occasion. Quantrill recognized him and asked if he were not the same doctor. Marshall answered, "I am the man. I have moved here."

"So have I," responded Quantrill, with grim humor.

The next day Terrill took Quantrill on into Louisville, where the Federal authorities placed him in the military prison hospital.[5]

The Louisville newspapers noted his arrival. The *Daily Union Press* was brief:

Quantrill.—The noted guerrilla who had been operating in Kentucky under the name of Quantrill and whose capture was noted Saturday, is in the Military Prison hospital. There is very little hope of his recovery, as his whole body is perfectly paralyzed.

The *Daily Courier*, however, provided fuller coverage:

Quantrill, the notorious Kansas guerrilla, arrived in this city yesterday morning about 11 o'clock. He was conveyed in a country wagon on a bed of straw, and a few pillows, and guarded by Terrill's men disguised as guerrillas. He is wounded through the left breast, and it is thought he will die. All the honor of his capture is due to Captain Terrill and his company—"Terrill's guerrillas."

On Wednesday, Terrill and his men surprised and charged on Quantrill's gang, five miles beyond Taylorsville, killing three of the outlaws and dispersing the remainder. They were also on the scent of Berry's guerrillas, and only one hour behind them when they received orders to report to the general commanding. Quantrill had been sailing under the name of Captain Clarke and it is supposed by many that it is not the veritable Kansas outlaw, but we understand that Terrill and part of his company are intimately acquainted with him. One fact that strongly corroborates their assertions is that a picture of a young lady was found in his possession, which one of the parties recognized as Miss Hickman, who resides within five miles of the Kansas line. Quantrill also stated that the three followers of his who were killed were from Missouri. The news of his capture will cause great joy throughout the Union. The inhuman outrages that he committed years ago, such as burning the town of Lawrence, etc., are still fresh in the memory of our people.

The *Daily Democrat*, on the other hand, denied that the prisoner actually was Quantrill:

Captain Terrill and his company arrived here yesterday from Taylorsville. They brought with them the guerrilla who bears the name of "Quantrill." It is not the Quantrill of Kansas notoriety, for we have been assured that he was at last accounts a colonel in the rebel army under Price. This prisoner was shot through the body in a fight in a barn near Taylorsville on Wednesday last. Five others were killed on the spot by Terrill's men, but what their names were we could not ascertain. The prisoner brought down is confined in the military prison hospital and is said to be in a dying condition.[6]

Terrill did not enjoy his triumph long. A few weeks later he was killed while "shooting up" the little town of Shelbyville.[7] Quantrill actually outlived him, and perhaps had the satisfaction of reading of his death in the newspapers.

A number of persons visited Quantrill as he lay paralyzed in the military prison hospital, among them some of his own men. But unfortunately for future historians and biographers, no newspaper reporter had the enterprise to interview him, nor did the military authorities obtain a statement from him—procedures which today would be a matter of course. Nor did Quantrill himself endeavor to write or dictate an account of his exploits. This mysterious man was destined to remain a man of mystery.

Quantrill, however, must have spent many a long day and night thinking back over his career. His father's death . . . mother and the boardinghouse . . . the little one-room schools . . . the journey to Kansas . . . his troubles with Beeson and Torrey . . . the expedition to Utah . . . Salt Lake City . . . Pike's Peak . . . Kansas and teaching again . . . the Lawrence ferry landing and Charley Hart . . . Stewart and Dean . . . Sam Walker . . . Morgan Walker . . . the Independence mob . . . the escape from Snyder . . . to Texas with Mark Gill . . . Wilson's Creek and Lexington . . . beginning of the gang . . . leader . . . Aubry, Olathe, Shawneetown . . . the Tate house fight . . . the terrible battle in the ravine with Gower's troopers . . . the capture of Independence . . . the captain's commission . . . the futile attack on Lamar . . . Arkansas . . . Richmond and the interview with Seddon . . . back to Missouri . . . the march to Lawrence . . . massacre . . . riding about in the buggy . . . the escape to Missouri . . . Order No. 11 . . . Baxter Springs . . . Texas . . . the Mineral Creek camp . . . Sherman . . . Anderson's desertion . . . the escape from McCulloch . . . the return to Missouri . . . humiliated by Todd . . . Kate King . . . Fayette . . . Price's raid . . . Todd and Anderson killed . . . Kentucky . . . Old Charley . . . Jim Little's death . . . Wakefield's barn . . . Terrill . . . and now? . . . Well, so be it.

Quantrill, although Canal Dover was but a short distance from Louisville, made no attempt to contact his family, who had not heard from him since 1860. As the end drew near, he turned to the last refuge left him, religion. He embraced the Catholic faith and received its last rites.

On June 6, at four o'clock in the afternoon, Quantrill died. A woman who visited him shortly before his death later claimed that his passing was hastened, if not caused, by neglect. Prior to dying he gave the Catholic priest at the hospital eight hundred dollars and directed him to use part of the money for his gravestone and then send the rest to "Kate Clarke."* According to Fletch Taylor in a statement made after the war, Kate used her share to establish a famous St. Louis brothel.

The Louisville papers published only short notices of the notorious guerrilla chieftain's demise. The *Journal* even insisted that he was not *the* Quantrill! Papers in Kansas and Missouri were similarly laconic in reporting the event.[8] Perhaps they felt that the news was too good to be true—after all, there had been so many rumors of his death or capture.† Besides, the war was over now. Already much of it was being forgotten. New names, new sensations, occupied the public's fickle attention.

Quantrill was buried in the Louisville Catholic Cemetery. The priest, however, disregarded his instructions concerning a tombstone. Instead, he ordered Mr. and Mrs. Scully, custodians of the cemetery, to empty their dishwater and slops over the grave so as to obliterate all trace of it. He believed that unless this were done, the body would be stolen.

The subsequent history of Quantrill's body was of a macabre nature quite in fitting with his life. In 1887 William W. Scott, who was gathering materials for his never-to-be-written history of Quantrill, visited Louisville in company with Quantrill's mother. During the war she refused to believe that the destroyer of

* Quantrill had previously left this money with a woman in Spencer County for safekeeping. See McCorkle, *Three Years With Quantrill*, p. 152.

† For instance, in the summer of 1864 there was a great joy in Lawrence, Kansas, when word arrived that Quantrill had been arrested and imprisoned in Indianapolis. A committee went to identify the prisoner and return him to Kansas for execution, but he proved to be merely a professional gambler who by some odd chance had adopted Quantrill's old alias of Charley Hart.

Lawrence was her son, but afterward not only accepted the fact but became very proud of his exploits and fame. Scott, on a previous trip to Louisville, had located his burial place, and she was now determined to secure the body and take it back to Canal Dover.

Scott and Mrs. Quantrill visited Mrs. Scully, who was now sole custodian of the cemetery, and induced her to let them open the grave for the purpose of placing the remains in a new casket. On a dismal, drizzly December afternoon Scott went by himself to the cemetery while Mrs. Quantrill stayed behind at their hotel, and with the assistance of a reluctant gravedigger unearthed the body.

Practically all vestiges of the coffin had disappeared. Part of the skeleton's spinal column and the ribs crumbled to dust on being touched, but the rest of the bones were in good condition. The hair, which had taken on a bleached yellow color, had slipped off in a half-circle around the skull. Several shirt buttons and a piece of army sock were all that survived of the clothes.

Scott had the bones placed in a box and reburied near the surface. Then, with Mrs. Scully's permission, he took the skull, wrapped in newspaper, back to the hotel. In the morning he showed it to Mrs. Quantrill, who cried on seeing it, and positively identified it as her son's by a chipped tooth in the lower right jaw.

When Scott said that he had promised to return the skull, she refused to let him do so, and insisted that all the bones be secured for burial beside her husband's grave. After some argument, Scott consented to a deception by which the rest of the remains were obtained from Mrs. Scully. Mrs. Quantrill then took the skeleton back to Canal Dover and reburied it there. Scott, however, secretly kept part of the skeleton, with the ironic result that several arm and leg bones eventually ended up in the Kansas State Historical Society, where they remained until buried in October 1992 in the Confederate cemetery at Higginsville, Missouri.[9]

Quantrill was not dead long before the myth-makers were hard at work. Here, as previously mentioned, John N. Edwards took the lead. In his book, *Noted Guerrillas,* he portrayed Quantrill as a gloriously romantic cavalier of the border, the bravest of the brave, going from one amazing exploit to still another even more amazing yet. Lesser writers imitated and repeated Edwards' colorfully written tales, so that throughout the South and West, and especially in Missouri, Quantrill became a truly lengendary figure of heroic proportions.

In the North, however, and particularly in Kansas, a different conception prevailed. Here the authority was Connelley. Aided by Scott's researches, Connelley presented the basic facts about Quantrill's career and exposed Edwards' juvenile absurdities. But, carried away by his pro-Union and pro-Kansas prejudices, he pictured him as a "degenerate" and "depraved" monster who was motivated solely by "blood-madness" and a lust for "plunder" and "fallen women."

Both Edwards and Connelley were half right and half wrong. Edwards exaggerated Quantrill's courage and prowess, and ignored or romanticized his cruelty and criminality. Connelley, on the other hand, was guilty of exactly the reverse. And neither presented or was capable of presenting a realistic, objective analysis of his career and of the Civil War on the border.

Quantrill, like all men, was an incalculable mixture of good and bad, of the admirable and the detestable. His admirable qualities were his military skill, cool courage, and power to command. His detestable characteristics were his brutality and callousness, his utter lack of scruples, and his treacherous opportunism. All in all, the latter tend to obscure the former.

Quantrill remains to this day a favorite subject for the mythmakers, as witness the movies, television plays, novels, and "true" articles in which he figures. And no doubt he long will be. For the very name "Quantrill" conjures up visions of galloping raiders, desperate battles, smoking six-shooters, daring deeds, and all the other ingredients of those two greatest American myths of all—the Civil War and the Wild West. In the former was he not the most spectacular and successful of the guerrilla leaders? And in the latter, was he not the mightiest of the outlaws, the mentor of the Younger brothers and of Frank and Jesse James?

Thus, in a certain sense, Quantrill did not really die in that Louisville military prison hospital on June 6, 1865. . . .

epilogue The Bandits

Every spring since 1861 had brought forth in West Missouri a new and bloodier outbreak of bushwhacking. Would the spring of 1865 do the same?

General Grenville M. Dodge, who had replaced Rosecrans as Union commander in Missouri, was determined that the answer to this question would be in the negative. Late in January 1865, shortly after assuming command, he instituted a program designed to crush out the bushwhackers once and for all. First, he called out thirty-one companies of Missouri Volunteer Militia, put them under experienced and competent officers, and stationed them at strategic points throughout the guerrilla-infested country. Next, he encouraged the regular civil and police authorities in northern and western Missouri to resume the exercise of their normal functions. Finally, he applied a modified form of Order No. 11 by directing that the families of all known bushwhackers and Confederate soldiers be sent south.

Editor Thacher of the *Western Journal of Commerce* was not impressed by Dodge's program. Past failures to suppress the guerrillas had made him cynical. "If the issuing of 'orders,'" he wrote, "would have put down bushwhacking, it would have ceased to exist long ago. General Dodge's orders don't amount to a row of pins unless they are enforced. . . . The bushwhackers don't scare worth a cent." [1]

It soon became evident, however, that Dodge intended to back up his orders with action. Thus, early in February, the military authorities told twenty-six bushwhacker families in Clay County to leave their homes within twenty days, announcing as they did so that this was to be only the "first installment." At the same time the civil authorities began taking a firmer stand against bushwhacking. Missourians of practically all shades of political opinion had come to feel that the guerrillas were merely prolonging the agony of the war and completing the ruination of the state. Consequently, many pro-Southerners joined with Unionists in a campaign to kill or arrest the bushwhackers, or to drive them away. This new attitude was expressed most vehemently by the Columbia *Statesman* early in April: "Let the sight of a guerrilla be a signal to shoot him. If he comes to your home shoot him. If you meet him on the road shoot him down."

During the winter only a few, small, scattered bands of partisans skulked in the hills and thickets, sallying forth now and then to murder a Union man or attack the workers on the Missouri Pacific Railroad. Colonel Chester Harding, commander of the Central District, which included Jackson and Lafayette counties, stated in February that there were hardly any guerrillas in his area, and that things were generally quiet.[2]

Everyone knew, however, that most of the bushwhackers had gone south with Price, and that the real test of Dodge's program would come when they returned. Lee's surrender and the collapse of the Confederacy encouraged some to predict that they would not resume operations, but others were not so sure. There was no way, really, of telling what these wild men might do. Maybe defeat would cause them to fight all the more desperately. . . .

Down in Texas the bushwhackers themselves were uncertain as to what they should and would do, now that the war was lost. Some elected to remain in Texas and take up ranching. Others, such as Thrailkill, joined Shelby's brigade in its fantastic, romantic march into Mexico. But most decided to head back once more to their old stamping grounds in Missouri. At their head rode Dave Poole, Jim Anderson, Ol Shepherd, and fiendish Archie Clement.

They marched northward by their usual route—up through the Indian Territory, into Southwest Missouri, and across the Osage and Grand rivers. Near the Osage they claimed their first victim—a Union militiaman whom Clement accused of having killed his brother and burnt his mother's house. While Jesse James, John

Maupin, and Theodore Castle held the screaming prisoner tightly, Clement cut his throat and then scalped him.[3]

After crossing the Grand, the bushwhackers headed into Johnson County, where on the morning of May 7 they proclaimed their return by a dramatic double raid. First, forty of them struck Holden, robbed the stores, and killed a civilian. Then, an hour later, over a hundred of them sacked near-by Kingsville, burning five houses and slaying eight men. Quite obviously the war was still on as far as they were concerned.

As soon as he learned of the Holden-Kingsville raids, General Dodge ordered all available troops into the region, and instructed Colonel Harding to spare neither men nor horses in pursuing the guerrillas. The *Western Journal of Commerce,* in reporting the raids, spoke for many other people when it asked whether these outrages would ever cease. Almost desperately it demanded that the Missouri regiments in Sherman's army be brought back immediately to halt the "ravaging of the border."

Clement and Poole led their bands up into Lafayette County, killing another fifteen men on their way, and took refuge in the Sni Hills. People who talked with the guerrillas reported that they scouted the news of Lee's surrender, maintaining that it was "just another damn Yankee lie." [4]

On May 11, Clement sent the Federal commander at Lexington, Major B. K. Davis, a note which must be regarded as a classic of sheer gall:

> This is to notify you that I will give you until Friday morning, May 12, 1865, to surrender the town of Lexington. If you surrender we will treat you and all taken as prisoners of war. If we have to take it by storm we will burn the town and kill the soldiers. We have the force and are determined to have it.

Davis ignored Clement's ultimatum as being the bluff it was. For several days now he had been receiving feelers from various bushwhackers on the subject of surrender. He was confident that "a large portion of them are anxious to give themselves up if they can be treated as prisoners of war." [5]

A few days after Clement's note, a totally different sort of message came from Poole. He informed Davis that he was in the

Sni Hills collecting his men in order to surrender, and that he wished to meet Davis and arrange terms.

On May 17 Davis, with five soldiers, met Poole, accompanied by an equal number of bushwhackers, at the Mound on the Warrensburg Road. He told the long-haired guerrilla chieftain that General Dodge had authorized him to assure all surrendering partisans that if they gave up their arms and obeyed the laws, the military would not take further action against them, but that they would have to take their chances insofar as the civil authorities were concerned. After asking several questions, Poole accepted these conditions and promised to surrender his band at Lexington on May 21.

Early on the afternoon of the twenty-first, Poole, at the head of eighty-five men, rode into Lexington. Spectators lined the streets and silently watched the fierce-looking young scourges of the border file by. In the town square a large body of troops stood drawn up in battle formation, ready for any trouble. Waiting to receive the surrender was Colonel Harding.

At a signal from Poole the bushwhackers halted in front of the courthouse and dismounted. He then ordered them to advance and lay down their weapons. After doing this, they took the oath of allegiance from a provost marshal, who in turn gave each of them a parole certificate. They then remounted, Colonel Harding told them to return to their homes and live in peace, and they rode out of town. That evening Harding telegraphed Dodge the laconic message: "Bushwhacking is stopped."

During the days and weeks that followed small groups of bushwhackers continued to surrender. By the end of May over two hundred had come into Lexington alone. Dave Poole, accompanied by a Federal officer, went out into the brush to urge the men to abandon bushwhacking and take the oath. Even he had a difficult time locating them, so rugged was the country and so clever had they become at concealment. As he rode about, he demonstrated to the Federal officer various bushwhacker tricks, such as spreading blankets over a road and then marching the horses over them to prevent any tracks being made.[6]

Late in May, Ol Shepherd, the best pistol shot in Quantrill's old band, wrote to the post commander at Liberty saying that he and six of his followers wished to surrender now that the war was over, but that they would do so only if they were permitted to retain their weapons. "We must keep our side arms," he declared, "for you know we have personal enemies who would kill us at the first opportunity. . . . Although we do not intend to insult any soldiers or civilians, we will not take any insults. We are willing to blot out the past and begin anew."

However, the commander at Liberty insisted that Shepherd and his men surrender under the same conditions as the other guerrillas. Eventually, and with much reluctance, they did so. The Clay County sheriff promptly arrested two of them on charges of murder and horse-stealing.

On June 2, Jim Anderson and Clement opened up negotiations with the Federal commander at Glasgow, who informed them that they would have to surrender unconditionally. Since they both knew that the Unionists hated them bitterly—and with good cause!—they concluded that to surrender on this basis would merely lead to a rope around the neck. Therefore they left the state and went back to Texas, Anderson permanently, Clement only until he felt it safe to return to Missouri.[7]

The last of the bushwhackers to call it quits were those who had followed Quantrill into Kentucky. On July 26—over three months after Appomattox—the following men surrendered at Samuel's Depot near Louisville: Frank James, Andy McGuire, Lee McMurty, Allen Parmer, Bill Hulse, Bud Pence, Ike Hall, Bob Hall, Jim Lilly, Dave Hilton, John Harris, John Ross, Ran Venable, and Payne Jones. If they can properly be considered as such, then they were the last Confederate troops to surrender. The Federal authorities released them as soon as they took the oath of allegiance.[8]

The surrender of the bushwhackers filled the editor of the Liberty *Tribune* with happiness. "The farmers," he wrote on June 2, "may now plant in security and gather in safety. The merchant will not need a convoy. Everything promises well. Let us hope that a few years will remove all traces of war, and so soothe and soften its memories, that we may feel once more the happiness of former times."

The physical signs of the war were everywhere. A Kansan who took a trip from Fort Scott to Kansas City in the summer of 1865 reported that western Missouri "presented a desolate appearance"

—the results mainly, he admitted, of the raids of Jennison, Anthony, Lane, and the Red Legs. "Now and then you could see a lone house that had escaped the bands of jayhawkers, but as far as the eye could reach in every direction you could see lone chimneys standing singly and in pairs, all that was left . . . of good homesteads." [9]

Yet, noted the Liberty *Tribune* on June 9, many people were returning to their farms, especially in the district depopulated by Order No. 11. The returnees, moreover, refused to sell their lands except at high prices, for they knew that "they can find no such homes elsewhere." And "although nothing remained save stone fences and chimneys the country looked beautiful in its ruins."

Far more serious and lasting than the physical effects of the war were the emotional scars. Much animosity continued to exist between pro-Union and pro-Confederate Missourians. In particular, the Unionists hated and resented former bushwhackers. They believed that these men should be punished for their wartime crimes. When the regular civil authorities failed to take any action, they formed vigilante bands which harassed the more notorious and obnoxious ex-guerrillas, and in some cases drove them from their homes or even killed them. In fact, for a time it seemed as if peace might prove more deadly to the bushwhacker than war.

The most famous of the victims of Unionist revenge was Clement, who returned to Missouri in the summer of 1866. Although officially an outlaw with a price on his head, he had no trouble at all remaining at large. In fact, he openly displayed himself in Lexington, where he visited frequently with his old friend, Dave Poole.

Then, on December 13, he and two dozen other ex-guerrillas came into town to register, as required by law, for the Missouri State Militia. As soon as they enrolled, the local military commander told them to leave town, which they did. But a short time later Clement and another bushwhacker returned and entered a saloon. A squad of soldiers went to arrest them. Clement dashed out a side door, jumped onto his horse, and galloped down the main street. Riflemen posted in the courthouse for just such an eventuality opened fire and he fell from his saddle riddled with bullets. Thus died the most vicious and depraved of all the bushwhackers.[10]

The wild young ex-partisans found it extremely hard to settle down to a humdrum, poverty-tinged existence on a farm after the adventuresome life and easy money of the war. This was especially true of those whose criminal tendencies had been developed and confirmed by bushwhacking. Therefore, it is little wonder that some of them, exasperated and made desperate by Unionist persecution, were unable to resist the temptation to make use of the techniques and skills they had learned so well under Quantrill, Todd, and Anderson.

On February 13, 1866—only eight months after the surrender—a gang of ex-bushwhackers robbed the Clay County Savings Bank at Liberty of nearly sixty thousand dollars and killed a William Jewell College student who got in their way. Recognized among the robbers were Ol Shepherd, Bud and Don Pence, and Frank Gregg—all prominent members of Quantrill's old band.

In October, four ex-guerrillas held up a bank in Lexington. Interestingly enough, they were pursued by a posse headed by Dave Poole! The local paper commented dryly that the pursuit was not especially vigorous.

On May 22, 1867, a gang numbering twelve to fourteen men robbed a bank at Richmond and then killed three citizens while making their getaway. Six former Quantrill followers participated in the raid: Allen Parmer, Tom Little, Andy McGuire, Ike Flannery, Payne Jones, and Dick Burns. McGuire and Little were subsequently captured and lynched.[11]

Four ex-bushwhackers who turned bandit soon became nationally, even internationally, famous. They were Frank and Jesse James, and Cole and Jim Younger.

Both the James boys belonged to the definitely criminal element among the bushwhackers. Frank, as we have noted, accompanied Quantrill's ill-fated expedition to Kentucky, and surrendered there in July. As for Jesse, he was, significantly, a buddy of Clement's, and like him never formally surrendered. According to some accounts of extremely low reliability he did try to surrender at Lexington in May but was treacherously shot by Federal troops while riding under a flag of truce. In any case, he was badly wounded toward the end of the war and spent the rest of 1865 being nursed back to health by his mother at Rulla, Nebraska, where she had been forced to go as a result of Union proscription.

During the next several years Frank and Jesse lived most of the time on their mother's farm near Kearney in Clay County. Unionists in the neighborhood regarded them with extreme suspicion and accused them of having taken part in the bank robbery at Liberty. In addition, some people charged that they were members of the gang that looted a bank at Russellville, Kentucky, in the spring of 1868.

Then, on December 7, 1869, bandits held up a bank at Gallatin, Missouri, killing in the process the cashier, who was a former officer in the Federal militia. General public opinion had it that the James boys were responsible for the crime, and although they strongly denied it, they refused to submit to arrest and stand trial, claiming that if they did, they would be lynched like Tom Little and Andy McGuire. As a consequence they became, if not so already, professional outlaws.

Cole Younger was in California when the war ended, and he did not return to Missouri until the fall of 1865. If we are to credit his own story, and that of his apologists, he settled down on the farm near Lee's Summit and tried to lead a lawful, peaceful life. But vindictive Unionists would not permit him to do so. Instead, they charged him with a murder committed during the war, and he was forced to go into hiding in order to evade arrest. Soon he and his brothers were being blamed, either fairly or falsely, for every holdup and shooting in the region. After a while they decided, in effect, to live up to their reputations.

By 1870 the Jameses and Youngers headed a gang which rapidly became the most notorious in the West. Among its members, at one time or another, were such guerrilla veterans as Allen Parmer, Ike Flannery, Bill Hulse, Bud Pence, William Chiles, Payne Jones, George Shepherd, and John Jarrette. Ranging from Kansas to Kentucky, from Iowa to Texas, the "James Gang" committed a series of highly sensational bank robberies and train stick-ups. The latter in particular excited the public's imagination, for it was such a novel and dramatic crime: A red lantern swinging in the darkness—burning ties piled across the tracks—masked bandits springing aboard the train as it slowed to a halt—crew and passengers covered by six-shooters—the express safe blown open—passengers forced to hand over their money and jewelry—the outlaws riding off into the night firing their pistols into the sky! Scarcely a month went by without the *Police Gazette* and similar magazines publishing vivid accounts, accompanied by garish drawings, of the latest thrilling exploits of Jesse James and Cole Younger. At the same time hack writers who had never been west of the Hudson River scribbled highly colored, highly imaginative "true stories" of the James boys and Younger brothers which were published in cheap, crudely illustrated paperbacks and sold at depots and aboard trains—sometimes the very trains which they had supposedly robbed!

Ever so often Jesse James and Cole Younger wrote letters to the newspapers denying that they had committed certain robberies and giving the names of respectable persons who could testify that they were nowhere near the scene of the crime at the time it occurred. And, in truth, they were undoubtedly accused of many deeds of which they were innocent. For instance, on several occasions the newspapers reported them holding up banks in towns hundreds of miles apart on the same day! Thus they became the victims of their own notoriety.

Sheriffs and police officers throughout the West and South, as well as the Pinkerton Detective Agency, vainly tried to apprehend the James boys and Younger brothers. But, along with their own bumbling ineptitude, they were severely handicapped by an old obstacle: namely, the fact that there were hundreds of people in Missouri, also in Kentucky, who fervently sympathized with, even admired, the bandits and were more than willing to help them evade the law. Consequently, Jesse, Frank, and Cole were able much of the time to live almost openly, yet in nearly perfect security, close to such towns as Lee's Summit, Liberty, and Independence, or even in Kansas City itself!

For the most part, pro-Southern Missourians believed that the Jameses and Youngers were the innocent victims of vicious Unionist-Republican prosecution. Moreover, banks and railroads were highly unpopular with the rural population in those days; hence, there were many who actually got a feeling of satisfaction whenever they read that the "boys" had knocked off another bank or emptied another train safe.

Early in 1875 public sympathy for the Jameses and Youngers reached its peak: On the night of January 25, a group of Pinkerton detectives sneaked up to the James home near Kearney and tossed a thirty-two-pound iron bomb, wrapped in kerosene-soaked rags, through the window. The explosion killed Frank's and Jesse's nine-year-old half-brother, Archie Samuel, and tore off their mother's right arm below the elbow.*

This atrocity, which was one of the worst deeds in the whole shabby history of the Pinkertons, aroused intense indignation throughout Missouri and led to the introduction of an amnesty bill in the legislature. Under its terms the James boys, the Younger brothers, and other outlawed ex-bushwhackers would be pardoned for their wartime activities and assured a fair trial for postwar crimes. But before the bill could be passed, Jesse allegedly murdered a man in Clay County, and public sentiment turned against the bandits.

By now the Jameses and Youngers were confirmed and hardened criminals, who probably would not have returned to a normal, lawful life even if they had had the chance (although in fairness it should be pointed out that they had never really known such a life to return to). Despite the folk tales to the contrary, there was nothing of the Robin Hood about them. They did not "rob from the rich to give to the poor," and they were not especially gallant or heroic. Although it would be wrong to say that they were lacking in courage and hardihood, nevertheless they preferred easy victims and always played it as safe as possible. Neither, again despite popular legend, were they particularly good shots or fast draws. They favored the shotgun over the revolver and did not hesitate to shoot men in the back from ambush. And although they originated a number of outlaw tricks, their tactics by the standards of a modern-day syndicate gangster were terribly crude.

This last statement is borne out by the Northfield, Minnesota, fiasco, which saw the beginning of the end of the James Gang.

On the morning of September 7, 1876, Frank James, Bob

* According to the Pinkertons, the object thrown into the house was not a bomb, but a "flare lamp," intended to light up the interior of the house so that the detectives and *local law officers* outside could see who was inside. The explosion was then caused by Dr. Samuel, the James boys' stepfather, throwing the "flare lamp" into a lighted fireplace (or stove). This version is far from satisfactory, but even supposing that it was not a "bomb" but a "flare lamp," the effect and consequences were the same.

Younger, and Charlie Pitts rode across the bridge spanning the Cannon River and dismounted in front of the First National Bank of Northfield. They wore long linen dusters which concealed their weapons, and they pretended to be casual loafers. Both Frank James and Bob Younger had braced themselves beforehand with whisky, and hence were feeling somewhat befuddled.

After a little while five more riders, similarly attired, crossed the bridge. Three of them, Jesse James, Jim Younger, and Bill Chadwell, halted at the end of it. The other two, Cole Younger and Clell Miller, continued on toward the bank. As they approached, Frank James, Bob Younger, and Pitts entered the bank—which was contrary to plans, as they were supposed to wait until joined by Cole Younger and Miller. These two, instead of going inside the bank, stopped outside the front door, which Frank James' group carelessly left open. On orders from Cole, Miller closed the door.

This queer action awakened the suspicions of J. S. Allen, proprietor of an adjoining hardware store, who had been eying the strangers with growing curiosity. He walked over to the bank to see what was up, but as he came near, Miller yelled at him to stay away. Immediately his suspicions became a certainty. Turning around, he ran up the street shouting, "Get your guns, boys! They're robbing the bank!" Within a matter of seconds dozens of armed men were converging from every direction on the bank.

Cole quickly realized that things had gone wrong. Therefore he fired his pistol into the air as a signal for those inside the bank to clear out. At the same time the party under Jesse began firing their revolvers and warning people off the street. One pedestrian, however, merely stood facing the raiders, a puzzled grin on his face. Exasperated by such stupid stubbornness, one of the bandits, either Cole or Jesse, shot him dead. It later developed that the victim was a newly arrived Swedish immigrant who did not understand a word of English.

Meanwhile, inside the bank, Frank James and his companions continued to botch up matters. First Frank placed a knife at the throat of the cashier, Joseph Heywood, and ordered him to open the vault. With suicidal bravery, Heywood refused. Frank then called on another bank employee, A. E. Bunker, to open the vault.

Bunker replied that he did not know the combination. The bandits started to kill him, but he broke away and ran out the back door. They fired at him, hitting him in the shoulder, but he kept going. Before they could do anything else, they heard Cole's shot, followed by his voice shouting through the front door, "Come out, boys! They're killing our men!"

Cole was not exaggerating. A rifle shot fired by a townsman pierced Chadwell's chest and he tumbled dead from his horse. Buckshot gouged Miller's face, then a bullet through the heart killed him. Cole himself was struck by a shot in the thigh, and another bullet shattered the upper jaw of brother Jim.

The outlaws rushed out of the bank, their pistols blazing. At the doorway, one of them turned and shot the cashier, Heywood, through the head, killing him instantly. Outside a sniper hit Bob Younger in the right elbow, breaking it. Bob shifted his revolver to his left hand and continued to fire. All the bandits were banging away with their pistols, but they failed to hit a single assailant.

Finally all of the would-be robbers succeeded in remounting, with Bob Younger, whose horse had been killed, riding double behind Cole. Just eight minutes after entering Northfield they galloped back across the bridge and out of the town, followed by a hail of bullets.

During the next two weeks western Minnesota was the scene of a gigantic manhunt. Grim-faced posses scoured the countryside, while the raiders sought desperately to make it back to Missouri. Their progress, however, was slowed by the badly wounded Bob and Jim Younger, and after several days heavy rains began falling, further delaying their flight. At this juncture Frank and Jesse James abandoned the others and went on alone. Eventually they made good their escape.

The Youngers and Pitt were not so lucky. On September 21, near Madelia, Minnesota, a six-man posse brought them to bay in a swamp. A short but violent gun battle ensued. When it was over, Pitts was dead, Jim Younger had four more bullets in him, Bob Younger was shot through the right lung, and Cole was wounded in eleven places. These men, reputedly the deadliest gunfighters in the West, had been unable to defeat an enemy which outnumbered them by only two, and they had moreover failed to hit a single one of their attackers.

As soon as they had sufficiently recovered, the Youngers stood trial for murder and attempted robbery. By pleading guilty, they escaped the hangman's noose, but were sentenced to life imprisonment in the Minnesota State Penitentiary at Stillwater. During the trial they steadfastly refused to admit that their escaped companions were Frank and Jesse James. Instead, they insisted that the two were named Howard and Woods. Not until long afterward, and then only in private, did Cole reveal their true identity.*

The Youngers began their sentences on November 20, 1876. The prison clerk put down the following on Cole's entrance record:

> Prison number—699
> Age—32 years
> Height—5 feet, 11½ inches
> Weight—230 pounds
> Occupation—farmer
> Native—Missouri State

The three brothers were all model prisoners, for they hoped someday to secure paroles. As the years passed, Missouri friends worked hard and persistently to secure pardons for them. The leader of this effort was Warren C. Bronaugh, a former Confederate soldier whose life Cole had saved at Lone Jack. Eventually, in 1901, success crowned his efforts, and the Governor of Minnesota granted conditional paroles to Cole and Jim. As for Bob, he had died in prison of tuberculosis in 1889.

Jim did not live long after his release. Despondent over failure to make a decent living, and discouraged by the refusal of the parole board to let him get married, he committed suicide in a St. Paul hotel room on October 19, 1902. In 1903, as a result of further efforts by Bronaugh, the Minnesota authorities gave Cole a

* In his book, *The Story of Cole Younger*, Younger categorically denied that Frank and Jesse were members of the Northfield holdup gang. With equal veracity he also claimed that the only robbery he ever participated in during his entire life was the Northfield one—which of course, he could not very well deny! Furthermore, Younger stated that Pitts killed the cashier, Heywood. Most accounts of the Northfield robbery charge Frank James or Jesse James with the slaying (in some versions Jesse, not Frank, was inside the bank).

complete pardon. He immediately went to his old home near Lee's Summit. He was now a fat, bald, old man. Only his hard, cold eyes, and cruel mouth bespoke the tough young bushwhacker and ruthless bandit of yore.

Frank and Jesse, following the Northfield disaster, lay low in Texas and Tennessee the next several years. Jesse lived under assumed names with his wife and children. Given the primitive identification devices and the almost nonexistent police communications of the time, it was not necessary for them to adopt elaborate disguises or take any special precautions. In fact, the law-enforcement agencies lacked photographs or even accurate descriptions of the brothers, so that on several occasions Jesse was able to converse with detectives who had sworn to track him down!

Probably the Jameses would have remained at large indefinitely had not some of their fellow bandits become disaffected.

In 1881 Jesse was living with his wife and two children on Woodlawn Avenue in Kansas City, having moved there from Nashville. While there he received word that a member of the gang, Jim Cummins, was becoming too talkative. Therefore he set out to find and kill him. At last he traced him to the farm of Bob and Charley Ford in Kentucky. When the Fords denied knowledge of his whereabouts, he took a fourteen-year-old brother of the Fords into the woods and slapped him around in a vain effort to find out where Cummins was hiding.

Sometime later, also in Kentucky, Wood Hite, a member of the gang, learned that his stepmother was carrying on an illicit affair with Dick Liddil, another bandit. Hite had already fallen out with Liddil over the division of the proceeds of a robbery, and this discovery thoroughly enraged him. On December 4, 1881, he tried to kill Liddil at the home of the Fords, but instead was himself slain by Bob Ford. Since Hite was a cousin and good friend of Jesse's the Fords and Liddil buried him in an unmarked grave and tried to keep his death a secret.

Bob and Charley Ford now had a reason to fear Jesse, and one to hate him: fear him because of their part in the killing of Hite, hate him because of maltreatment of their kid brother.

Consequently they were in a receptive mood when Sheriff Timberlake of Clay County contacted them and asked their help in apprehending Jesse. After being assured that the state authorities would grant them immunity, they agreed to co-operate. Besides fear and revenge, they were no doubt strongly influenced by the ten-thousand-dollar reward the Governor of Missouri was offering for Jesse, dead or alive.

Late in 1881 Jesse moved with his family to St. Joseph, Missouri, where under the name of Thomas Howard he resided in a seven-room frame house which commanded a view of the town in three directions. In March, 1882, Bob and Charley Ford joined him and agreed to take part in a bank robbery he was planning. For several weeks they lived in the James home, constantly on the outlook for a favorable opportunity to kill the always wary, extremely dangerous Jesse. Neither they nor Timberlake, apparently, so much as considered trying to take him alive. Perhaps they considered this task either impractical or too risky.

On the morning of April 3, Mrs. James, who was pregnant, felt ill, so Jesse obligingly assumed the house-cleaning chores. Since it was rather warm, he removed his coat, revealing a brace of pistols in shoulder holsters. Not wishing to excite the unwelcome attention of any passers-by who might happen to glance through the windows, he removed his harness and laid it on a bed.

Then, with a feather duster, he climbed up on a chair to clean a picture. Bob and Charley Ford were present in the room. The instant Jesse mounted the chair they exchanged quick looks, then Bob drew a pistol and cocked it; it was a pistol which Jesse had given him just the day before. The familiar click of a hammer going back caused Jesse to start to turn around. As he did so, Bob fired from about six feet away and the bullet tore through the back of his skull behind the right ear and out over the left eye near the temple. Without uttering a sound he crashed to the floor, dead.

The story of the bushwhackers comes to a fitting end with the slaying of Jesse James. All of the followers of Quantrill, Todd, and Anderson by then were dead, in jail, missing or living as common, everyday farmers, laborers, and businessmen. Frank James, the only important one still on the loose, voluntarily "came in" after Jesse's death. Twice, once at Gallatin, Missouri, and again at Muscle Shoals, Alabama, he stood trial for his alleged crimes, and each time the court acquitted him for lack of evidence. In fact, strange as it may seem, it has never been proved in a strictly legal sense that the James boys, the most famous outlaws in American history, ever committed so much as a single robbery!

During the remainder of his life Frank James enjoyed the privileged status of a living legend. After Cole Younger returned to Missouri, he joined him in operating a Wild West show in which they were the star attractions, but the venture failed. In 1915 he died at Kearney, and the following year Cole passed away at Lee's Summit. All the big names were now gone.[12]

Beginning in 1888 the surviving members of Quantrill's band held annual reunions. Initially these were modest and informal but by 1898 they had become elaborate two-day picnics held usually at Independence or Blue Springs. A reporter from the Kansas City *World* described the 1898 reunion, held at Blue Springs on October 10, as follows:

> Thirty-eight men lined up as a company of soldiers along an old worn rail fence at the Blue Springs picnic Saturday looked up startled as they heard the cry "Blue Coats!" several times repeated. They for a moment seemed to be led back again into '63 when that cry was a warning of life and death. What they saw when they looked up was Hi George running in high jumps toward them and yelling the old warning which has often sent them to their horses. There was a laugh and Frank Gregg finished calling the roll. Frank James stood near the center of the line and was the center of interest with his old comrades as well as with others at the picnic.[13]

At these yearly get-togethers the old-timers reminisced about the war days, argued moot points, and gave unreliable interviews to the reporters. They considered themselves Confederate veterans and were quite proud of having served under Quantrill, whose picture they always displayed prominently at their meetings.*

* The following is an account of the Eighth Annual Reunion at Independence on August 25-26, 1905:

"Among those registered Friday morning were Captain Ben Morrow of Lake City, Lieutenant Lee Miller of Knobnoster, Hi George of Grain Valley, Sylvester Akers of Levasy, William Greer of Lexington, John A. Workman of Wellington, George [Jim] Noland of Kansas City [this is the Negro spy Quantrill sent to Lawrence], A. J. Liddil of Independence [the man whom Wood

Time had softened and romanticized the memories of the war, so that most people now regarded the ex-guerrillas as heroic figures to be honored and venerated. There are many people today in Missouri who can recall the awe they felt as children when their parents pointed out to them a white-haired, stoop-shouldered old man, and said in hushed tones: "He was one of Quantrill's raiders."

In 1929 the last reunion took place. A few years later all the bushwhackers were dead.[14]

Hite tried to kill], J. M. Campbell of Lee's Summit, Levi Potts of Grain Valley, Henry Frazier of Mount Washington, D. Hughes of Hughes, Ark.; Tyler Burris [or Burns] of Mount Washington, D. S. Lane of Armourdale, William Gaugh of Jackson County and J. C. Ervin of Marshal, Mo.

"The visitors are given badges of bright red ribbon on which are pinned a medallion portrait of Quantrell [*sic*]. Underneath are the words: 'Eighth Annual Reunion of Quantrell's Guerrillas, Independence, Mo., August 25 and 26, 1905.'

"Cole Younger is the central figure. His burly figure may constantly be seen towering above a crowd of admirers seeking to shake his hand, congratulating him on his freedom, and talking over old times with him."

The above account appeared in the Miami *Weekly News* of Miami, Missouri, September 1, 1905. Mr. A. H. Edmonds of Kansas City, Missouri, very graciously supplied the author with a copy.

Notes

In order to avoid a hopelessly large number of notes, I have followed the practice of collecting the references necessary to a particular passage in a single note. Certain oft-cited sources are abbreviated as follows in the notes:

OR—*The War of the Rebellion: A Compilation of the Official Records of the Union and Confederate Armies*, 128 vols., plus atlas, Washington, 1881-1901.
KCDJ—Kansas City *Daily Journal of Commerce.*
KCWJ—Kansas City *Weekly Journal of Commerce.*
KHC—*Kansas Historical Collections.*
KHQ—*Kansas Historical Quarterly.*
MHR—*Missouri Historical Review.*

PROLOGUE

The story of the Kansas-Missouri, antislavery-proslavery struggle of the 1850's had been told many times. The following standard sources were consulted for this version.

Brewerton, George D. *The War in Kansas*, New York, 1856.
Carr, Lucien. *Missouri: A Bone of Contention*, Boston, 1888.
Cordley, Richard, *Pioneer Days in Kansas*, Boston, 1903.
Eldridge, Shalor W. *Recollections of Early Days in Kansas*, Topeka, Kansas, 1920.
Gihon, John H. *Geary and Kansas*, Philadelphia, 1857.
Gladstone, Thomas H. *The Englishman in Kansas; or Squatter Life and Border Warfare*, New York, 1857.
Goodlander, C. W. *Memoirs and Recollections of the Early Days of Fort Scott*, Fort Scott, Kansas, 1900.
Haskell, John G. "The Passing of Slavery in Western Missouri," KHC, VII (1901-1902), 28-39.
Herklotz, Hildegarde R. "Jayhawkers in Missouri, 1858-1863," MHR, XVII (April, 1923), 266-84.
Malin, James C. *John Brown and the Legend of Fifty-Six*, Philadelphia, 1942.
——— "The Proslavery Background of the Kansas Struggle," *Mississippi Valley Historical Review*, X (December, 1923), 285-305.
Phillips, William A. *The Conquest of Kansas by Missouri and Her Allies*, Boston, 1856.

Robinson, Charles. *The Kansas Conflict*, New York, 1892.
Robinson, Sara. "The Wakarusa War," KHC, X (1907-1908), 457-71.
Shoemaker, Floyd C. "Missouri's Proslavery Fight for Kansas, 1854-1855," MHR, XLVIII (April-July, 1954), 222-40; XLIX (October, 1954), 41-54.
Spring, Leverett W. *Kansas: The Prelude to the War for the Union*, Boston, 1885.
Stephenson, Wendell H. *The Political Career of General James H. Lane*, Topeka, Kansas, 1930.
Thayer, Eli. *The Kansas Crusade*, New York, 1889.
Tomlinson, William P. *Kansas in Eighteen Fifty-Eight*, New York, 1859.
Villard, Oswald Garrison, *John Brown, 1800-1859*, Boston, 1910.

CHAPTER I

1. Holland Wheeler, "Quantrill a Suspicious Loafer," KHC, VII (1901-1092), 224-26.
2. Manuscript Memoirs of Frank Smith (copy of original in possession of author), pp. 6-8.
3. Wheeler, "Quantrill a Suspicious Loafer," KHC, VII (1901-1902), 226; Edwin R. Smith, "How Quantrill Became an Outlaw," *ibid.*, pp. 214-18; Sidney S. Herd, "Always under an Alias and without Visible Means of Support," *ibid.*, pp. 226-28.

CHAPTER II

1. D. P. Hougland, "Voting for Lincoln in Missouri in 1860," KHC, IX (1905-1906), 509-20.
2. John S. McElroy, *The Struggle for Missouri* (Washington, 1909), pp. 60-66.
3. Liberty *Tribune*, May 17, 24, 1861; KCWJ, January 17, 1861; St. Louis *Republican*, quoted in KCDJ, May 25, 1861.
4. OR, Ser. I, III, pp. 4-5, 371-72; McElroy, *Struggle for Missouri*, pp. 68-78; Edward Conrad Smith, *The Borderland in the Civil War* (New York, 1927), pp. 236-38.
5. Liberty *Tribune*, May 17, 1861; KCWJ, June 5, 1861.
6. St. Louis *Republican*, quoted in *ibid.*, May 29, 1861; Smith, *Borderland*, pp. 238-51; Thomas L. Snead, *The Fight for Missouri* (New York, 1886), pp. 197-200.

7. Leavenworth *Daily Times*, June 25, 1861; Liberty *Tribune*, October 11, 25, November 1, 1861; KCDJ, June 5, 1861.
8. KCDJ, June 6, 12, 13, 14, 16, 1861; *History of Jackson County, Missouri* (Kansas City, Mo., 1881), p. 469.
9. KCDJ, July 2, 1861; Liberty *Tribune*, June 14, 1861.
10. KCDJ, June 15, 1861.
11. *Ibid.*, June 18, 20, 23, July 25, August 12, 1861; Albert Castel, *A Frontier State at War: Kansas, 1861-1865* (Ithaca, N. Y., 1958), pp. 45-46.
12. KCDJ, July 31, 1861.
13. *Ibid.*, August 21, 1861.
14. *Ibid.*, August 17, 1861.
15. OR, Ser. I, III, pp. 67-69, 100, 105, 746; *Battles and Leaders of the Civil War* (4 vols., New York, 1884), I, 290-306; Snead, *Fight for Missouri*, pp. 243-94.
16. Smith, *Borderland*, p. 250.
17. Castel, *Frontier State*, pp. 52-57; Leavenworth *Daily Conservative*, October 9, 1861.
18. St. Louis *Republican*, quoted in Liberty *Tribune*, November 22, 1861.
19. Castel, *Frontier State*, pp. 57-62, 214; Albert Castel, "Kansas Jayhawking Raids into Western Missouri in 1861," MHR, LIV (October, 1959), 1-11; Liberty *Tribune*, November 22, 1861; War Diary of Fletcher Pomeroy (typewritten copy of the original MS, Kansas State Historical Society, Topeka, Kansas), p. 18; George Caleb Bingham to James S. Rollins and Will A. Hall, February 12, 1862, MHR, XXXIII (October, 1938), 52.
20. William L. Webb, *Battles and Biographies of Missourians* (Kansas City, Mo., 1900), p. 324.
21. Leavenworth *Daily Conservative*, September 20, 1861
22. Webb, *Battles and Biographies*, p. 324
23. Virgil Carrington Jones, *Gray Ghosts and Rebel Raiders* (New York, 1956), pp. vii-viii, xi.
24. Castel, *Frontier State*, p. 63.
25. OR, Ser. I, VIII, 463-64.

CHAPTER III

1. Connelley, pp. 196-200; Edwards, *Noted Guerrillas*, p. 51.
2. Statements of Andrew Walker in Connelley, pp. 201-3; Smith MS.
3. *Ibid.*; Daniel Geary, "War Incidents at Kansas City," KHC, XI (1907-10), 284.

4. Smith MS.
5. *Ibid.*; Walker's Statement, Connelley, p. 203.
6. William H. Gregg Manuscript, Missouri State Historical Society, Columbia, Missouri.
7. Smith MS.
8. Cole Younger, *The Story of Cole Younger, by Himself* (Chicago, 1903), pp. 9-20; W. C. Bronough, *The Youngers' Fight for Freedom* (Columbia, Mo., 1906), p. 112.
9. OR, Ser. I, VIII, 57.
10. Gregg MS; Smith MS.
11. Gregg MS; Statements of Randlett and Ellis, in Connelley, pp. 225-28; OR, Ser. I, VIII, 335.
12. Eldridge, *Early Days in Kansas,* p. 182.
13. Connelley, pp. 229-34.
14. Liberty *Tribune*, March 31, 1862. (It is possible that the Liberty raid was carried out by some other band than Quantrill's as none of the bushwhacker memoirs mentions this affair); Smith MS; Gregg MS; KCDJ, March 23, 1862.
15. Smith MS.
16. *Ibid.*; Gregg MS: OR, Ser. I, VIII, 347; KCDJ, March 26, 27, 1862.
17. Smith MS; Gregg MS.
18. *Ibid.*; Smith MS; OR, Ser. I, VIII, 358-60.
19. Smith MS; Gregg MS; OR, Ser. I, XIII, 58.
20. Gregg MS; Smith MS; Edwards, *Noted Guerrillas,* pp. 72-75.
21. Gregg MS; Smith MS; OR, Ser. I, XIII, 154-55.

CHAPTER IV

1. Connelley, pp. 260-61.
2. Smith MS.
3. OR, Ser. I, XIII, 15.
4. Gregg MS; Smith MS; KCDJ, August 13, 14, 1862; OR, Ser. I, XIII, 226-27; Statement of Morgan T. Mattox in Connelley, pp. 262-63.
5. Smith MS.
6. *Ibid.;* Wiley Britton, *Memoirs of the Rebellion on the Border—1863* (Chicago, 1882), pp. 136-39; George Miller, *Missouri's Memorable Decade, 1860-1870* (Columbia, Mo., 1898), pp. 81-83.
7. Bronough, *Youngers' Fight for Freedom,* p. 112; Younger, *The Story of Cole Younger*, pp. 28-29.

8. OR, Ser. I, XIII, 15, 225-30, 235-39, 513-19, 535, 557-58; John N. Edwards, *Shelby and His Men* (Cincinnati, 1867), pp. 69-71.
9. OR, Ser. I, XIII, 254-55.
10. Gregg, MS; McCorkle, *Three Years with Quantrill*, pp. 34-35, gives a somewhat different version of Copeland's murder. According to him, Copeland was a Kansas jayhawker guilty of atrocities in Jackson County.
11. *Ibid.*; Leavenworth *Daily Conservative*, September 9, 1862.
12. Connelley, p. 272.
13. Gregg MS.
14. OR, Ser. I, XIII, 267-88.
15. *Ibid.*, pp. 779, 803; Gregg MS; Connelley, pp. 273-74.
16. Gregg MS; Connelley, pp. 274-75.
17. Gregg MS; OR, Ser. I, XIII, 347.
18. *Ibid.*, p. 796; Gregg MS; McCorkle, *Three Years with Quantrill*, pp. 43-44.
19. OR, Ser. I, XIII, 33; Gregg MS; Edwards, *Noted Guerrillas*, p. 133; McCorkle, *Three Years with Quantrill*, pp. 44-45.

CHAPTER V

1. Smith MS; Gregg MS; McCorkle, *Three Years with Quantrill*, p. 45.
2. Connelley, pp. 281-82.
3. Smith MS; Gregg MS; Edwards, *Shelby*, p. 116; McCorkle, *Three Years with Quantrill*, pp. 45-47.
4. OR, Ser. I, XXII, Part 1, 320.
5. KCWJ, May 16, 23, 1863; Council Grove *Press*, May 11, 1863; Leavenworth *Daily Conservative*, May 7, 30, 1863; Leavenworth *Daily Times*, August 30, 1863; George Pilson Morehouse, "Diamond Springs, the Diamond of the Plains," KHC, XV (1915-1918), 799-800; David Hubbard, "Reminiscences of the Yeager Raid, on the Santa Fe Trail, in 1863," *Ibid.*, VIII (1903-1904), 169-70.
6. Smith MS; KCWJ, May 30, June 27, 1863.
7. Smith MS; KCWJ, May 30, 1863.
8. *Ibid.*, April 25, May 2, July 4, 1863; Liberty *Tribune*, April 17, 1863; John McCorkle, *Three Years with Quantrill*, p. 75.
9. KCWJ, May 30, 1863.
10. Smith MS.
11. KCWJ, June 13, 1863.
12. *Ibid.*, May 2, 23, 30, June 13, 1863.

13. The above account of bushwhacker arms and tactics is based upon a study of all known material bearing on this topic. Particularly useful was the Smith MS and Connelley, pp. 316-22.
14. Statement of Ike Hall, in *ibid.*, pp. 302-3.
15. McCorkle, *Three Years with Quantrill*, pp. 6-24.
16. Smith MS.
17. Connelley, p. 430.
18. KCWJ, June 20, 1863; McCorkle, *Three Years with Quantrill*, pp. 68-69.
19. Castel, *Frontier State*, pp. 25-26, 110-11; KCWJ, June 13, 20, 1863.
20. *Ibid.*, July 4, 1863; OR, Ser. I, XXII, Part 2, 388-92; Leavenworth *Daily Conservative*, July 21, 22, 31, August 2, 1863.
21. OR, Ser. I, XXII, Part 2, 419-20; KCWJ, July 25, 1863, quoting Lexington *Union*.
22. OR, Ser. I, XXII, Part 2, 428-29, 450-51, 460-61; KCWJ, June 27, July 25, 1863.
23. KCDJ, August 14, 1863; McCorkle, *Three Years with Quantrill*, pp. 76-78; Richard Brownlee, *Gray Ghosts of the Confederacy* (Baton Rouge, La., 1958), p. 119; Connelley, pp. 299-303, 316.
24. A. T. Andreas (Comp.), *History of the State of Kansas* (Chicago, 1883), p. 800; Brownlee, *Gray Ghosts of the Confederacy*, pp. 137-39.

CHAPTER VI

1. Gregg MS; Smith MS; F. W. Hinsey, "The Lawrence Raid," Kansas City *Star*, July 19, 1903.
2. *Ibid.*; Edwards, *Noted Guerrillas*, pp. 188-89; Connelley, p. 310.
3. Gregg MS; Smith MS; McCorkle, *Three Years with Quantrill*, pp. 79-80.
4. Gregg MS; Smith MS; OR, Ser. I, XXII, Part 1, 580, 583; "Statement of Captain J. A. Pike concerning the Quantrill Raid," KHC, XIV (1915-1918), 311-18; H. E. Lowman, *Narrative of the Lawrence Massacre* (Lawrence, Kansas, 1864), 42, 47-56; Connelley, pp. 323-28, 335-36; Andreas, *History of Kansas*, p. 321.
5. The above account of the Lawrence Massacre is based upon the following sources: Gregg MS; Smith MS; McCorkle, *Three Years with Quantrill*; C. M. Chase to Sycamore, Illinois, *True Republican and Sentinel*, August 22, 1863, C. M. Chase Letters, Kansas State Historical Society, Topeka, Kansas; R. G. Elliott, "The Quantrill Raid as Seen from the Eldridge House," in Eldridge,

Early Days in Kansas; Lowman, *Narrative of the Lawrence Massacre;* John C. Shea (Comp.), *Reminiscences of Quantrill's Raid upon the City of Lawrence, Kansas* (Kansas City, Mo., 1879); Adolph Roenigk (Comp.), *Pioneer History of Kansas* (Published by Roenigk, n.p., c. 1913); H. D. Fisher, *The Gun and the Gospel* (4th ed., Kansas City, Mo., 1902); Richard Cordley, A *History of Lawrence, Kansas, from the First Settlement to the Close of the Rebellion* (Lawrence, Kansas, 1895); Robinson, *Kansas Conflict;* Richard Cordley and Others, "The Quantrell Raid" (a pamphlet published in Lawrence in 1884, based mainly on a letter by Cordley to the Congregational Record written a few days after the raid and later published in Boughton & McAllister's *Directory of Lawrence for 1865*); Connelley, *Quantrill and the Border Wars.* In addition, contemporary accounts appearing in the Kansas and Missouri newspapers were also consulted. The above constitutes a complete list, insofar as the author knows, of sources containing firsthand and reliable information on the Lawrence Massacre.

6. Smith MS; Gregg MS; McCorkle, *Three Years with Quantrill,* pp. 81-84; KCWJ, August 29, 1863, containing account of Samuel Boies, who was taken prisoner by the guerrillas at Lawrence and later escaped from them; OR, Ser. I, XXII, Part 1, 580-82, 589-90 *ibid.,* Part 2, pp. 479-80; Edwards, *Noted Guerrillas,* p. 200; Connelley, pp. 352-57, 378-420; Cordley, *History of Lawrence,* pp. 229-30.
7. Cf. Brownlee, *Gray Ghosts of the Confederacy,* pp. 120-21.
8. McCorkle, *Three Years with Quantrill,* p. 78.
9. Testimony of William L. Bullene, in Shea (Comp.), *Reminiscences of Quantrell's Raid,* p. 14.
10. Castel, *Frontier State,* pp. 136-37.
11. Lloyd Lewis, "Propaganda and the Kansas-Missouri War," MHR, XXXIV (October, 1939), p. 11.

CHAPTER VII

1. Connelley, pp. 417-18; John M. Schofield, *Forty-six Years in the Army* (New York, 1897), pp. 79-80; OR, Ser. I, XXII, Part 2, 473.
2. KCWJ, September 19, November 23, 1863, January 30, 1864; Liberty *Tribune,* September 11, 1863; Edwards, *Shelby and His Men,* p. 218; Vivian K. McLarty (ed.), "The Civil War Letters of Colonel Bazel Lazear," MHR, XLIV (July, 1950), 390; OR,

Ser. I, XXII, Part 2, 570-71, 591, 753; *ibid.*, XXXIV, Part 2, 326, 375.

3. KCWJ, September 5, October 3, October 10, 1863, quoting St. Louis *Republican* and Lexington *Union;* C. B. Rollins (ed.), "Letters of George Caleb Bingham to James S. Rollins," MHR, XXXIII (October, 1938), 62.
4. KCWJ, August 29, 1863.
5. Castel, *Frontier State*, pp. 146-49; Ewing to Guitar, August 27, 1863, Guitar Papers, Missouri State Historical Society; Guitar to R. Leonard, August, 28, 1863, Abiel Leonard Papers, Missouri State Historical Society.
6. Smith MS; KCWH, September 5, 1863.
7. Smith MS; Statement of Fletch Taylor, in Connelley, p. 451.
8. Smith MS.
9. *Ibid.*; Gregg MS; McCorkle, *Three Years with Quantrill*, pp. 89-95; KCWJ, October 24, 1863; OR, Ser. I, XXII, Part 1, 688-701; W. H. Warner, "The Battle and Massacre at Baxter Springs, October 6, 1863," in Andreas (Comp.), *History of Kansas*, pp. 1152-53; James G. Blunt, "General Blunt's Account of His Civil War Experiences," KHQ, I (May, 1932), 261-65; Connelley, pp. 421-34.
10. OR, Ser. I, XXII, Part 1, 700-1; Smith MS.

CHAPTER VIII

1. Smith MS.
2. OR, Ser. I, LIII, 908; *ibid.* XXVI, Part 2, 339-40; KCWJ, September 26, 1863, quoting Richmond *Examiner*.
3. OR, Ser. I, XXVI, Part 2, 348, 379, 382-83, 430-31; *ibid.*, XXII, Part 2, 1072-73.
4. Gregg MS; Connelley, 436-37; Brownlee, *Gray Ghosts of the Confederacy*, pp. 136-37.
5. Smith MS; Statements of Sylvester Akers and W. L. Potter, in Connelley, pp. 439-43.
6. *Ibid.*, XXXIV, Part 2, 957-58.
7. Smith MS; OR, Ser. I, XXII, Part 2, 855; *ibid.*, LIII, 907-8; Statement of Sylvester Akers, in Connelley, pp. 443-44.
8. Smith MS; Statement of Sylvester Akers, in Connelley, pp. 444-45; OR, Ser. I, XXXIV, Part 3, 742.
9. Smith MS.
10. OR, Ser. I, XXII, Part 2, 693-94, 702-3, 713-14; *ibid.*, XXXIV,

Part 2, 79-81, 89; KCWJ, November 21, 1863, January 23, 30, May 14, 1864.

11. Smith MS; Gregg MS; Statement of W. L. Potter in Connelley, pp. 447-48; *ibid.*, 449-50, citing interviews by W. W. Scott with various members of Quantrill's band.
12. *Ibid.*, p. 436.
13. Smith MS; Gregg MS; Statement of Fletch Taylor, in Connelley, p. 451; McCorkle, *Three Years with Quantrill*, pp. 103-4. McCorkle merely states that Quantrill went to Howard County in the summer of 1864, gives no reasons for his doing so. He also states that Quantrill was accompanied by Jim Little, John Barker, Tom Harris, Dave Hilton, and Tom Evans. Edwards, interestingly enough, does not mention whatsoever the quarrel between Quantrill and Todd, but states (*Noted Guerrillas*, pp. 308-9) that Quantrill spent the summer in Howard County because he was ill, wounded, and worn out. Furthermore, Edwards does not describe the internal squabbles among the bushwhackers in Texas. To have done so would have spoiled the legend of the always heroic and knightly guerrillas that he was trying to create.

CHAPTER IX

1. KCWJ, March 19, 1864.
2. *Ibid.*, June 11, July 2, 9, 23, 1864; St. Joseph *Herald*, July 19, 1864.
3. KCWJ, June 18, July 16, 1864.
4. *Ibid.*, June 18, 1864.
5. OR, Ser. I, XXXIV, Part 1, 1018-24; KCWJ, June 25, 1864.
6. Smith MS; McCorkle, *Three Years with Quantrill*, pp. 104-5. KCWJ, July 16, 1864; OR, Ser. I, XLI, Part 2, 73-74.
7. KCWJ, July 16, 23, 30, August 13, 1864; OR, Ser. I, XXXIV, Part 2, 254; *ibid.*, Part 3, pp. 526, 576, 596; *ibid.*, Part 4, pp. 92-553 *passim*.
8. KCWJ, July 16, August 6, 1864; OR, Ser. I, XXIV, Part 3, 406; *ibid.*, Part 4, pp. 25, 54-55; *ibid.*, XLI, Part 2, 896; Julia Lovejoy to Her Family, May 10, 1864, KHQ, XVI (May, 1948), 207-8.
9. Liberty *Tribune*, July 5, 1864.
10. KCWJ, July 23, July 30, August 6, 1864; Liberty *Tribune*, July 15, 22, 1864; OR, Ser. I, XLI, Part 1, 52-55; *ibid.*, Part 2, 160, 175, 185, 245-51.
11. Smith MS; OR, Ser. I, XLI, Part 2, 310-11, 337, 347.
12. *Ibid.*, pp. 75-77.

13. Liberty *Tribune*, August 12, 1864; KCWJ, July 30, August 6, 13, 1864; OR, Ser. I, XLI, Part 1, 55, 251-52; *ibid.*, Part 2, pp. 38, 209, 216-17, 235, 423, 824-25, 839-41, 959; *ibid.*, Part 3, p. 395; Brownlee, *Gray Ghosts of the Confederacy*, pp. 203-5.

CHAPTER X

1. Jennie Edwards (Comp.), *John N. Edwards, Life, Writings and Tributes . . . Including His Shelby's Expedition to Mexico* (Kansas City, Mo., 1889), pp. 233, 283; Smith MS; OR, Ser. I, XLI, Part 1, 424-29.
2. Smith MS; Hamp B. Watts, *The Babe of the Company* (Fayette, Mo., 1913), pp. 17-21; Connelley, pp. 452-53; McCorkle, *Three Years with Quantrill*, pp. 110-12; OR, Ser. I, XLI Part 1, 415-16, 440-41.
3. *Ibid.*, pp. 309, 440-43, 448, 91, 521-22, 693; Smith MS; Watts, *Babe of the Company*, pp. 22-32; KCWJ, October 1, 8, 1864; Liberty *Tribune*, September 30, 1864; McCorkle, *Three Years with Quantrill*, pp. 113-16; Harry A. Houston (ed.), "*A True Narrative*" *by Sergeant Thomas M. Goodman* (Des Moines, Iowa, 1868, typewritten copy of MS, Kansas City, Mo., Public Library), pp. 8-15; R. I. Holcombe, "Massacred Soldiers," Washington, D.C., *National Tribune*, August 28, 1884; C. R. Barns (ed.), *Switzler's Illustrated History of Missouri from 1541 to 1877* (St. Louis, 1879); Brownlee, *Gray Ghosts of the Confederacy*, p. 220. The statements concerning the atrocities are taken from the official report of Lt. Col. Dan. N. Draper, in OR, Ser. I, XLI, Part 1, 440-41, and from Goodman and Switzler.
4. Watts, *Babe of the Company*, pp. 23, 32; KCWJ, October 1, 1864.
5. Houston (ed.), "A *True Narrative*," pp. 17-25; Watts, *Babe of the Company*, p. 24; Smith MS.
6. OR, Ser. I, XLI, Part 3, 454-55.
7. *Ibid.*, Part 1, pp. 417-24.
8. *Ibid.*, Part 3, p. 741.
9. *Ibid.*, Part 1, pp. 632, 718, 888; *ibid.*, Part 3, 893; *ibid.*, Part 4, p. 354; KCWJ, November 12, 1864.
10. OR, Ser. I, XLI, Part 1, 439; Brownlee, *Gray Ghosts of the Confederacy*, p. 225.
11. Smith MS; Connelley, pp. 454-55; McCorkle, *Three Years with Quantrill*, pp. 123-24; KCWJ, November 5, 1864; OR, Ser. I, XLI, Part 4, 194, 206.

12. Brownlee, *Gray Ghosts of the Confederacy*, p. 228.
13. OR, Ser. I, XLI, Part 1, 442; Watts, *Babe of the Company*, pp. 23-40; Liberty *Tribune*, November 11, 1864; KCWJ, November 5, 1864.
14. OR, Ser. I, XLI, Part 4, 354.
15. McCorkle, *Three Years with Quantrill*, pp. 124-48; Smith MS; KCWJ, November 5, 1864; Albert Castel, "Sterling Price and the Civil War in the West" (M.A. Thesis, University of Wichita, 1951), pp. 98-101.

CHAPTER XI

1. Smith MS; OR, Ser. I, XLI, Part 4, 715, 782, 960; McCorkle, *Three Years with Quantrill*, pp. 129-33; Connelley, pp. 456-59, citing information obtained from Sylvester Akers, M. T. Mattox, and other Quantrill veterans. See also Edwards, *Noted Guerrillas*, pp. 383-89.
2. OR, Ser. I, XLIX, Part 1, 657; McCorkle, *Three Years with Quantrill*, pp. 133-40; Connelley, pp. 459-60.
3. OR, Ser. 1, XLIX, Part 1, 17-18, 35-37, 512, 626, 634-35, 673-77, 684, 694, 698, 788; McCorkle, *Three Years with Quantrill*, pp. 141-42; Connelley, pp. 461-64.
4. *Ibid.*, pp. 464-65; McCorkle, *Three Years with Quantrill*, pp. 143-50.
5. Connelley, pp. 466-80, using information obtained by himself and W. W. Scott from various Kentuckians and bushwhacker veterans; McCorkle, *Three Years with Quantrill*, pp. 150-52, gives a somewhat different version. However, he was not, according to his own statement, with Quantrill on May 10 at Wakefield's and he makes such basic errors as calling Terrill "Captain Mead."
6. Newspapers quoted in Connelley, pp. 481-82.
7. *Ibid.*, pp. 468, 477.
8. *Ibid.*, pp. 35, 451, 477, 480-82; Leavenworth *Daily Times*, June 9, 1865; Leavenworth *Daily Conservative*, June 9, 1865; KCWJ, June 12, 1865.
9. Memorandum of W. W. Scott, in Connelley, pp. 35-36.

EPILOGUE

1. OR, Ser. I, XLI, Part 4, 89; *ibid.*, XLVIII, Part 1, 330; KCWJ, January 28, February 18, March 18, 25, 1865.
2. OR, Ser. I, XLVIII, Part 2, 286; KCWJ, January 7, February 11,

18, 25, April 15 (quoting Columbia *Statesman*), 1865; Liberty *Tribune*, March 31, April 7, 1865.

3. Edwards, *Noted Guerrillas*, pp. 390-447; Harrison Trow, *Under the Black Flag* (Vega, Texas, 1923), pp. 223-29; KCWJ, May 13, 1865.
4. OR, Ser. I, XLVIII, Part 2, 342, 353-63; KCWJ, May 13, 20, 1865.
5. OR, Ser. I, XLVIII, Part 2, 370-71.
6. *Ibid.*, pp. 341-42; 408-9, 470, 545, 705-6; Liberty *Tribune*, May 26, 1865; Trow, *Black Flag*, p. 230.
7. Liberty *Tribune*, June 2, 9, 1865; OR, Ser. I, XLVIII, Part 2, 737-38, 785, 848, 872; Trow, *Black Flag*, p. 230.
8. Connelley, pp. 478-79.
9. C. W. Goodlander, *Memoirs and Recollections of the Early Days of Fort Scott* (Fort Scott, Kansas, 1900), p. 107.
10. Brownlee, *Gray Ghosts of the Confederacy*, pp. 242-43; A. C. Appler, *The Younger Brothers* (New York, 1955), pp. 42ff., 194.
11. Carl W. Breihan, *The Complete and Authentic Life of Jesse James* (New York, 1953), pp. 93-104; Brownlee, *Gray Ghosts of the Confederacy*, pp. 243-44; Edwards, *Noted Guerrillas*, pp. 448-60.
12. The above account of the career of the Jameses and Youngers is based on the works of Edwards, Breihan, and Appler already cited, plus the following books: Jesse James, Jr., *Jesse James My Father* (New York, 1957); Burton Rascoe, *Belle Starr, "The Bandit Queen"* (New York, 1941); Younger, *The Story of Cole Younger*; Robertus Love, *The Rise and Fall of Jesse James* (New York, 1925); Homer Croy, *Jesse James Was My Neighbor* (New York, 1949); Croy, *Last of the Outlaws;* James D. Horan, *Desperate Men* (New York, 1949). There is very little really authentic information on the Jameses and Youngers, and none of the above works are very reliable—not even those by Cole Younger and Jesse James, Jr.! In writing my account, I tried to stick to the definitely known facts, and where that was impossible, to choose that version of the James-Younger legend which seemed most in keeping with probability and reality.
13. Quoted in B. James George, Sr., "The Q-Men of Jackson County," The Oak Grove (Mo.) *Banner*, October 9, 1959, a copy of which was very kindly supplied the author by Mr. George, son of the George mentioned in the quotation.
14. *Ibid.*

Index